I0810055

IMAGES
of America

BUILDING THE CALDECOTT TUNNEL

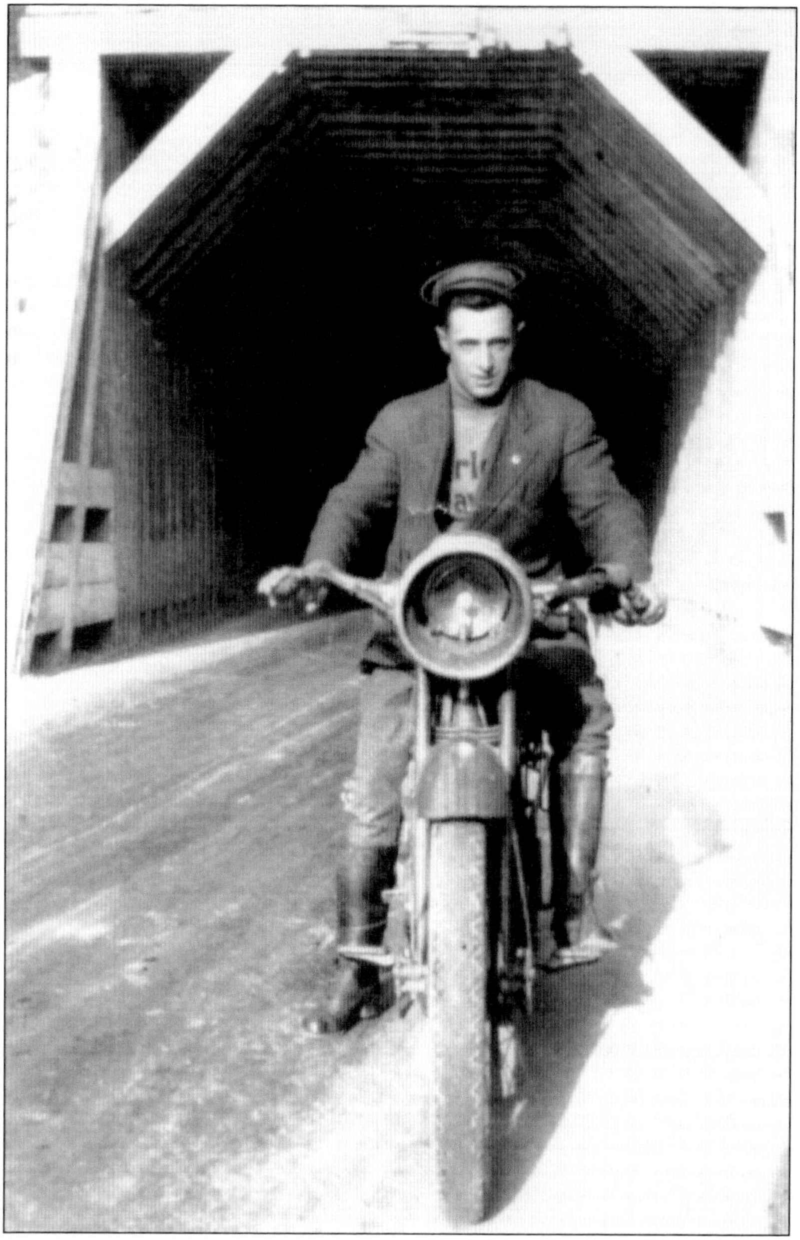

Ernest Guido, secretary of the Oakland Motorcycle Club, is shown on his Harley-Davidson motorcycle at the Kennedy Tunnel in 1917. Two months before this photograph was taken, the United States entered World War I. Corporal Guido was drafted and served in France, where he was killed in action at the front in September 1918. (Courtesy Contra Costa County Historical Society.)

On the Cover: The East Portal of the Broadway Low Level Tunnel is shown shortly after it opened in late 1937. This new tunnel had two bores, one for each direction of traffic, and replaced the Kennedy Tunnel, which was located some 300 feet above it. The completion of this project greatly expedited travel and commerce between Alameda and Contra Costa Counties. (Courtesy Lafayette Historical Society.)

IMAGES
of America

BUILDING THE CALDECOTT TUNNEL

Mary Solon and Mary McCosker

ARCADIA
PUBLISHING

ISBN 978-1-4671-3181-0

Published by Arcadia Publishing
Charleston, South Carolina

Printed in the United States of America

Library of Congress Control Number: 2013954622

For all general information, please contact Arcadia Publishing:
Telephone 843-853-2070
Fax 843-853-0044
E-mail sales@arcadiapublishing.com
For customer service and orders:
Toll-Free 1-888-313-2665

Visit us on the Internet at www.arcadiapublishing.com

This book is dedicated to Bhaskar Thapa, PE, PhD (9/7/1963–6/19/2013), chief engineer of the Caldecott Fourth Bore Project, and to those who lost their lives building the tunnels through the Oakland/Berkeley hills.

CONTENTS

ACKNOWLEDGMENTS

Thanks to Ivy Morrison, public information officer for the Caldecott Fourth Bore Project, and Ray Mailhot, retired Caltrans superintendent for tunnels and bores for District Four, for their invaluable assistance with gathering information and knowing who to ask when we had questions; to Nathan Kerr of the Oakland Museum of California and Dorothy Lazard, Martha Bergmann, and Elia Shelton of the Oakland Main Public Library History Room for sharing photographs of the construction of the Second and Third Bores; to Priscilla Couden, Lee and Avice Taylor, and Janet Stapleton of the Contra Costa County Historical Society for their assistance with historical photographs; to Nildo Rego for her historical reference work; to Mary Elings and Susan Snyder of the Bancroft Library at the University of California, Berkeley, for historical photographs and information; to Joseph Barkley and Richard Reeves for sharing photographs and stories of family members who were part of the tunnel construction; to Bill Hall, John Huseby, and Isaac Garcia for sharing the Caltrans District Four photographic archives; to Lucy Hupp Williams of the Orinda Historical Society, Elsie Mastick of the Moraga Historical Society, Ralph Cozine and Beverly Lane of the Museum of San Ramon Valley, and our colleagues at the Lafayette Historical Society for their support of this project; to Janet Coles of the California Department of Transportation Library in Sacramento for help in our research; to Mark DuFrene, Denis Cuff, and Chris Treadway for their help with *Oakland Tribune* archives; to Brian Smith for sharing his tunnel photographs and signs; to Elpidio Perez for his help with the geology of the dig; to Thomas P. Caldecott for family photographs and information; and, especially, to Randy Anderson of the California Department of Transportation for his technical expertise and patience when we kept asking tunnel questions, and to Lisa Albert for her editing skills and thoughtful suggestions. Much gratitude is due as well to our long-suffering husbands, who humor us when we get harebrained ideas, and to Susie, who graciously listened to tunnel talk many mornings while walking at the Lafayette Reservoir. Appreciation and thanks to all of the employees of Caltrans who improve our transportation and get us safely to our destinations.

Introduction

For centuries, the natural barrier provided by geography divided the California counties on either side of the Oakland/Berkeley hills. Although Alameda County was initially part of Contra Costa County, it had become a separate county by 1853. Alameda County, which has access to the San Francisco Bay and is in close proximity to San Francisco itself, grew as an urban area at the end of the 19th century. Contra Costa County remained a less-populated agricultural area due, in great part, to the hills separating it from Alameda County. In the 19th century, one route of travel over the hills between Alameda County and Contra Costa County went along the Oak Springs Creek through Claremont Canyon. This road was first called Harwood's Road, but when the Alta Telegraph Company built a telegraph line between Oakland and Martinez in 1859, Harwood's Road—along which the line was strung—was renamed Telegraph Road. Telegraph Road went along today's Telegraph Avenue from downtown Oakland to the Temescal area, then along Claremont Avenue to the summit, where it became Fish Ranch Road. Travelers going east could also use Tunnel Road, a perilous route that traversed the top of the hills with 1,300-foot drops on either side. As traveling between the counties became more desirable and necessary, residents needed a faster, more convenient route.

In 1861, the California Legislature approved a bill for the construction of a tunnel between the counties by the Oakland and Contra Costa Tunnel Company, but the company did not begin the work until 1873. Excavation resulted in only 200 feet of progress from the Alameda County side and only 100 feet from the Orinda side before a lack of funds closed down the project. In February 1879, a tunnel 16 feet wide and 16 feet high was begun under a new contractor, but in June 1880, "the weight of rock and earth on the Oakland end of the Oakland and Contra Costa Road Company's tunnel crushed the timbering and let down the material above; the tunnel was said to have run about 900 feet from each of the opposite openings," according to the *Contra Costa Gazette* of June 12, 1880. In 1897, the project started again, and the Contra Costa Tunnel (also known as Kennedy Tunnel) opened in November 1903. It was built above the location of the present-day Caldecott Tunnel with the approach to it along Tunnel Road, which started at the top of Ashby Avenue. The tunnel was 1,100 feet long, narrow (17 feet wide), and unpaved. The bore was reinforced only with timber, which made it prone to landslides during the rainy season. There were no lights in the tunnel until the 1920s, and farmers taking products through the tunnel in wagons often lit torches or carried lanterns to better light the way. Travelers through the bore often paid a toll to William Kennedy, on whose land the tunnel had been constructed. The final cost of the tunnel—$46,000—was paid for with taxes, public subscription, and proceeds from a "Tunnel Day" at an East Bay racetrack.

Although often inadequate, this first tunnel conveniently linked the two counties of the East Bay. For the next 20 years, it made the small, rural, and mostly agricultural towns on the eastern side of the hills easier to reach and provided the farmers of those towns with safer access to the markets of Alameda County and San Francisco.

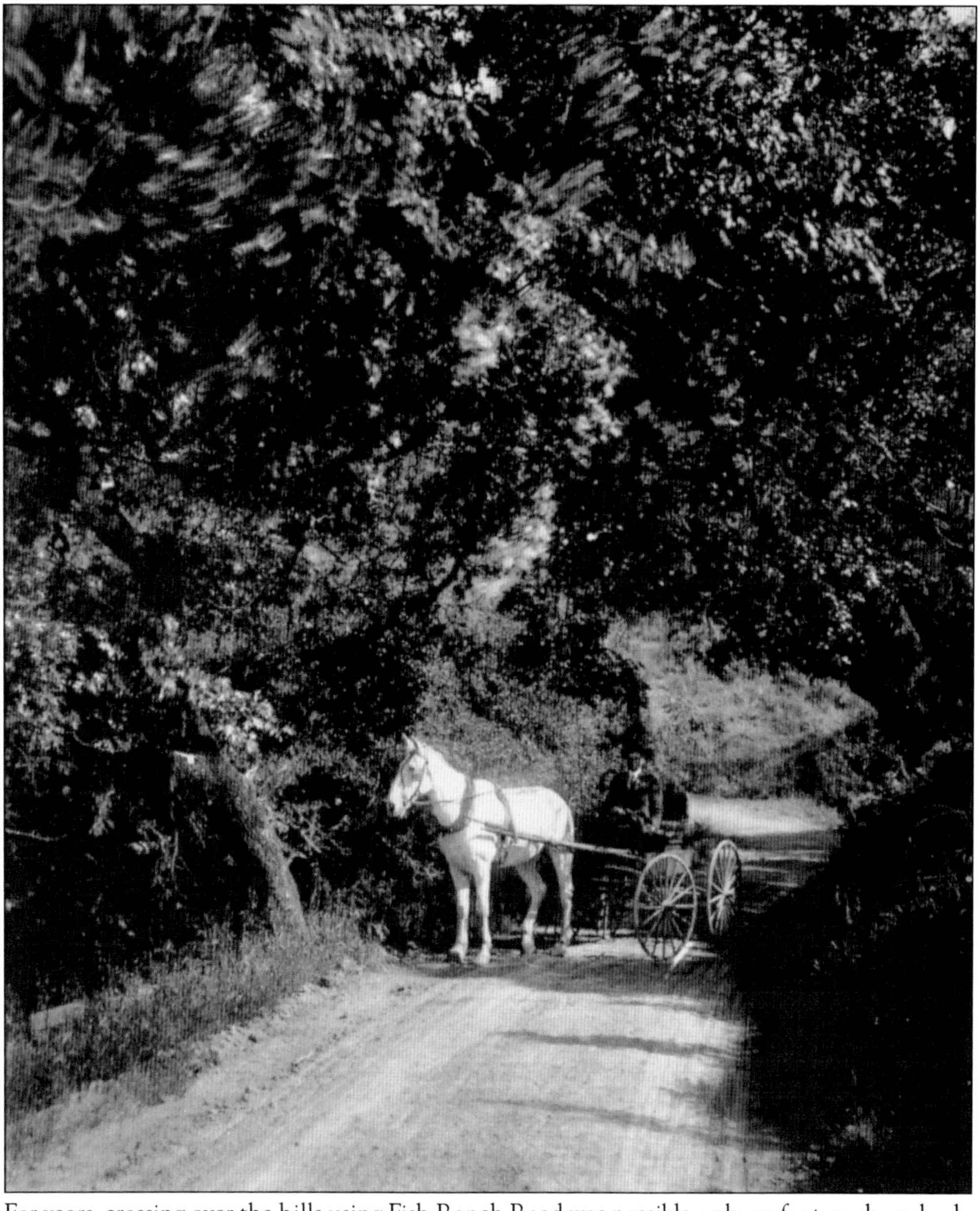

For years, crossing over the hills using Fish Ranch Road was possible only on foot, on horseback, or using a horse-drawn carriage. The road was so steep, winding, and often rutted that horses had to be led or pushed to reach the summit. A Miss Miner of Orinda wrote about a trip from Oakland to Orinda in the late 1800s: "The drive home went like this: out Telegraph Avenue, past the Three-Mile House at Shattuck and Telegraph Avenue, then the Four Mile House at College and Claremont, out along Claremont Avenue. Then there was the long, slow climb up to the summit. Here stood the Summit House, a reminder of the days when the stages ran to Mt. Diablo and changed horses there. From the summit, we trotted down the grade. At the foot where we turned into the Fish Ranch Canyon was the Buckley Ranch. Mr. Buckley was always talking about a tunnel through the hills. People just thought of him as mildly demented." (Courtesy Contra Costa County Historical Society.)

One

Trails and Roads

Before the Spanish, the Mexicans, and the Yankee settlers arrived in the East Bay, the native people followed paths and trails over the hills between present-day Alameda and Contra Costa Counties. These paths generally followed the stream and creek beds of the area. Natives used the trails for hunting, gathering plants, and trading with other Miwok tribes of the East Bay and the coast near present-day Marin County.

Early settlers on horseback or with horse-drawn wagons or buggies used trails and primitive roads to cross the hills. Although the first roads were little more than dirt trails, Contra Costa County was divided into road districts as early as July 20, 1850, and a few main roads were declared public highways. Once roads had been established, people could travel more frequently between the counties. Farmers from Contra Costa County brought their agricultural goods to Alameda County to sell to local residents at the Oakland Produce Mart or to send to other places by ship.

In 1859, the Alta Telegraph Company constructed a telegraph line between Oakland and Martinez, and the existing road that ran alongside it was renamed Telegraph Road. The segment of Telegraph Road that ran from downtown Oakland to the Peralta Estate in Temescal was first known as Peralta Road. The segment that ran to and up Harwood's (now Claremont) Canyon was first known as Harwood's Road. Telegraph Road followed the route of the present-day Telegraph Avenue from downtown Oakland to Temescal, then ran along what is now the route of Claremont Avenue up to the summit of the Berkeley hills, where it became Fish Ranch Road.

Pony Express riders used the route along Telegraph Road, passing through Lafayette and Orinda when the early westbound trips missed the boat from Sacramento to San Francisco and used the Benicia ferry instead.

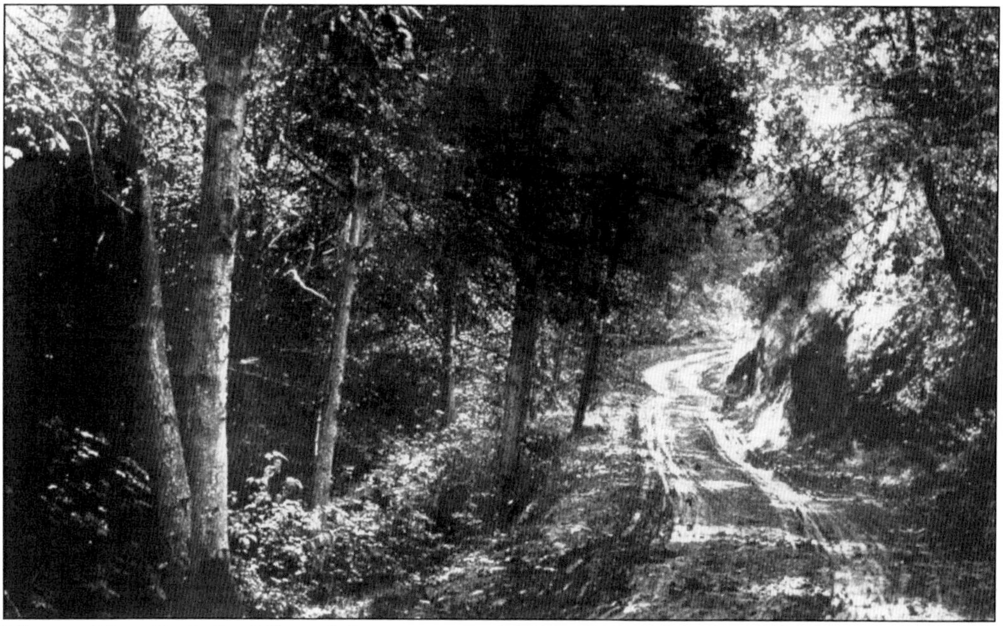

The road from Berkeley followed the present-day Telegraph Avenue route from Oakland to where it connected with Claremont Avenue and then went over the hills, following the approximate path of the present-day Fish Ranch Road towards Orinda and Lafayette. (Courtesy Contra Costa County Historical Society.)

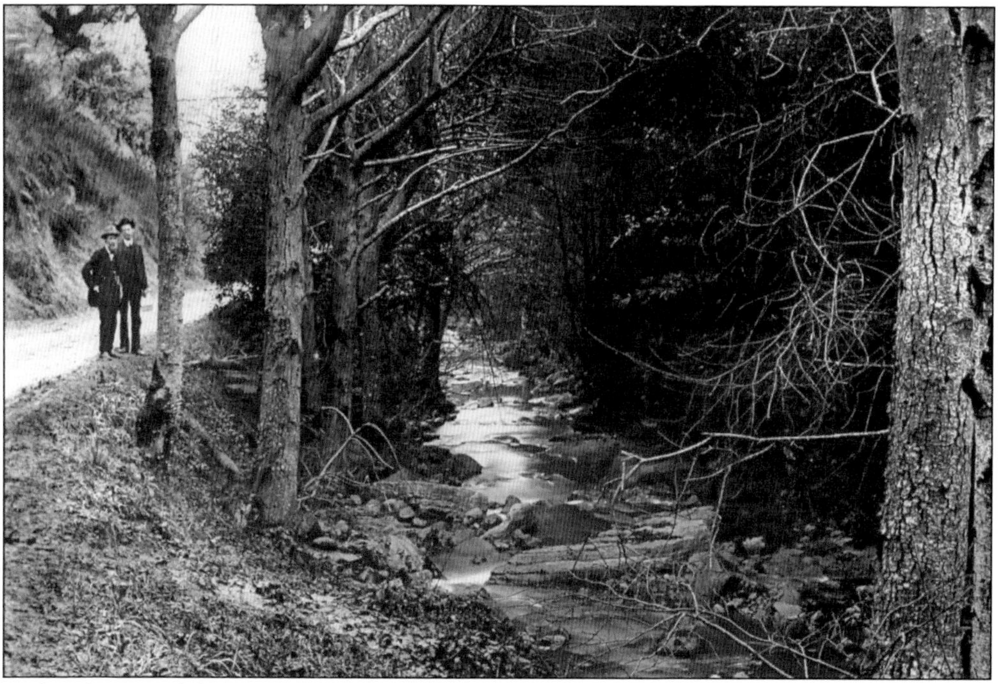

In this photograph from January 1904, Vic Post (on the left) and C. Ayer stand by the Oak Springs Creek located along Fish Ranch Road up Claremont Canyon. This road was often impassable during winter months, when rain would cause the creek to overflow its banks, which created muddy conditions for horse-drawn vehicles. (Courtesy Contra Costa County Historical Society.)

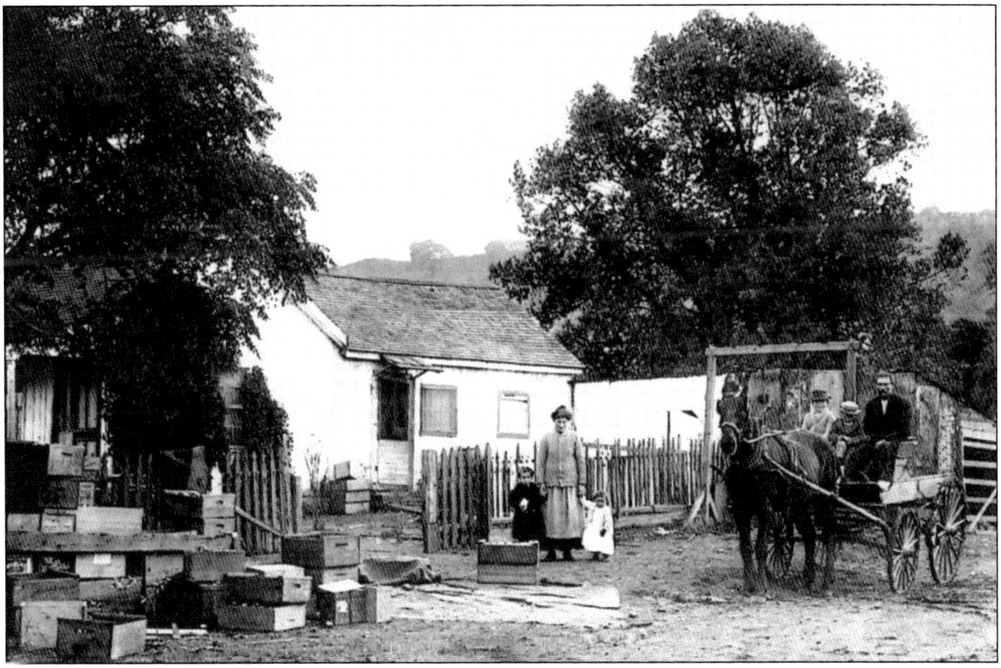

Before the construction of a tunnel, farmers in Contra Costa County used horses and wagons to carry agricultural products over the hills to sell in Alameda County. Farmers transported milk, butter, fruit, and hay to Oakland and Berkeley—a trip that could take several hours. (Courtesy Lafayette Historical Society.)

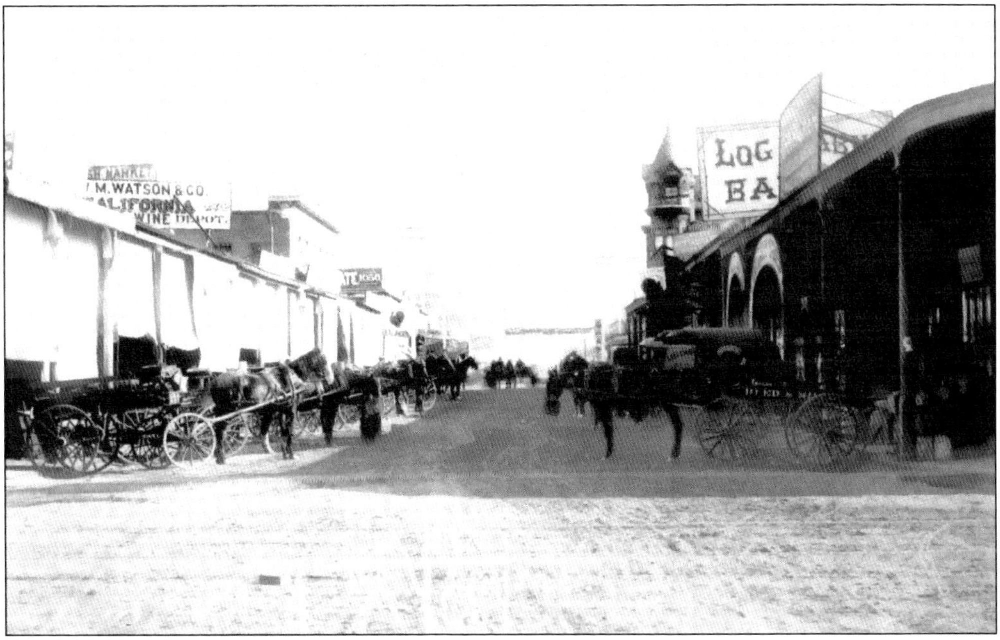

In this 1880s photograph, horses and wagons parked at the Oakland Produce Mart on Eleventh Street north of Broadway are ready to load produce to deliver to local neighborhoods. Much of the produce was grown east of the Oakland/Berkeley hills and delivered to the produce mart in the wagons of Contra Costa County farmers. (Courtesy Bancroft Library, University of California.)

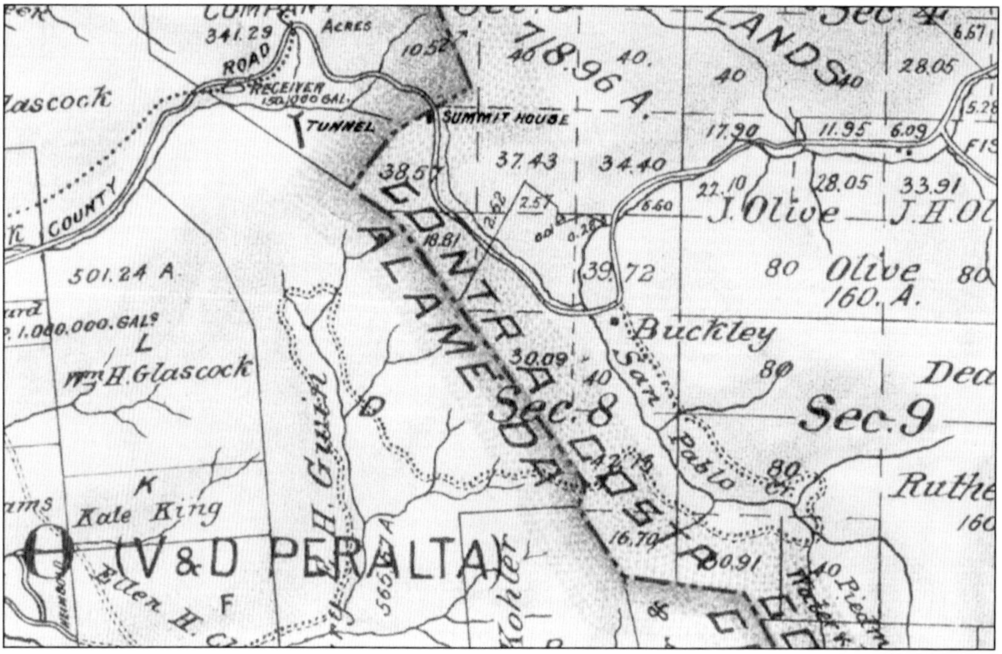

The Theodore Wagner map of Alameda and Contra Costa Counties (above) is from 1894 and shows the stage line, a dirt road called the County Road, which wound through the Claremont Canyon and over the hill to Contra Costa County. The Summit House, the Buckley property, and John Olive's ranch are visible on this map. The Pony Express medallion (below) commemorates the 18 months of overland mail delivery service, from April 1860 to October 1861, when Pony Express riders traveled over the hills to Oakland and Berkeley if the mail missed ferry connections to San Francisco. (Above, courtesy Library of Congress; below, courtesy Lafayette Historical Society.)

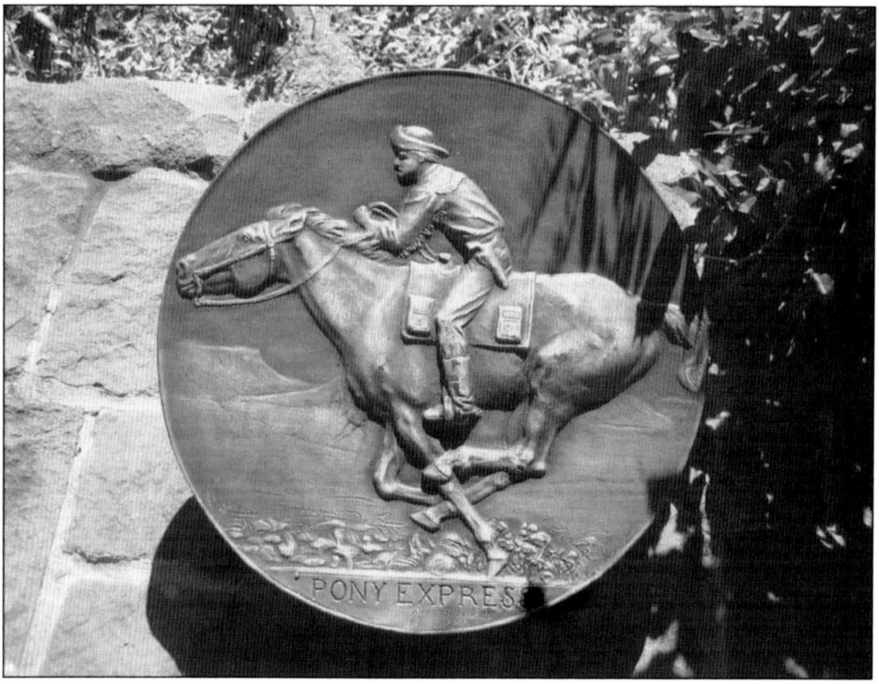

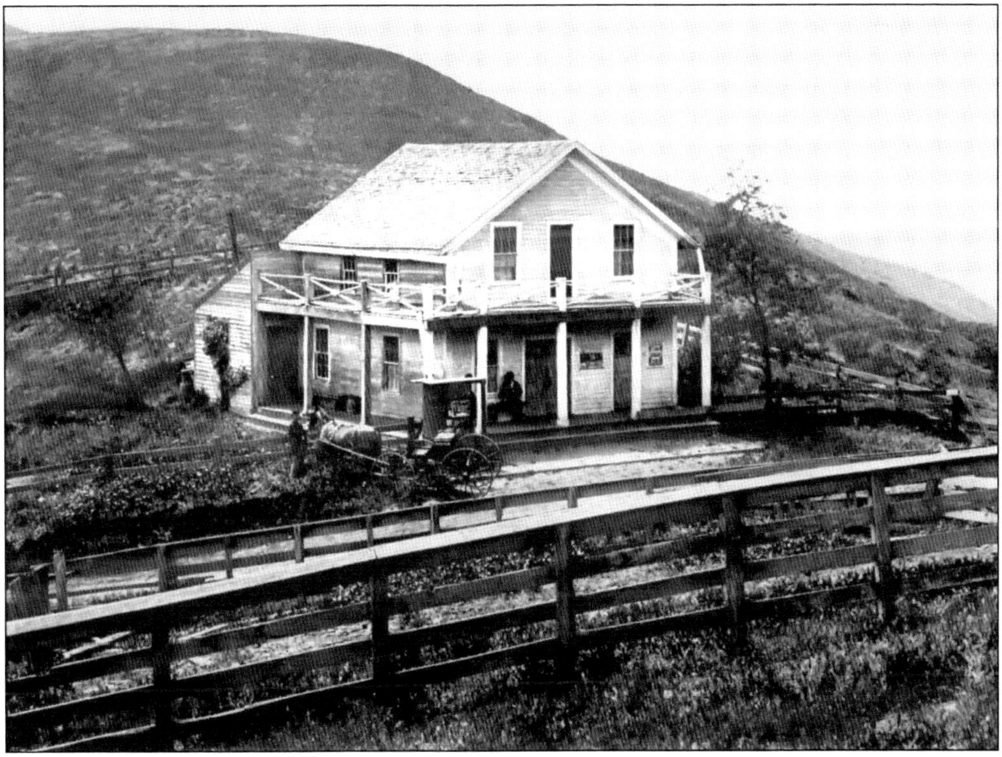

The Summit House was a stopping place that stood at the top of Fish Ranch Road in the late 1880s. Those traveling between Alameda and Contra Costa Counties would stop here to change horses, have a meal, or spend the night. Drinking and gambling were favorite activities after the arduous journey by wagon up from the east or west. Westbound travelers who came upon hay wagons going to Oakland found the dust from the wagons so thick that they wore linen dusters to protect their clothing. (Courtesy Bancroft Library, University of California.)

In the late 1880s, trips over the Berkeley hills went up Claremont Avenue to the summit. After the long climb, the downgrade to the east ended at the Oakland Trout Company, managed first by George Winslow and later by his son-in-law John Olive, where there was a small saloon, large stables, and a stage stop near the road. The property eventually became known as the Fish Ranch and the road as Fish Ranch Road. (Courtesy Bancroft Library, University of California.)

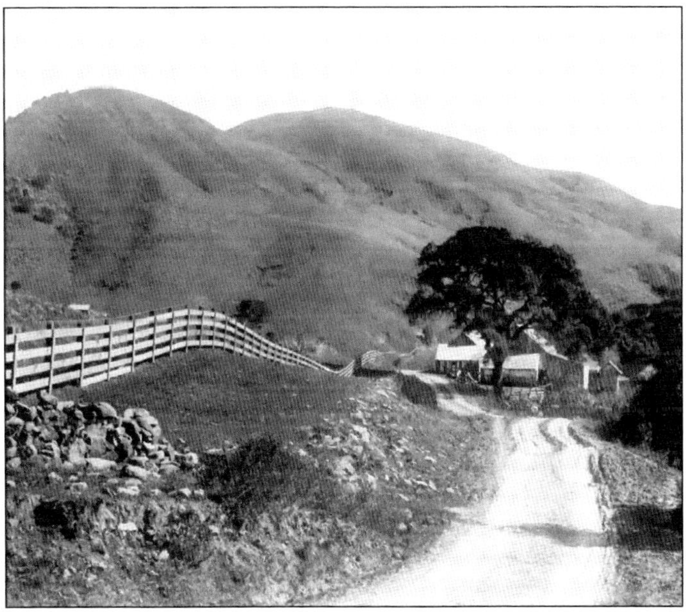

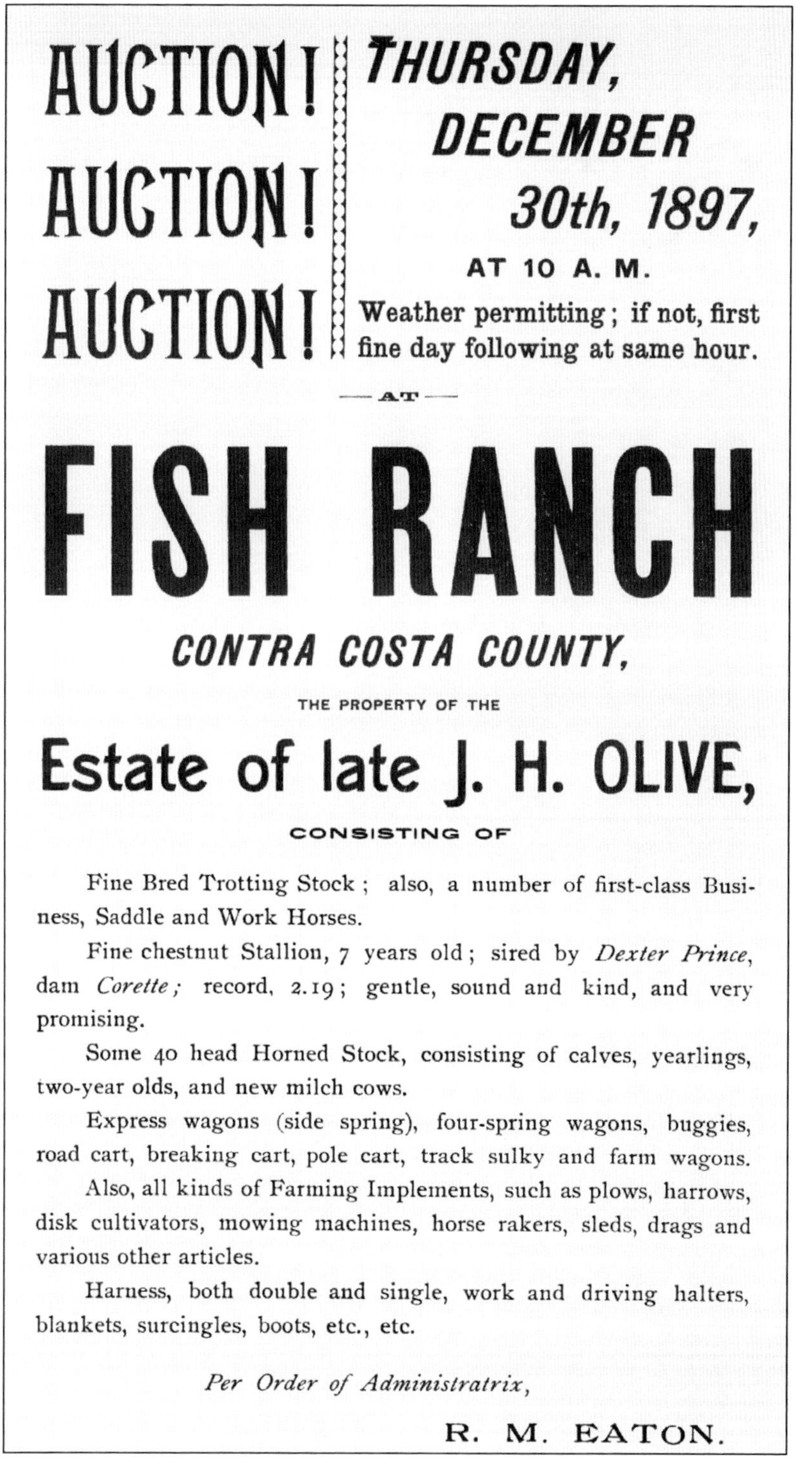

AUCTION! AUCTION! AUCTION!

THURSDAY, DECEMBER 30th, 1897,

AT 10 A. M.

Weather permitting; if not, first fine day following at same hour.

— AT —

FISH RANCH

CONTRA COSTA COUNTY,

THE PROPERTY OF THE

Estate of late J. H. OLIVE,

CONSISTING OF

Fine Bred Trotting Stock; also, a number of first-class Business, Saddle and Work Horses.

Fine chestnut Stallion, 7 years old; sired by *Dexter Prince*, dam *Corette;* record, 2.19; gentle, sound and kind, and very promising.

Some 40 head Horned Stock, consisting of calves, yearlings, two-year olds, and new milch cows.

Express wagons (side spring), four-spring wagons, buggies, road cart, breaking cart, pole cart, track sulky and farm wagons.

Also, all kinds of Farming Implements, such as plows, harrows, disk cultivators, mowing machines, horse rakers, sleds, drags and various other articles.

Harness, both double and single, work and driving halters, blankets, surcingles, boots, etc., etc.

Per Order of Administratrix,

R. M. EATON.

This 1897 poster advertises an auction of livestock, farm vehicles, and implements at the Fish Ranch. J.H. (John) Olive had managed the property. Olive was said to be an expert on horses and boarded many carriage horses for Oakland residents. (Courtesy Orinda Historical Society.)

Two

The Kennedy Tunnel

There was interest in building a tunnel between Alameda and Contra Costa Counties as early as 1860, but the idea was initially rejected by citizens of both counties. The project would be too costly, and a route could not be agreed upon, so these initial efforts to build a tunnel were abandoned.

The idea of digging a tunnel was revived in the 1890s, when money from the two counties and funding from private citizens financed a new tunnel. The route would run from the end of Broadway following the route of today's Caldecott Tunnel. The proposed tunnel would be about 500 feet long and would exit on the eastern side in the San Pablo Creek watershed with a road leading into Lafayette. A franchise was granted to a group of developers who passed the franchise on to another group. The proposal stalled until the turn of the century.

In 1903, a tunnel was built above the current location of the Caldecott Tunnel in the next canyon south of Claremont Canyon. This tunnel was approached by a new road called Tunnel Road, which started at the top of Ashby Avenue in Berkeley. The tunnel was called the Broadway Tunnel for the road that accessed it or the Kennedy Tunnel for the old toll road and the local farm near the west portal. It was located about 220 feet above the current Caldecott Tunnel and 320 feet below the summit. It was 1,040 feet long, 17 feet wide, and built with timber supports. It could barely accommodate two-way traffic.

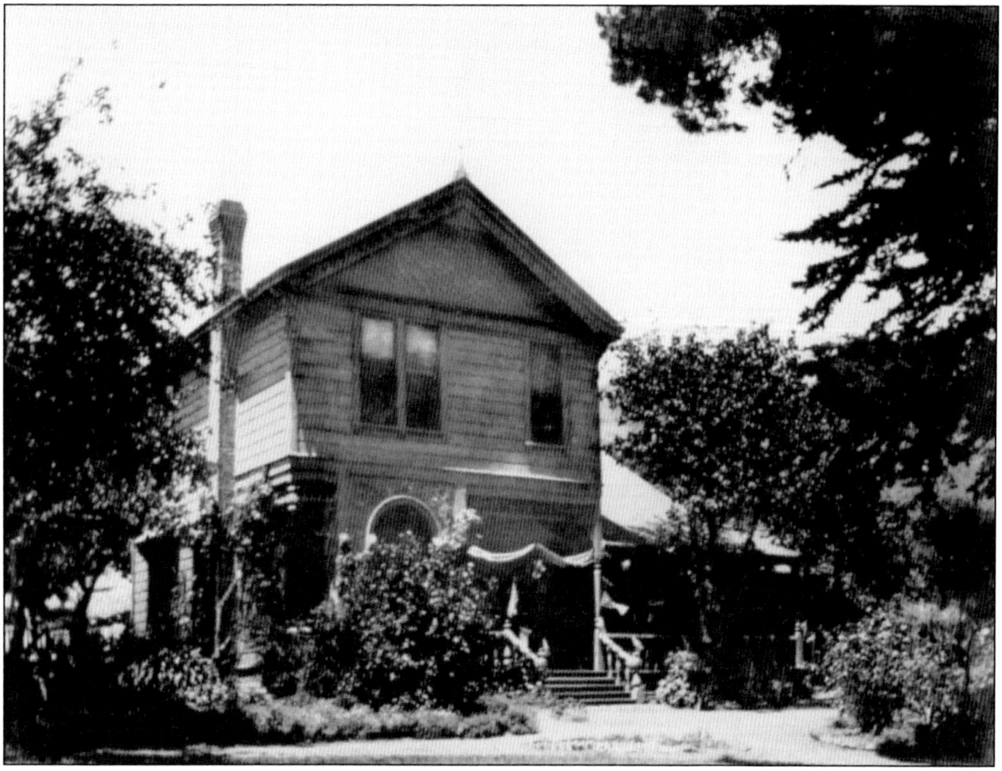

William Buckley built his first home on property near Tunnel Road on the east side of the tunnel. Representatives from both Alameda and Contra Costa Counties attended a barbecue on his property on May 23, 1897, where they sold subscriptions to fund a new tunnel. Buckley's house was torn down in 1935 to make room for the east portal of the Broadway Low Level Tunnel. In this photograph, the house is decorated for a Fourth of July celebration. (Courtesy Contra Costa County Historical Society.)

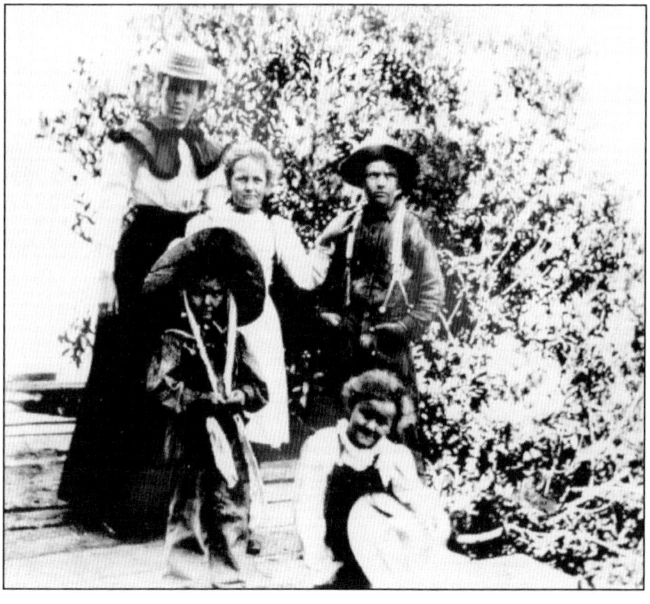

Local families—such as the McNeil family of Lafayette—set up camps at the Buckley Ranch so the men could work to construct the tunnel. Gertrude McNeil (at left in back) is said to have been the first woman to pass through the tunnel when it was just two days from completion. Some years later, she was driving a team of horses through the dark, timber-braced tunnel when a man leaped from behind a piling directly into her path. She was so startled that she made a complete U-turn and galloped back to Lafayette. (Courtesy Lafayette Historical Society.)

The cost of the tunnel construction was to be shared by Alameda and Contra Costa Counties, but a survey showed that three-fifths of the work would be located on the Contra Costa side. As law would not allow Alameda to pay for work in the other county, the project was in danger of being abandoned when the Merchant Exchange of Oakland raised the needed one fifth of the cost, $15,000, and the project resumed. Work then continued on the tunnel approach and the entrance as shown in this photograph. (Courtesy Contra Costa County Historical Society.)

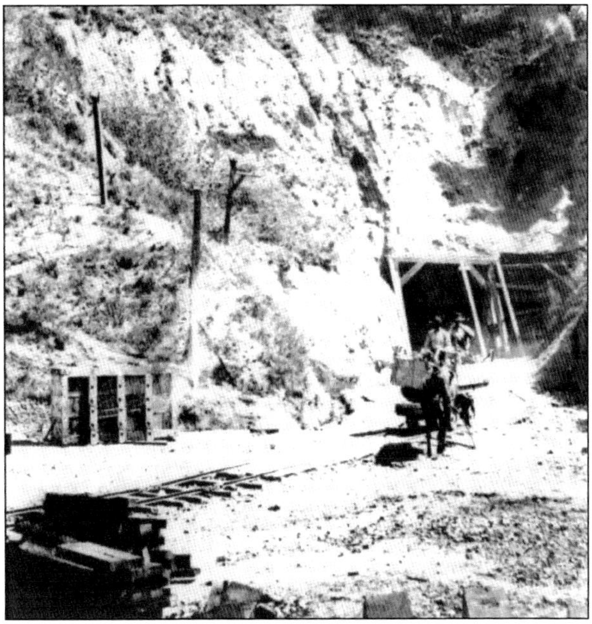

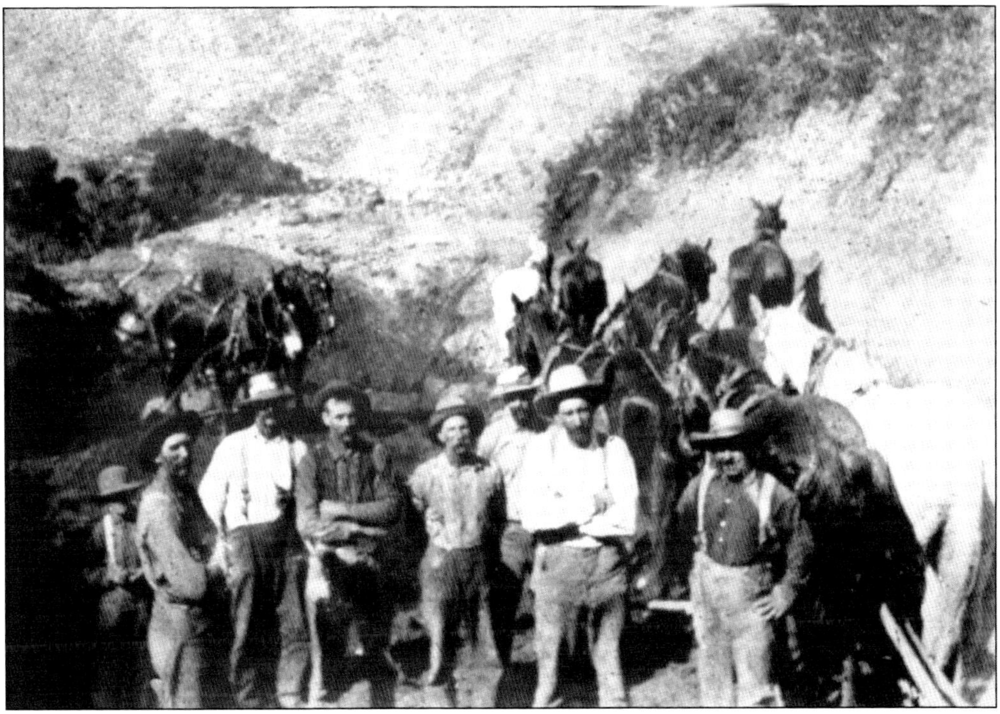

Workers, shown above, had to climb steep hills to the tunnel site, where they excavated using picks and shovels. Horses pulled carts on rails to haul out the dirt. Day laborers did the work on the Contra Costa County side; Alameda County hired a contractor to do the work. One workman commented that if the bore had been much farther up the hill, it would have been necessary to haul dirt to the spot in order to have something through which to tunnel. The tunnel on the Contra Costa side was dug at a rate of three feet per day. (Courtesy Contra Costa County Historical Society.)

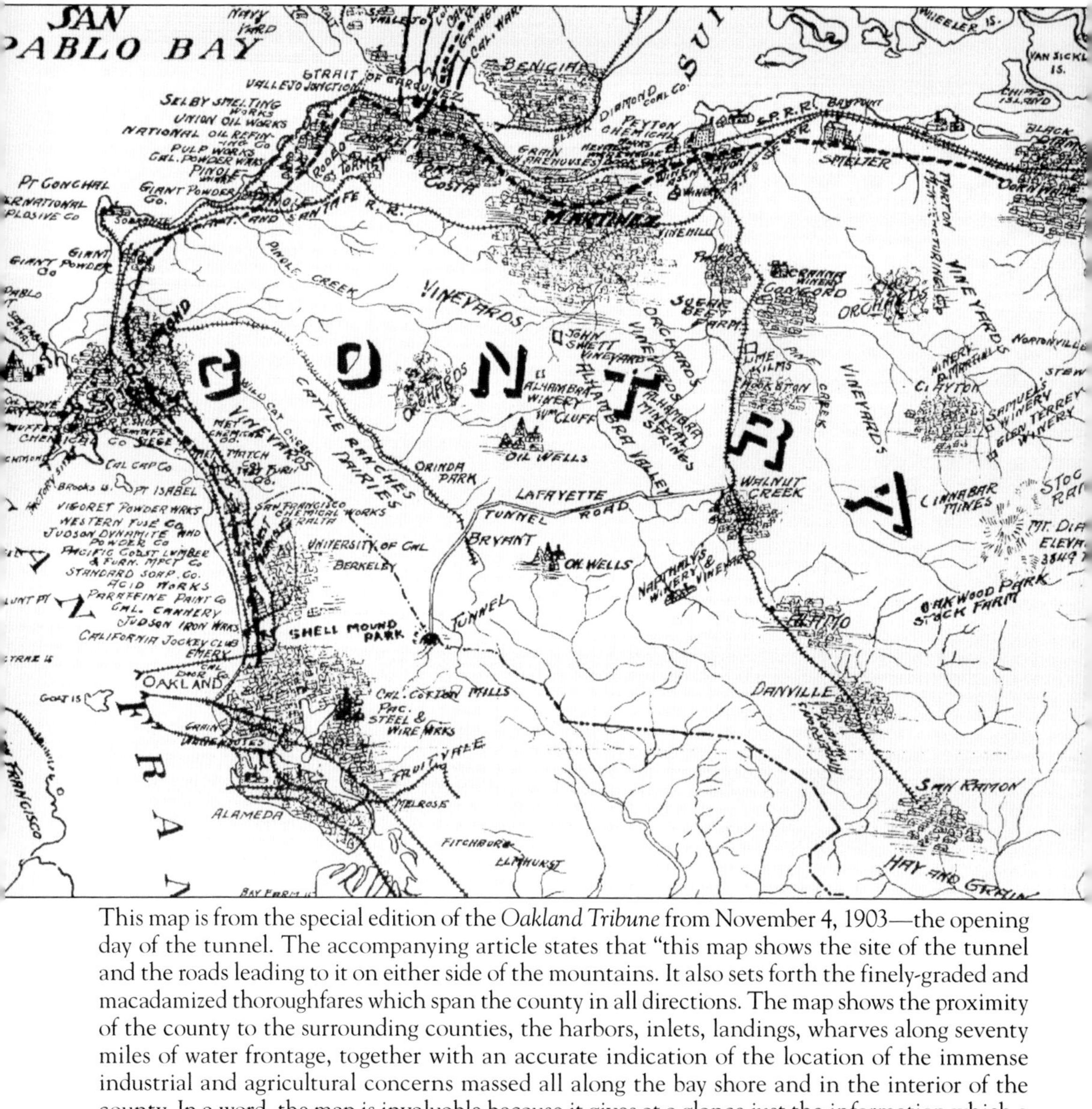

This map is from the special edition of the *Oakland Tribune* from November 4, 1903—the opening day of the tunnel. The accompanying article states that "this map shows the site of the tunnel and the roads leading to it on either side of the mountains. It also sets forth the finely-graded and macadamized thoroughfares which span the county in all directions. The map shows the proximity of the county to the surrounding counties, the harbors, inlets, landings, wharves along seventy miles of water frontage, together with an accurate indication of the location of the immense industrial and agricultural concerns massed all along the bay shore and in the interior of the county. In a word, the map is invaluable because it gives at a glance just the information which a practical man will want of the great County of Contra Costa." (Courtesy *Oakland Tribune*.)

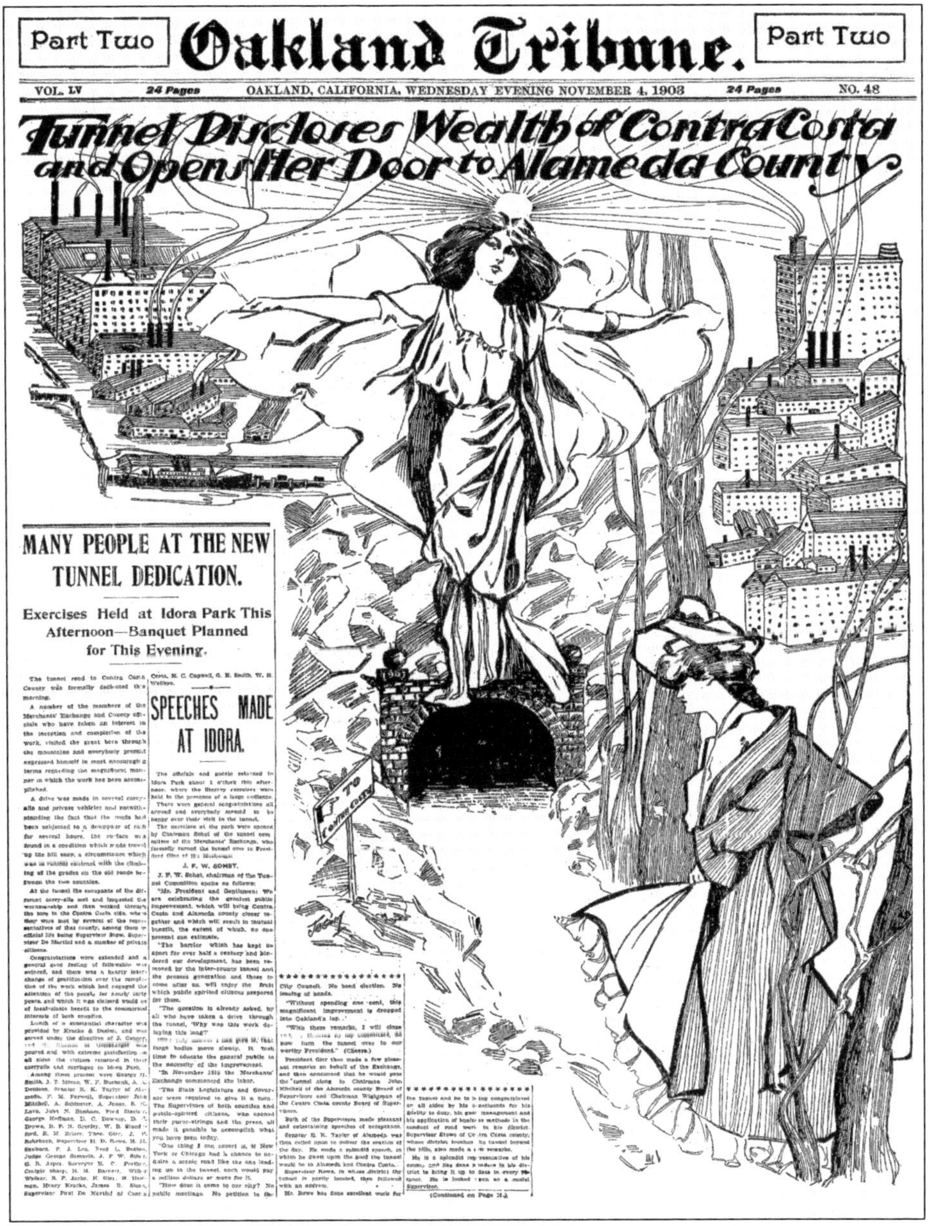

Part Two **Oakland Tribune.** Part Two

VOL. LV 24 Pages OAKLAND, CALIFORNIA, WEDNESDAY EVENING NOVEMBER 4, 1903 24 Pages NO. 48

Tunnel Discloses Wealth of Contra Costa and Opens Her Door to Alameda County

MANY PEOPLE AT THE NEW TUNNEL DEDICATION.

Exercises Held at Idora Park This Afternoon—Banquet Planned for This Evening.

SPEECHES MADE AT IDORA.

J. F. W. SOHST.

The second part of the *Oakland Tribune*'s November 4, 1903, edition included illustrations and information on the new tunnel. The dedication exercises were held at Idora Park, a 17.5-acre trolley park in North Oakland built on the north banks of the Temescal Creek. The paper reported that "a number of members of the Merchant's Exchange and County officials who have taken an interest in the inception and completion of the work, united the great bore through the mountain and everybody present expressed himself in most encouraging terms regarding the magnificent manner in which the work has been accomplished. A drive was made in several carry-alls and private vehicles and notwithstanding the fact that the roads had been subjected to a downpour for several hours, the surface was found in a condition which made travel up the hill easy, a circumstance which was in radical contrast with the climbing of the grades on the old roads between the two counties." (Courtesy *Oakland Tribune*.)

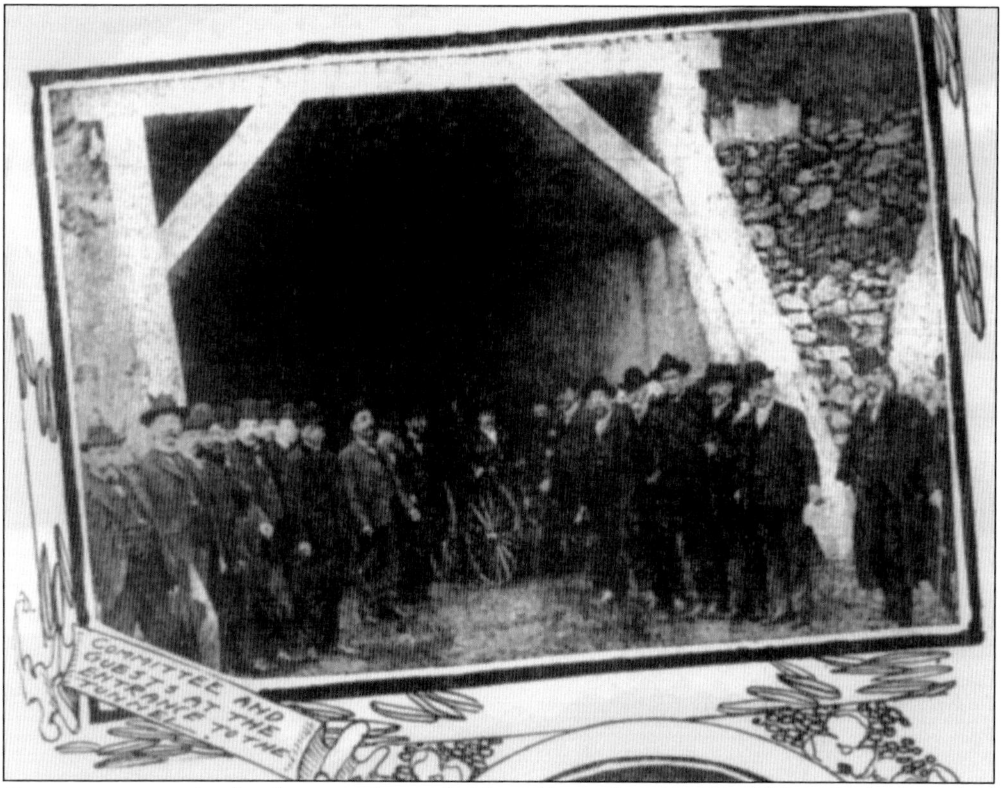

Opening ceremonies for the tunnel were held on November 4, 1903. Although the bore had been completed, the tunnel was unpaved, unlit, and prone to mudslides. J.F.W. Sohst, chairman of the Tunnel Committee, commented to the *Oakland Tribune* that "the barrier which has kept us apart for over half a century and hindered our development has been removed by the inter-county tunnel." (Courtesy *Oakland Tribune.*)

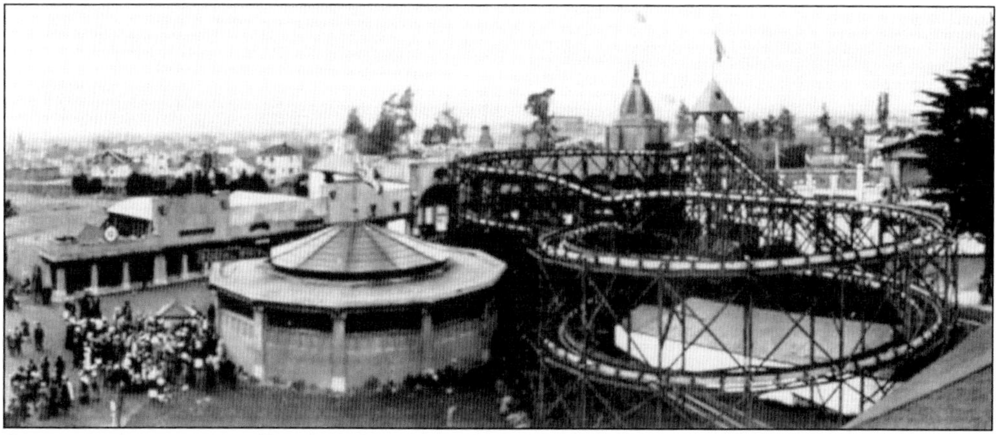

On November 4, 1903, officials and guests gathered at 1:00 p.m. in Idora Park to witness literary exercises held in the presence of a large audience. The exercises at the park were opened by J.F.W. Sohst, chairman of the Tunnel Committee of the Merchant's Exchange, who, after some remarks, turned the tunnel over to John Mitchell, chairman of the Alameda County Board of Supervisors, and J.A. Wightman, chairman of the Contra Costa County Board of Supervisors. (Courtesy Oakland Public Library History Room.)

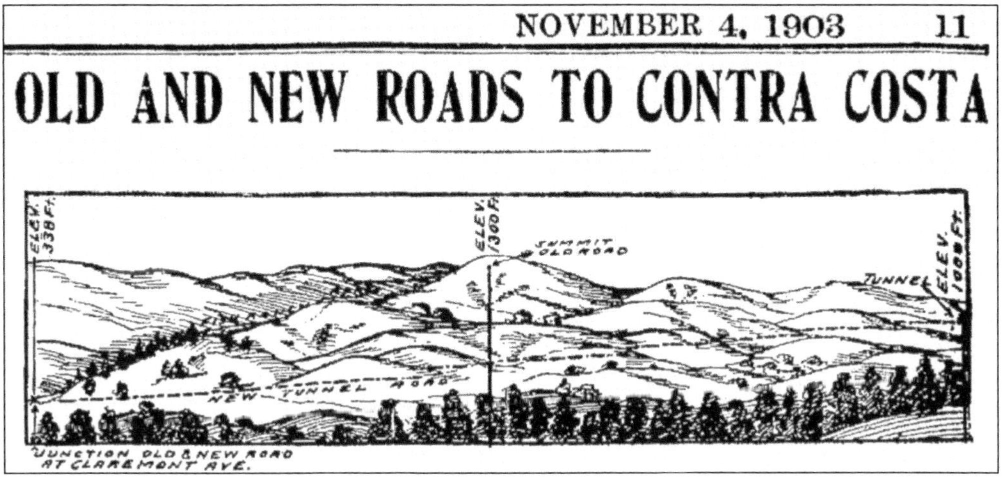
NOVEMBER 4, 1903 11

OLD AND NEW ROADS TO CONTRA COSTA

This graphic printed in the *Oakland Tribune* on the opening day of the tunnel shows a topographical drawing made by county surveyor Edward Prather that includes both the old road to Contra Costa County and the new tunnel. The caption stated: "the new road saves individuals and horses a climb to the summit of 320 feet, a distance which is ten feet greater than the height of the Call Building in San Francisco." (Courtesy *Oakland Tribune*.)

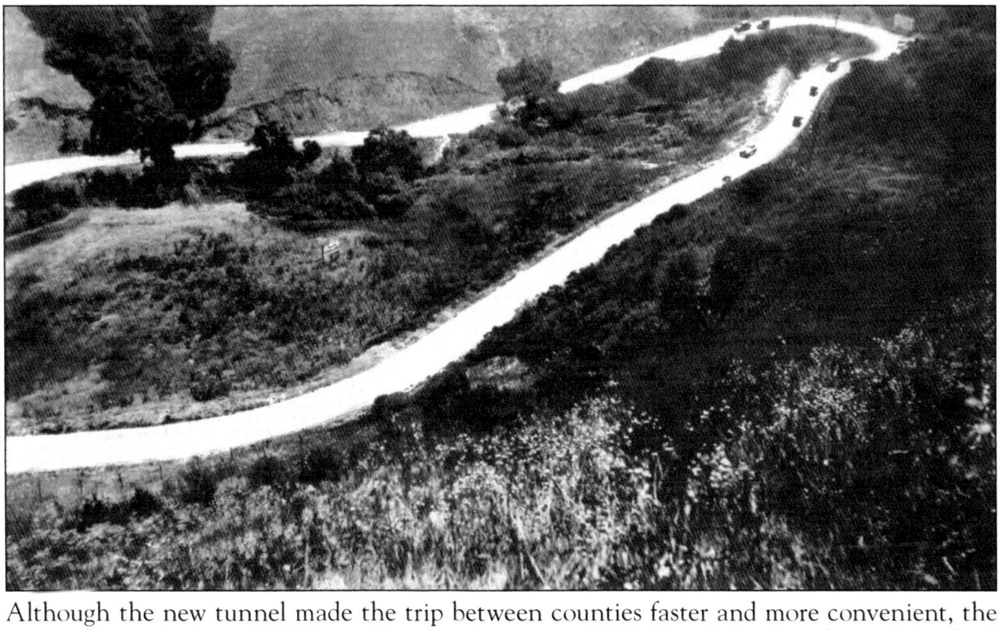

Although the new tunnel made the trip between counties faster and more convenient, the approaches to the bore (Old Tunnel Road to the west and Fish Ranch Road to the east) involved steep roads with many hairpin turns and dangerous cliffs, making the route difficult for four- and six-horse teams. The eastern approach to the Kennedy Tunnel is shown in this 1925 photograph. (Courtesy Contra Costa County Historical Society.)

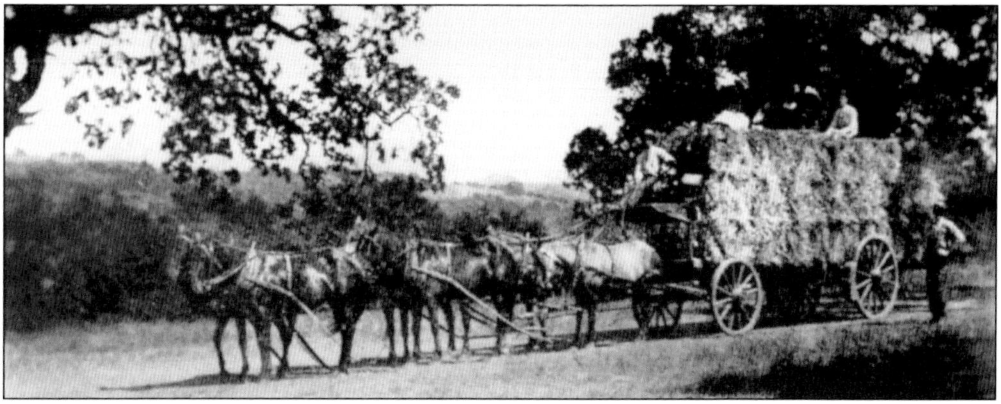

Large hay wagons, which could carry as much as two tons of hay, were sometimes too tall or wide for two-way traffic traveling through the tunnel. Drivers on either side would light rolled-up newspapers or hold up lanterns to signal drivers on the other side to wait for them to pass through. After a road slide on the western approach in the winter of 1912, the tunnel was closed for six months. While waiting for the road to be repaired, the tunnel was excavated two feet lower and was reopened in June of that year. (Courtesy Contra Costa County Historical Society.)

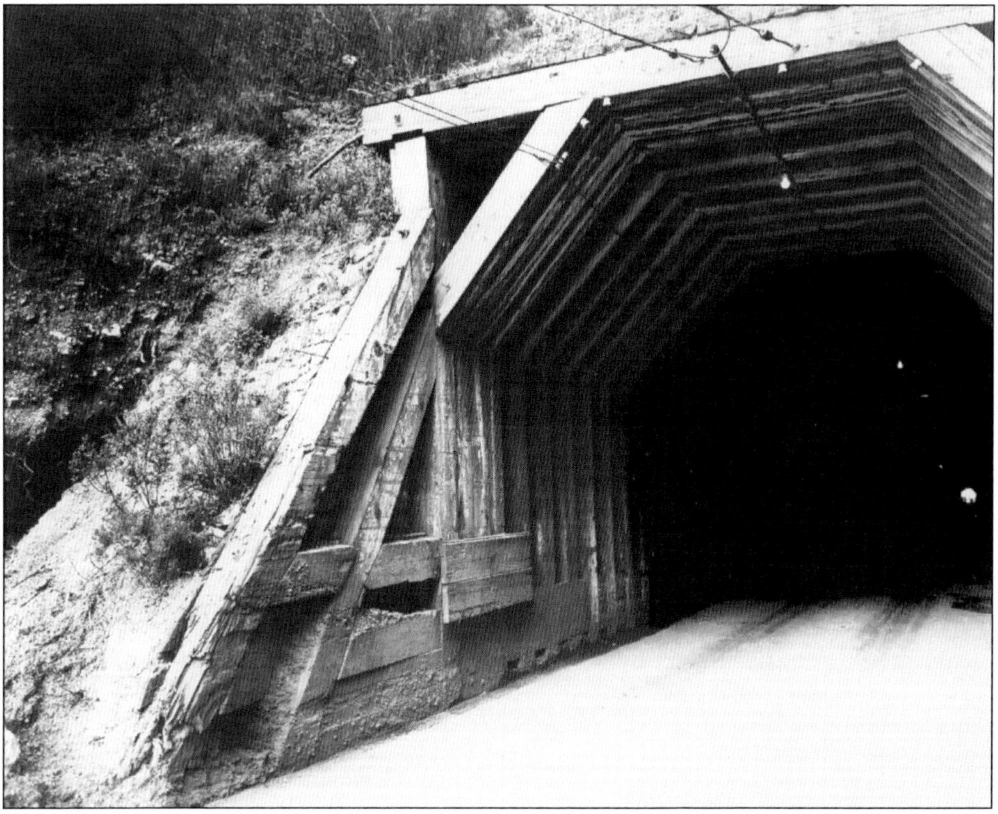

The west portal of the Kennedy Tunnel is shown in this 1920s photograph. The tunnel was originally very dark inside, and the roads leading into it were prone to mudslides. In 1914, electricity became available and lights were installed in the tunnel, while light poles were added outside. Workers changed light bulbs by standing atop hay wagons as they traveled through the tunnel. (Courtesy California Department of Transportation.)

Construction of the Kennedy Tunnel did not solve all the transportation issues in the area. Slides inside the tunnel—often a result of winter rainstorms—would force the closure of the tunnel until the slides were cleared and the tunnel shored up again. In this image, a man points to a dark spot on the ceiling of the tunnel where timbers fell after they had been weakened by years of water damage. (Courtesy *Oakland Tribune*.)

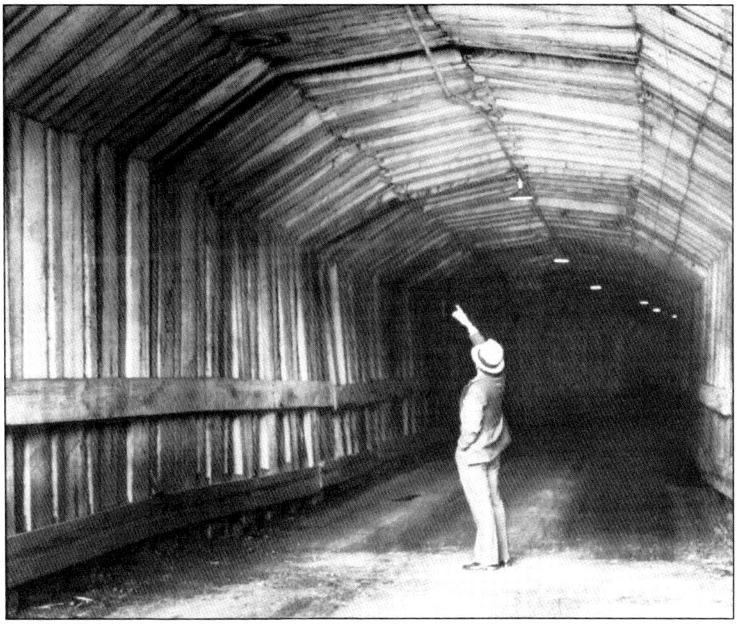

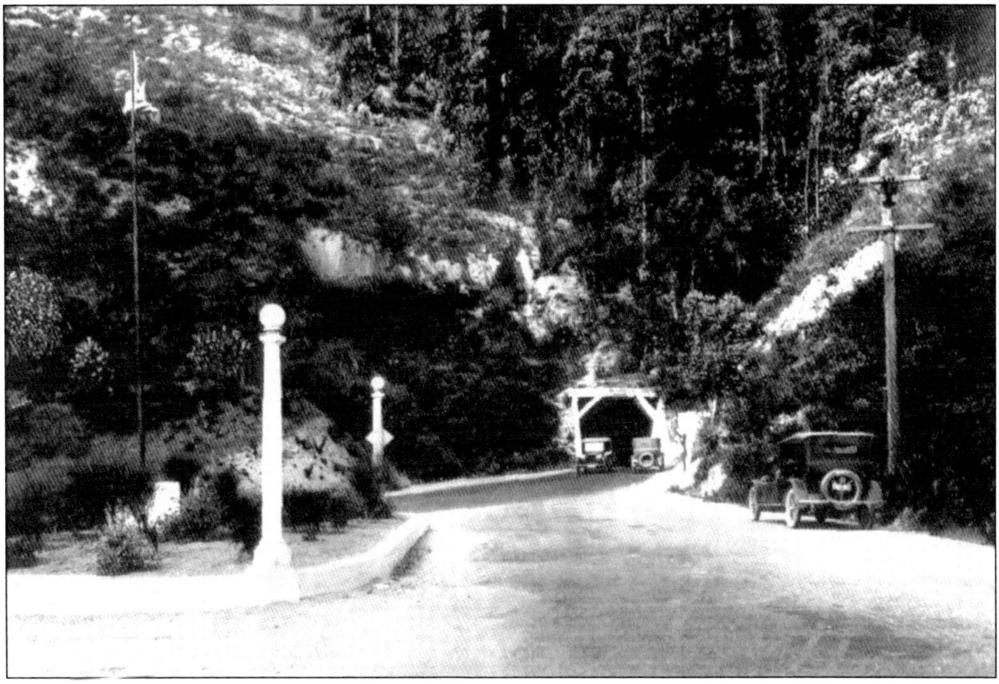

There was a $300 surplus from the money raised by subscriptions for the construction of the tunnel. W.A. Knowles, who safeguarded the money that had been raised, blocked all attempts to spend it on anything else, so the money sat in a trust fund for 30 years and grew to $900. The money was used to purchase a triangular plot of ground in front of the Oakland portal upon which a flagpole was erected. (Courtesy Lafayette Historical Society.)

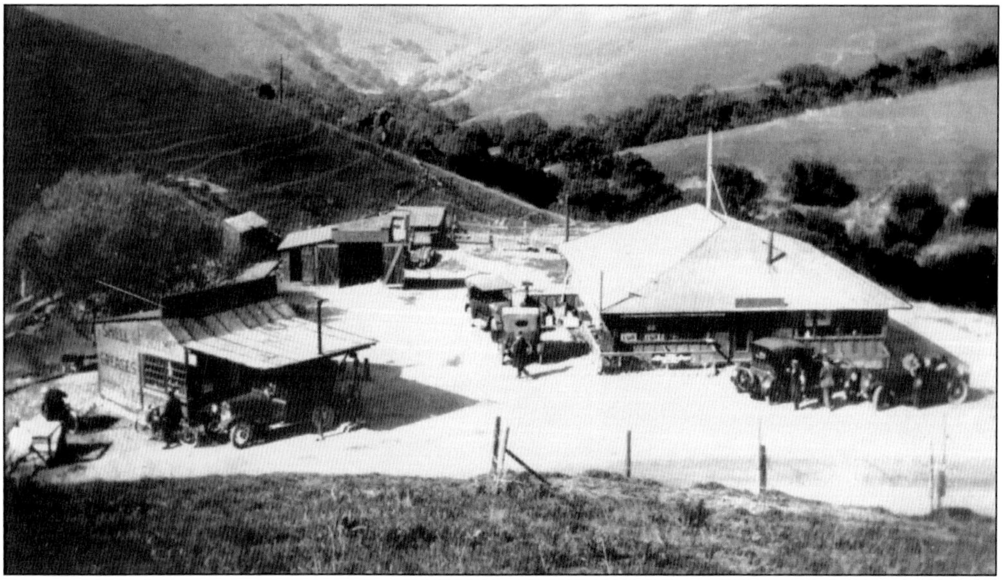

Canary Cottage, located on Henry Buckley's property near the east portal of the tunnel, provided a place to stop for food and fuel. When Frank Enos purchased the property in 1918, he convinced the Shell Oil Company to paint the buildings yellow when it was repainting the gas pumps, giving the place its nickname. (Courtesy Contra Costa County Historical Society.)

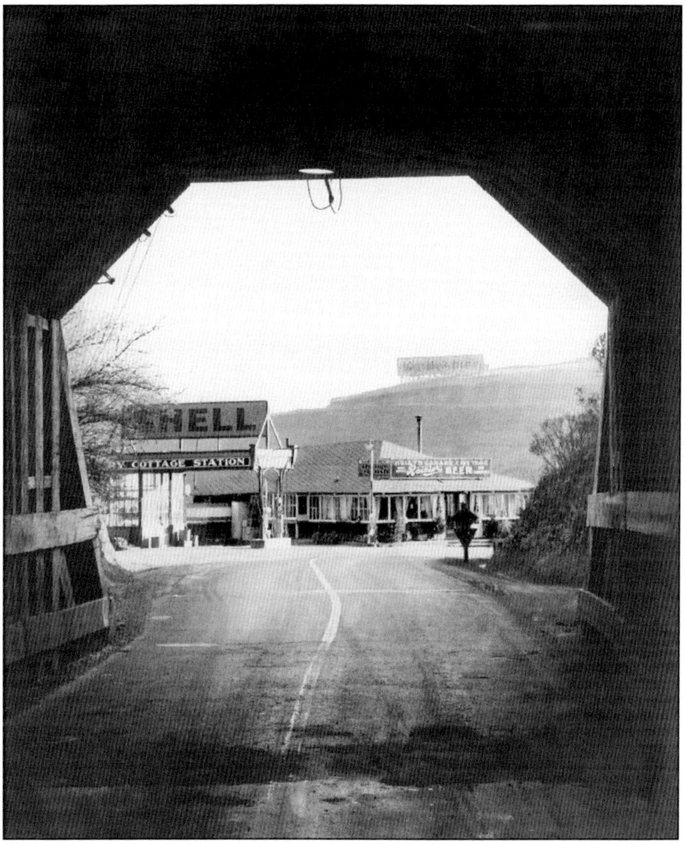

After the installation of electric lights in the tunnel in 1914, Frank Enos made a deal with the power company and tended the lights in the tunnel in exchange for lights at the Canary Cottage. The walls of the tunnel were initially whitewashed for improved visibility. This photograph of Canary Cottage was taken from inside the Kennedy Tunnel when it was closed for repairs after support timbers fell inside the tunnel in May 1934. (Courtesy *Oakland Tribune*.)

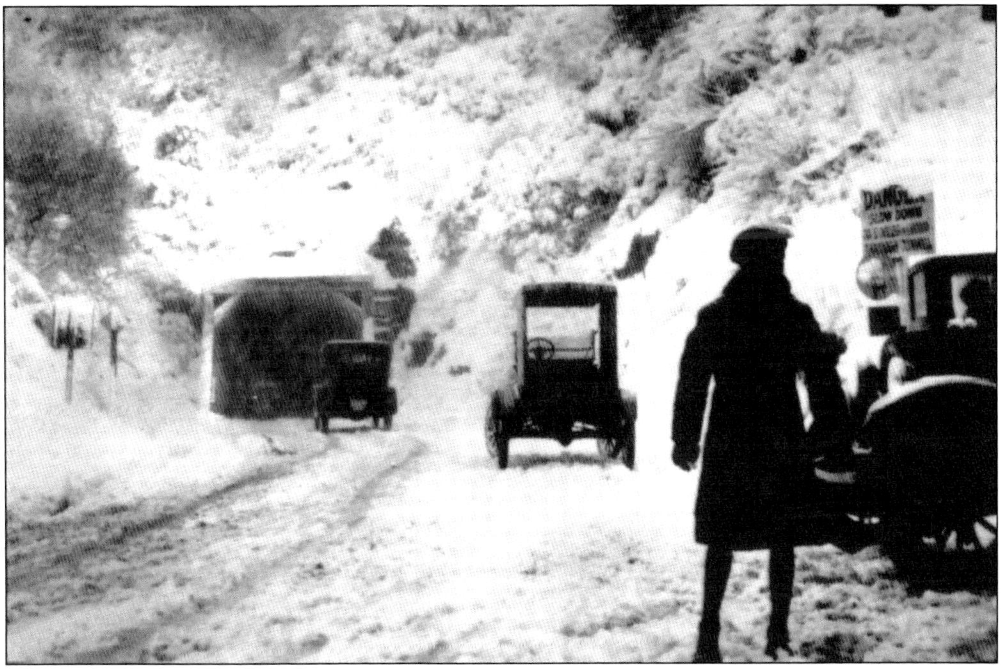

In January 1922, a sizeable snowstorm made travel difficult on the roads approaching the tunnel. Irene Bunker, in a Lafayette Historical Society oral history, remembered that "in wintertime there was quite a heavy rainstorm, then it turned cold and froze and we had icicles all the way through that tunnel the size of people's arms hanging down quite low in the tunnel. It took two and a half hours to go into Oakland." (Courtesy Contra Costa Historical Society.)

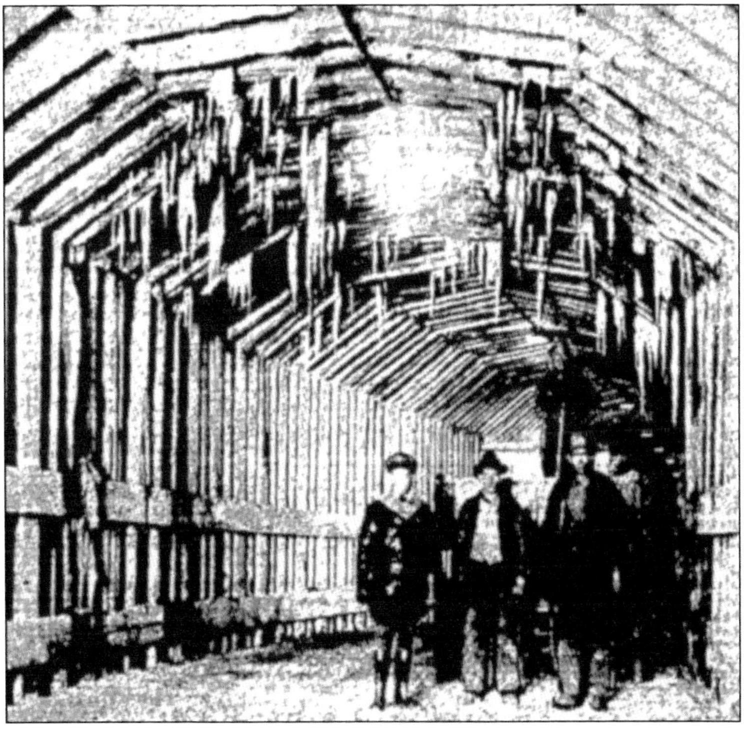

In this February 1929 photograph, huge icicles are shown hanging from the roof of the Kennedy Tunnel. Thousands of motorists were astonished by the three- and four-foot icicles created via seepage from the roof. Many people broke them off and brought them into Oakland to display. (Courtesy *Oakland Tribune*.)

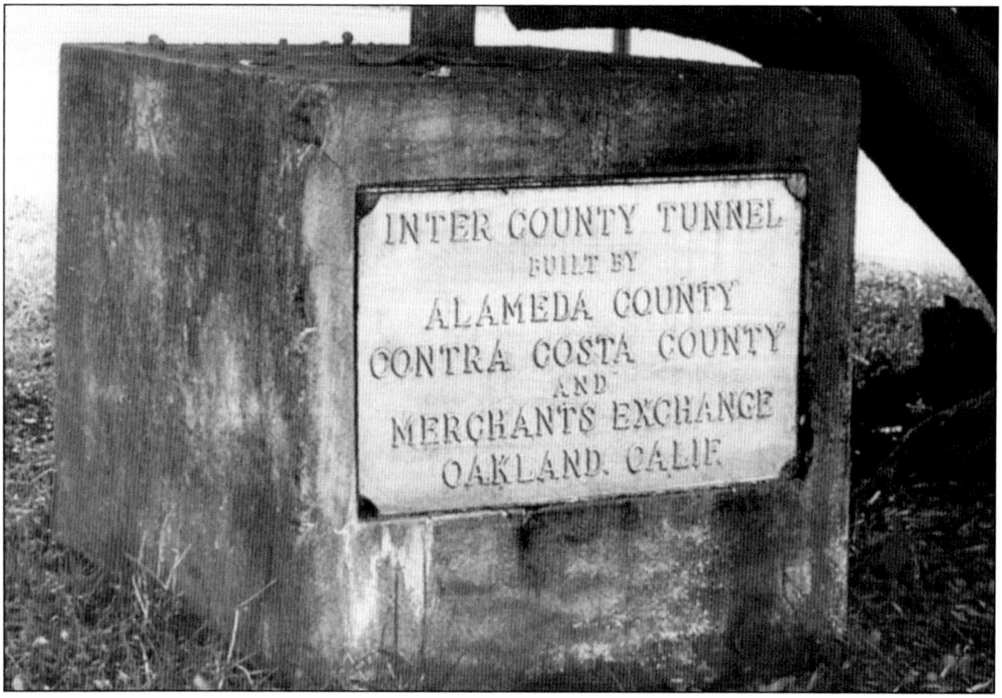

This original marker for the Kennedy Tunnel was located near the west portal. By the early 1930s, more than 4,000 vehicles traveled through the narrow tunnel each day on a faster and safer route between Alameda and Contra Costa Counties that offered easier access to San Francisco. (Courtesy Brian Smith, www.caltrafficsigns.com.)

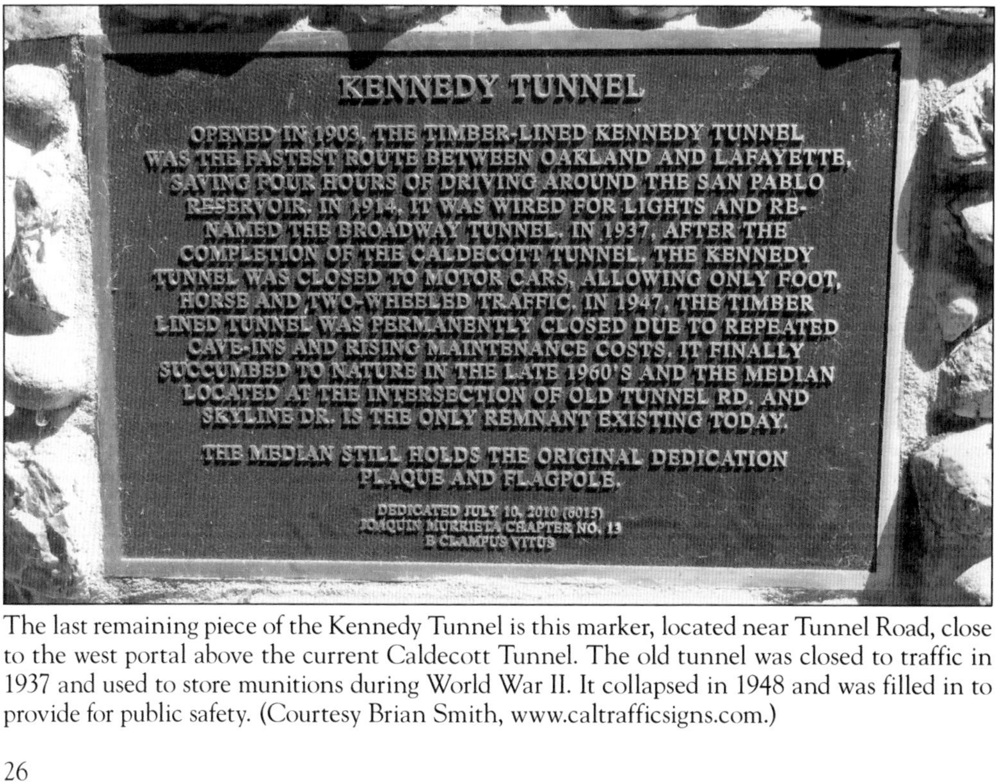

The last remaining piece of the Kennedy Tunnel is this marker, located near Tunnel Road, close to the west portal above the current Caldecott Tunnel. The old tunnel was closed to traffic in 1937 and used to store munitions during World War II. It collapsed in 1948 and was filled in to provide for public safety. (Courtesy Brian Smith, www.caltrafficsigns.com.)

Three

The Broadway Low Level Tunnel

By the mid-1920s, the Kennedy Tunnel had improved access between Alameda and Contra Costa Counties, but travel was difficult due to the tunnel's steep approaches and narrow width. In 1926, Alameda County, Contra Costa County, and the City of Oakland formed a joint commission to study the idea of moving the tunnel to a lower elevation. By 1929, the two counties had organized Joint Highway District No. 13 to build the Broadway Low Level Tunnel.

Several individuals were important in organizing the joint highway district: Thomas Caldecott, Alameda County supervisor and president of Joint Highway District No. 13; George Addison Posey, county surveyor in Alameda County and chief engineer for Joint Highway District No. 13, who is best remembered for designing the tunnel between Oakland and Alameda that bears his name; and Henry H. Meyers, Alameda County architect. When Posey died in 1932, Wallace B. Boggs, one of Posey's assistants, took over the final design responsibilities and supervised construction.

The original approaches to the tunnel were to extend from Broadway at its intersection with Keith Avenue in Oakland to Walnut Creek in Contra Costa County. In 1931, the district decided not to build the Contra Costa approach, but it still had to design and build 2.82 miles of roadway, .6 miles of which was in the tunnel. The project cost $3.75 million—$1.1 million came from a grant from the federal Public Works Administration, $700,000 from state gasoline tax money, and the remaining amount from local sources.

The successful construction bid came from Six Companies of California, which began construction in late 1934 but was unable to complete the project in a timely manner. With 68 percent of the work completed, the job was advertised again, and the George Pollock Company successfully won the bid to complete the tunnel lining, along with six smaller contracts for paving the road, building the ceiling for the tunnel, installing ventilation and electrical systems, and finishing the detail work on the portal buildings.

The tunnel formally opened and was turned over to the California Division of Highways on November 13, 1937. Its completion coincided with the opening of the San Francisco–Oakland Bay Bridge, which provided a more direct and convenient commute by automobile from Contra Costa County to Oakland and San Francisco.

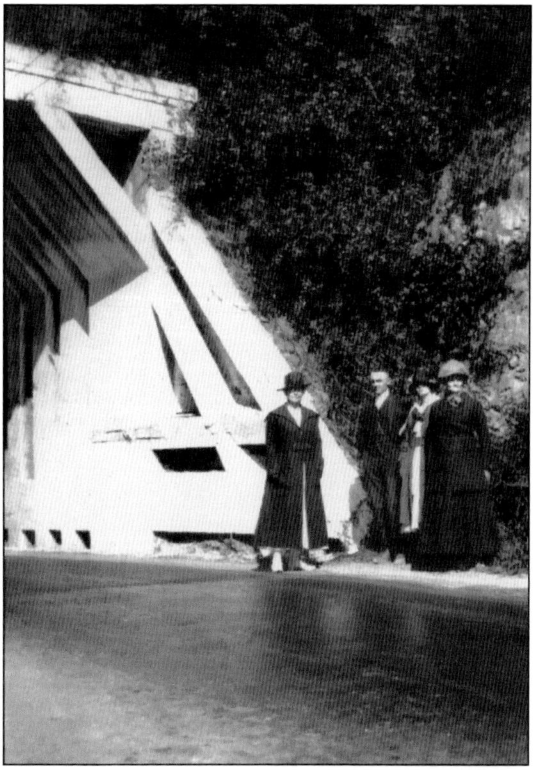

In the early 1920s, there was discussion about building another tunnel to connect Alameda and Contra Costa Counties. The Kennedy Tunnel and the roads leading to it were often impassable in inclement weather due to snow, mudslides, and water, as shown in the lower photograph. In September 1928, 28,000 automobiles per week used Tunnel Road to enter the Kennedy Tunnel. People often left their automobiles to pose for a photograph near the tunnel portals. Options were suggested for the site of a new tunnel: a toll road through Shepherd Canyon along Park Boulevard to Moraga Valley; a tunnel at the eastern end of Thirty-fifth Avenue near Lyona Heights; a low-level tunnel near the Claremont Hotel; and a new low-level tunnel under the current Tunnel Road. In October 1925, a committee was named by Contra Costa and Alameda Counties to study the various proposals. (Left, courtesy Lafayette Historical Society; below, courtesy Contra Costa County Historical Society.)

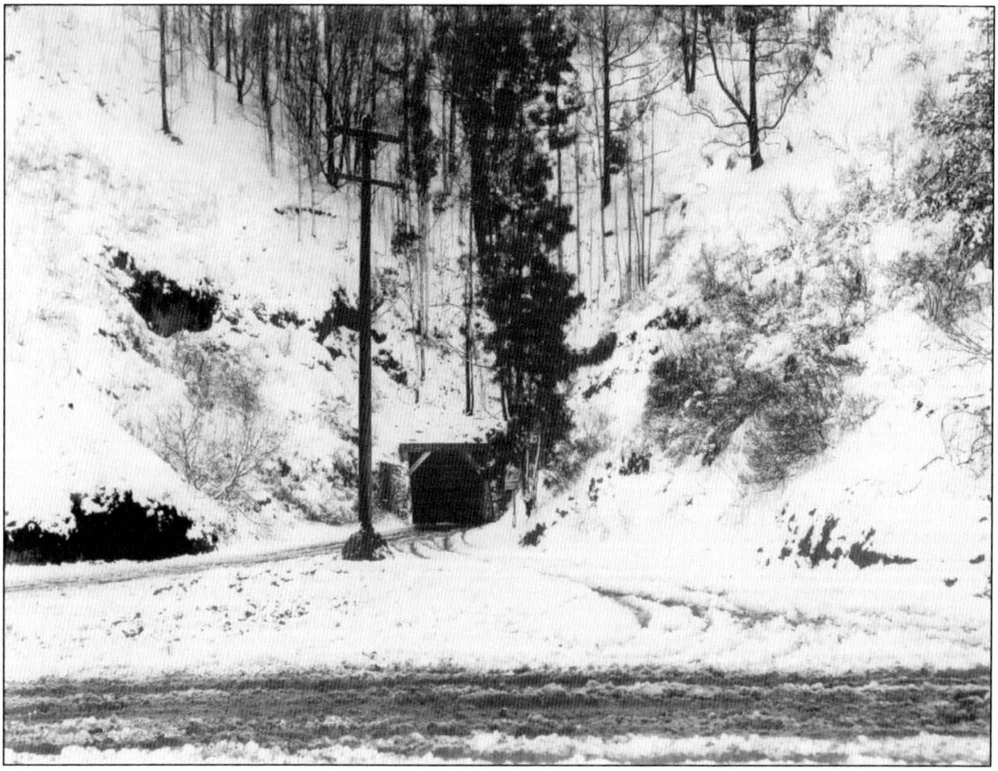

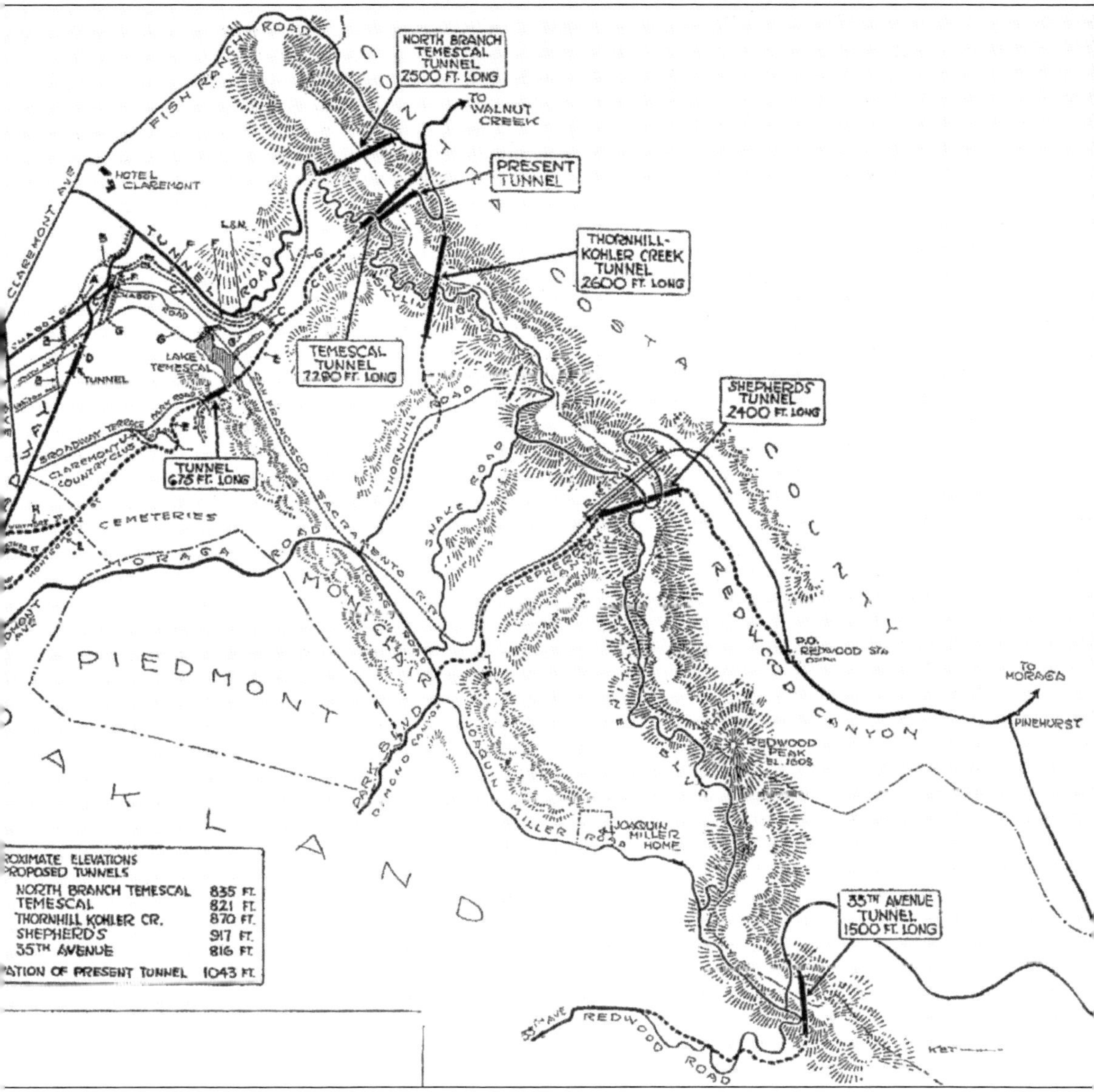

By June 1928, as shown on this map, the Joint Tunnel Engineering Commission of Alameda and Contra Costa Counties had narrowed the choice of new tunnel sites to two: the Temescal Creek route near the Kennedy Tunnel and the Shepherd Canyon toll route along Park Boulevard to Moraga Valley. East of the tunnel site, either of the tunnels would provide an outlet northerly and easterly to Contra Costa County leading to Walnut Creek. West of the tunnels to Alameda County, they would lead into Oakland over widely different routes. The tunnel was to be included in the transcontinental Victory Highway system, a road dedicated to US forces that died in World War I. Other proposed routes and tunnel sites were rejected because of excessive grades and the prohibitive lengths of tunnels. In all estimates of cost, the tunnel commission presented estimates for single and double bores and recommended that rights of way be obtained for a double bore at whatever sites were agreed upon in anticipation of future traffic demands. At the time, the commission made no recommendation favoring one route over another. (Courtesy *Oakland Tribune*.)

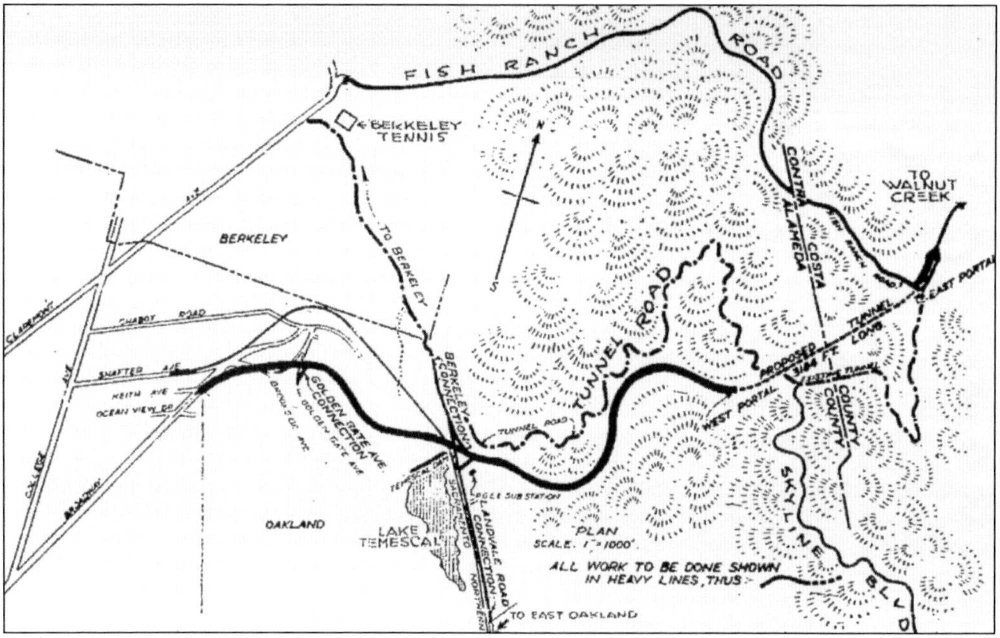

In November 1931, the directors of Joint Highway District No. 13 submitted plans for the Temescal Creek route to the boards of supervisors of the two counties and to the state director of public works with a recommendation that work be started immediately on the project (with an estimated cost of $4,487,060). This map shows the route of the tunnel and the approaching highways, which were designed to offer direct approaches from East Oakland and Berkeley—as well as the downtown area—at easy grades and with few curves. (Courtesy *Oakland Tribune*.)

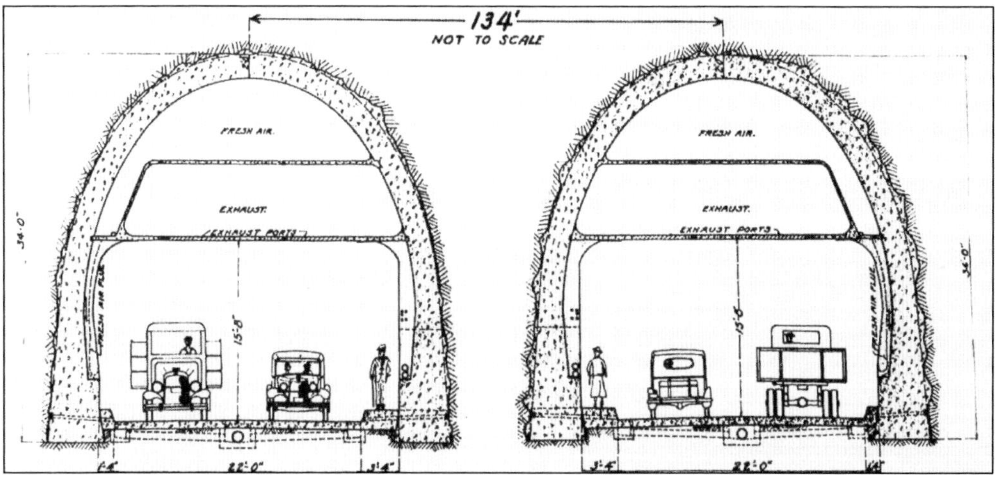

On the recommendation of Charles Derluth Jr., a civil and consulting engineer at the University of California, Berkeley, the proposed tunnel would consist of twin horseshoe-shaped bores that each provided two lanes, which met the requirements for ventilation equipment, and which provided an arch that would best fit the lines of stress. The floor slab, properly designed and reinforced, would act as a strut or tie between the side walls of the tunnel. The bores would provide four traffic lanes and a sidewalk and would be located 220 feet lower than the existing Kennedy Tunnel. (Courtesy Oakland Public Library History Room.)

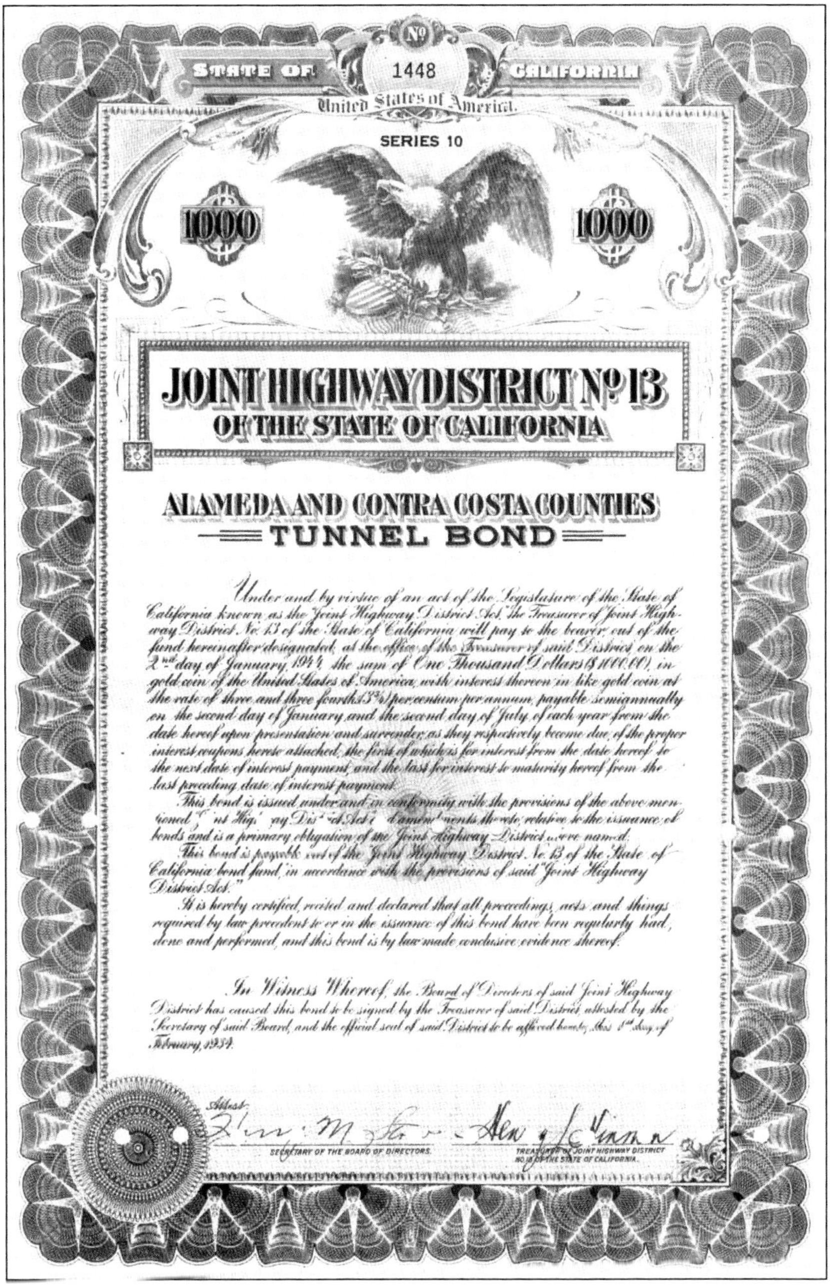
No 1448
STATE OF CALIFORNIA
United States of America.
SERIES 10
1000 1000

JOINT HIGHWAY DISTRICT No 13
OF THE STATE OF CALIFORNIA

ALAMEDA AND CONTRA COSTA COUNTIES
TUNNEL BOND

Under and by virtue of an act of the Legislature of the State of California known as the Joint Highway District Act, the Treasurer of Joint Highway District No. 13 of the State of California will pay to the bearer, out of the fund hereinafter designated, at the office of the Treasurer of said District on the 2nd day of January, 1944 the sum of One Thousand Dollars ($1000.00) in gold coin of the United States of America, with interest thereon in like gold coin at the rate of three and three fourths (3¾) per centum per annum, payable semiannually on the second day of January and the second day of July of each year from the date hereof upon presentation and surrender, as they respectively become due, of the proper interest coupons hereto attached, the first of which is for interest from the date hereof to the next date of interest payment, and the last for interest to maturity hereof from the last preceding date of interest payment.

This bond is issued under and in conformity with the provisions of the above mentioned "Joint Highway District Act" and amendments thereto relative to the issuance of bonds and is a primary obligation of the Joint Highway District above named.

This bond is payable out of the Joint Highway District No. 13 of the State of California bond fund, in accordance with the provisions of said "Joint Highway District Act."

It is hereby certified, recited and declared that all proceedings, acts and things required by law precedent to or in the issuance of this bond have been regularly had, done and performed, and this bond is by law made conclusive evidence thereof.

In Witness Whereof, the Board of Directors of said Joint Highway District has caused this bond to be signed by the Treasurer of said District, attested by the Secretary of said Board, and the official seal of said District to be affixed hereto, this 1st day of February, 1934.

Attest:
SECRETARY OF THE BOARD OF DIRECTORS.
TREASURER OF JOINT HIGHWAY DISTRICT NO. 13 OF THE STATE OF CALIFORNIA.

The Broadway Low Level Tunnel was initially financed by a bond issue of Joint Highway District No. 13 in the amount of $2,378,000 to be paid in allotments from the gas tax money allocated to Alameda and Contra Costa Counties. Alameda County was to pay 90 percent of this amount and Contra Costa 10 percent. Subsequently, the state made a grant of $300,000 to Joint Highway District No. 13, and, later, an additional $400,000 paid in installments over a term of years. With the organization of the Public Works Administration (PWA) came a grant of $1,950,000 for the tunnel project. The tunnel was one of the first major projects in the west to receive such aid, although civic leaders declared that the project would have been completed even without state and federal funds. (Courtesy Brian Smith, www.caltrafficsigns.com.)

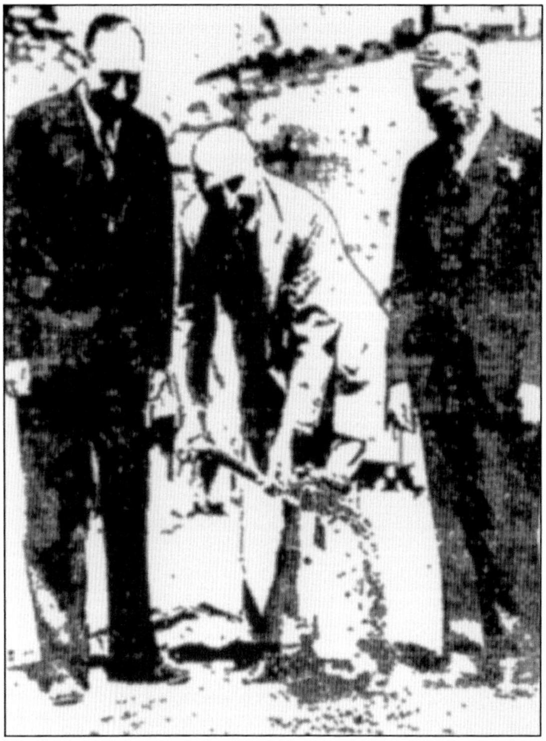

Ground-breaking ceremonies for the new low-level tunnel were held on June 17, 1934. A crowd, estimated at 6,500, saw Gov. Frank F. Merriam (center), assisted by Earl Lee Kelley (left), state director of public works, and Alameda County supervisor Thomas E. Caldecott (right), chairman of Joint Highway District No. 13, turn the first earth with a silver spade to formally launch work on the project. Before the ceremony, which was held near the western portal of the tunnel, was a luncheon at the Hotel Claremont for 300 civic and business leaders and public officials. The ground-breaking activities included aerial stunts, skywriting, music by three bands, a cross-country race, and a drum and bugle presentation. Speeches followed the ceremony. Although Pres. Franklin D. Roosevelt's name was listed in the program as a guest of honor, he was not in attendance. (Left, courtesy *Oakland Tribune*; below, courtesy Orinda Historical Society.)

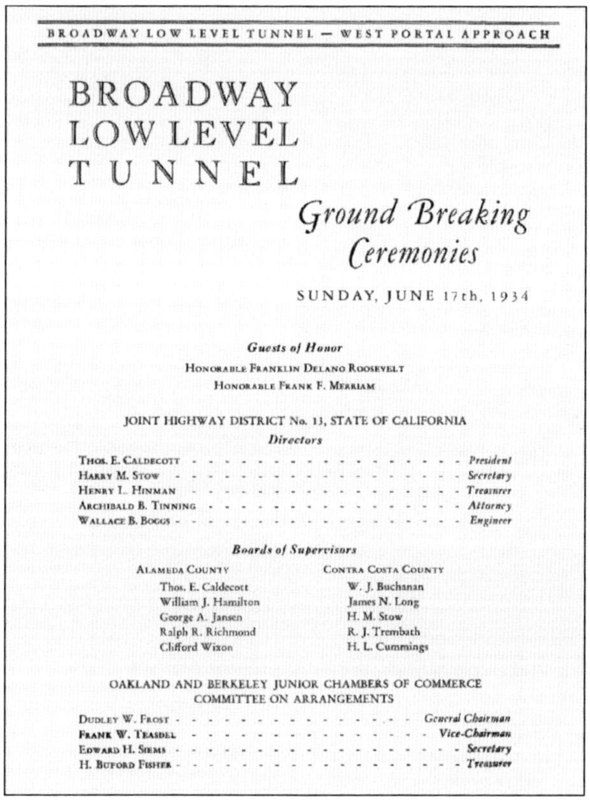

BROADWAY LOW LEVEL TUNNEL — WEST PORTAL APPROACH

BROADWAY
LOW LEVEL
TUNNEL

Ground Breaking Ceremonies

SUNDAY, JUNE 17th, 1934

Guests of Honor

Honorable Franklin Delano Roosevelt

Honorable Frank F. Merriam

JOINT HIGHWAY DISTRICT No. 13, STATE OF CALIFORNIA

Directors

Thos. E. Caldecott - - - - - - - - - - - - - - - - - - *President*
Harry M. Stow - - - - - - - - - - - - - - - - - - - *Secretary*
Henry L. Hinman - - - - - - - - - - - - - - - - - - *Treasurer*
Archibald B. Tinning - - - - - - - - - - - - - - - - - *Attorney*
Wallace B. Boggs - - - - - - - - - - - - - - - - - - *Engineer*

Boards of Supervisors

Alameda County	Contra Costa County
Thos. E. Caldecott	W. J. Buchanan
William J. Hamilton	James N. Long
George A. Jansen	H. M. Stow
Ralph R. Richmond	R. J. Trembath
Clifford Wixon	H. L. Cummings

OAKLAND AND BERKELEY JUNIOR CHAMBERS OF COMMERCE
COMMITTEE ON ARRANGEMENTS

Dudley W. Frost - - - - - - - - - - - - - - - - *General Chairman*
Frank W. Teasdel - - - - - - - - - - - - - - - *Vice-Chairman*
Edward H. Siems - - - - - - - - - - - - - - - - - *Secretary*
H. Buford Fisher - - - - - - - - - - - - - - - - - *Treasurer*

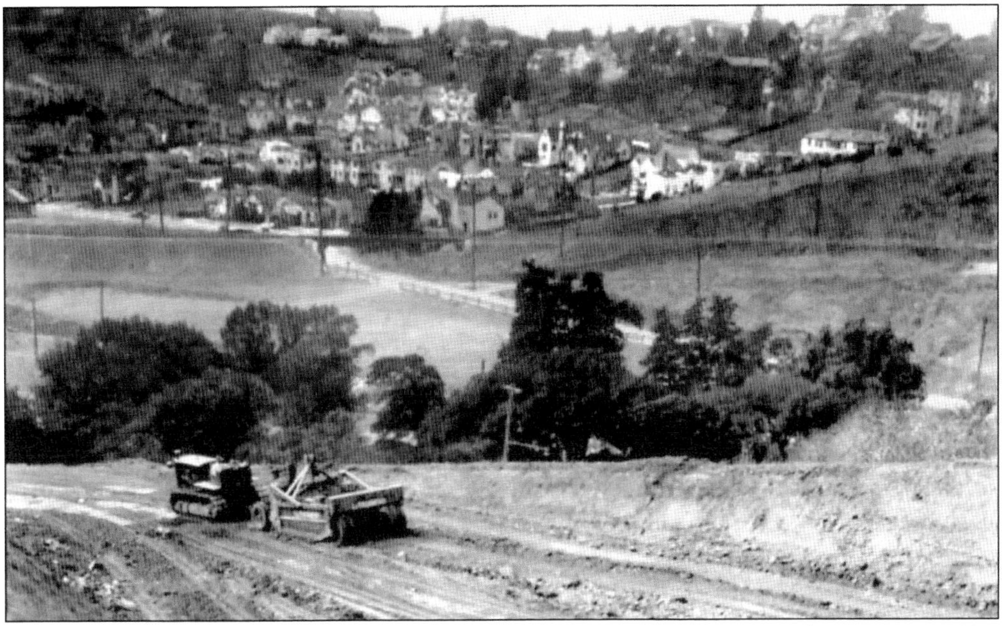

Tractors are shown grading the approach to the western portal. Joint Highway District No. 13 acquired the rights of way for the new highway and tunnel at a cost of nearly $400,000. Engineering plans were completed after two years at a cost of nearly $100,000. The contract to build the tunnel and the approaches was awarded to Six Companies, Inc. (Courtesy Contra Costa Historical Society.)

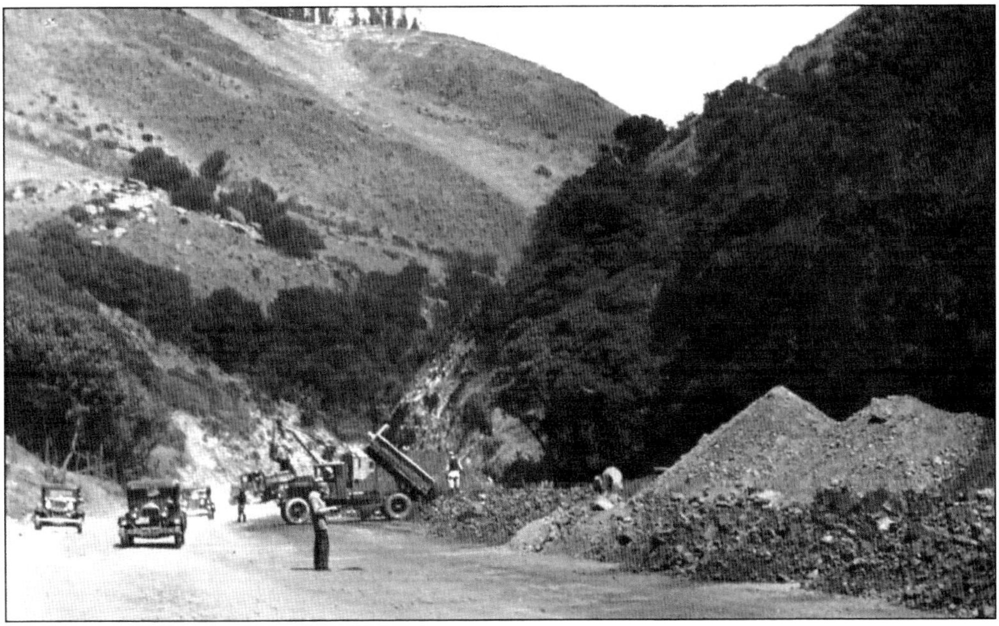

Spoil from the excavation of the tunnel is seen outside the eastern portal in 1934. Excavation went through shale, mudstone, sandstone, and an earthquake fault and was predominately done by hand. More than three million cubic yards of dirt and rock were moved during the grading and excavation. The rocks from the excavation were ground and used as part of the aggregate in the concrete mix for the tunnel construction. (Courtesy Contra Costa County Historical Society.)

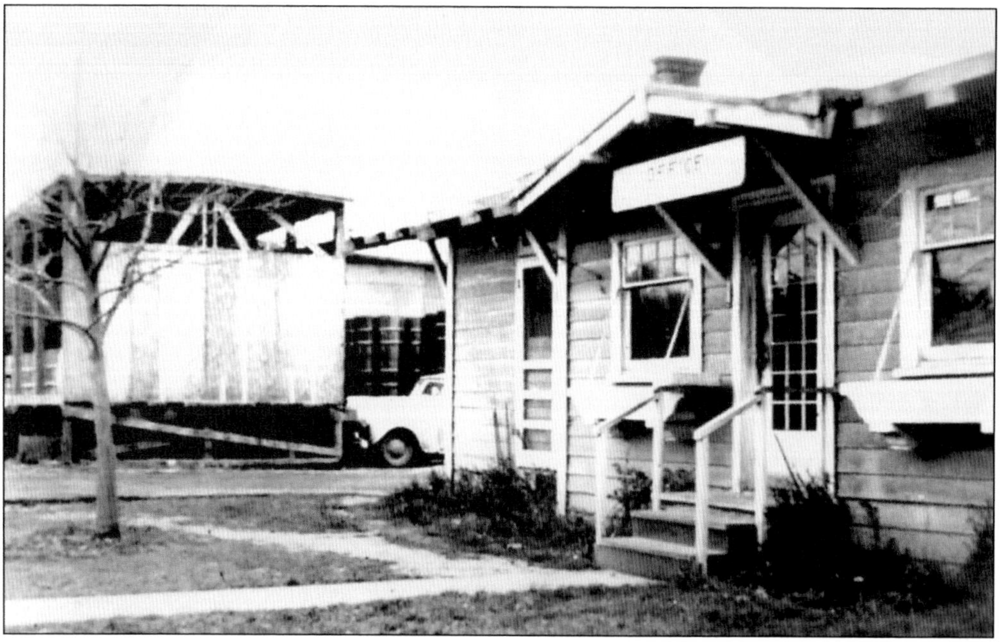

The construction offices for the Broadway Low Level Tunnel project are shown above. Six Companies, Inc., of California was a consortium formed in 1931 by eight smaller general contractors to submit a bid for the Hoover Dam project, which they completed two years ahead of schedule in 1935. Six Companies built many other large-scale public works projects during the 1930s. The company successfully bid on the tunnel project and began construction in late 1934. Dr. M.A. Shade's first aid station for the site is shown below with air-monitoring equipment lined up in front of it. (Above, courtesy Contra Costa County Historical Society; below, courtesy California Department of Transportation.)

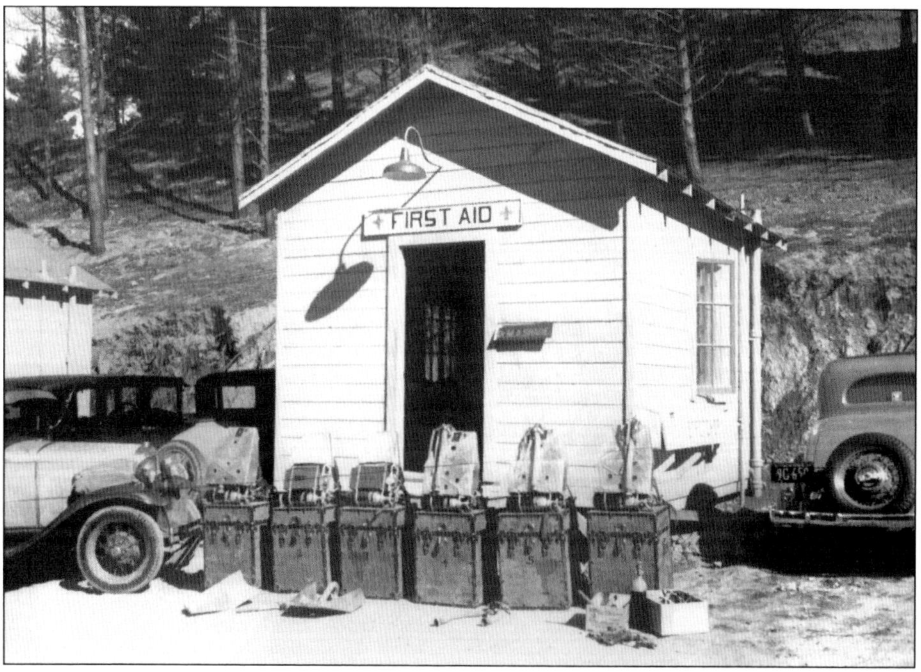

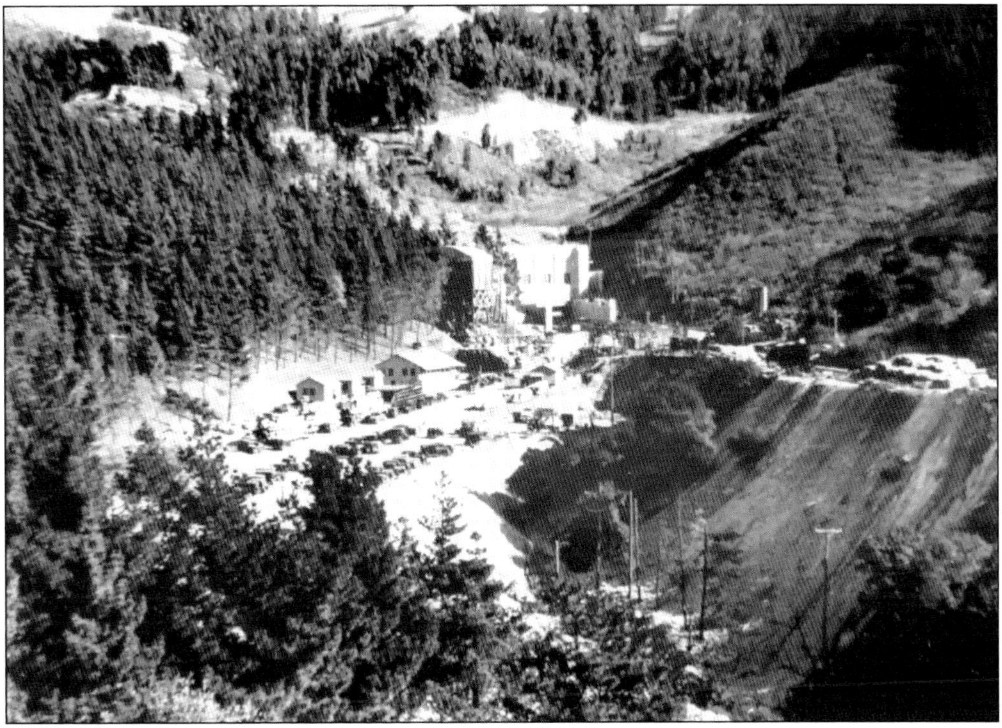

The low-level tunnel project was one of the first major projects of the Public Works Administration (PWA) of Pres. Franklin Roosevelt's New Deal. The PWA provided employment for many out-of-work men during the Depression, and scores of unions provided men for the project. Among them were carpenters, miners, laborers, teamsters, and surveyors. Wallace B. Boggs, engineer of Joint Highway District No. 13, was in charge of tunnel construction. Joseph W. Barkley served as assistant engineer of the project. Other members of the engineering staff included Arthur F. Gelston, resident field engineer; Merton C. Collins, who designed the ventilation; and Lorin W. Hunt, superintendent of the concrete work. (Above, courtesy Oakland Public Library History Room; below, courtesy California Department of Transportation.)

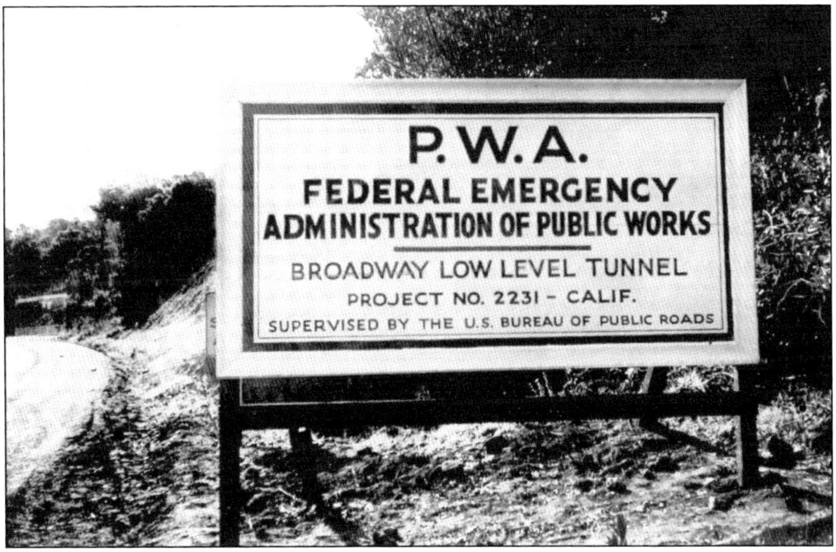

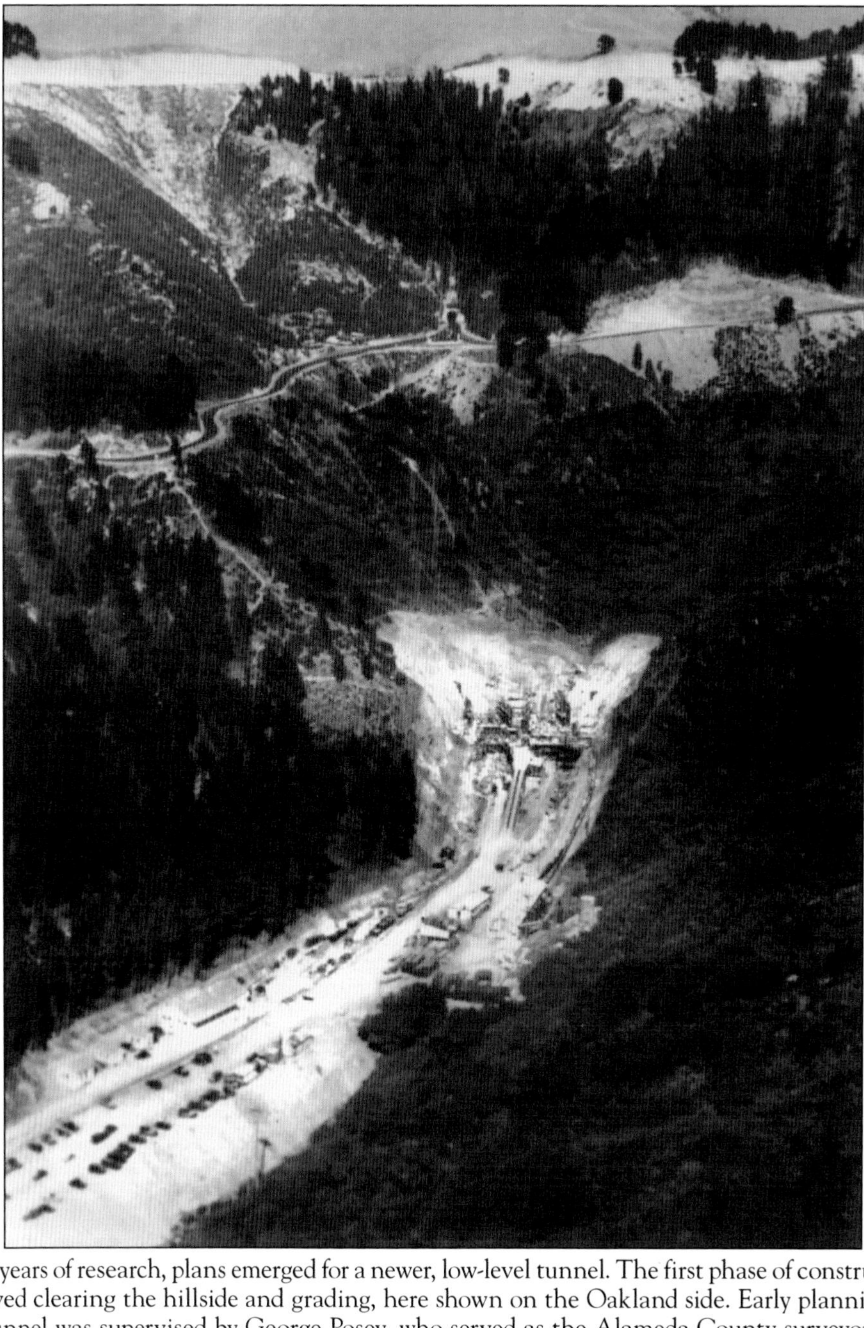

After years of research, plans emerged for a newer, low-level tunnel. The first phase of construction involved clearing the hillside and grading, here shown on the Oakland side. Early planning for the tunnel was supervised by George Posey, who served as the Alameda County surveyor from 1921 to 1932. He served as chief engineer for Joint Highway District No. 13. Posey completed the major preliminary studies on the low-level tunnel before his death in 1932. He was succeeded by Wallace B. Boggs, one of his assistants, who took over the final design responsibilities and supervised the construction. The Kennedy Tunnel and the original roads leading to it are visible in the upper part of this photograph. The lower location of the new tunnel meant a shorter climb but a greater distance for construction workers to bore. (Courtesy California Department of Transportation.)

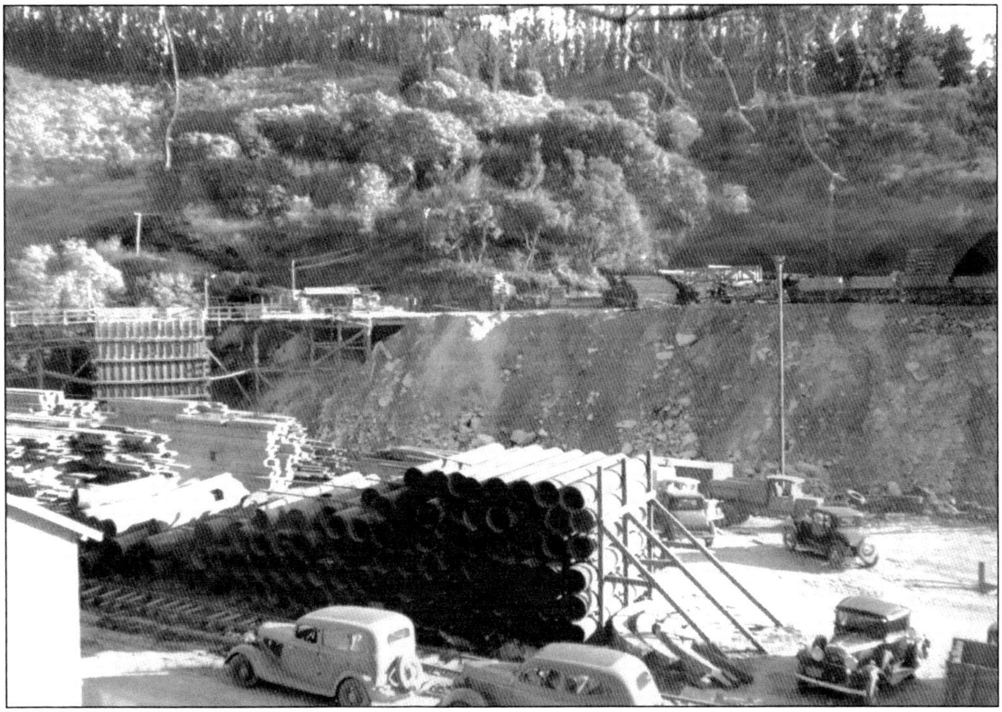

Large quantities of construction materials were stored on site for use in the tunneling process. Pipes were used to provide ventilation inside the bores and to build the drainage system. Lumber was used to build the forms for the exterior concrete pours for the roadways, portals, ventilation, and superintendent's buildings. Within the tunnel, lumber was used to build the forms to support the excavation of the tunnel crown and walls prior to concrete pours. Lumber from the forms was said to have been used to construct houses in Contra Costa County after the completion of the tunnel. (Both, courtesy California Department of Transportation.)

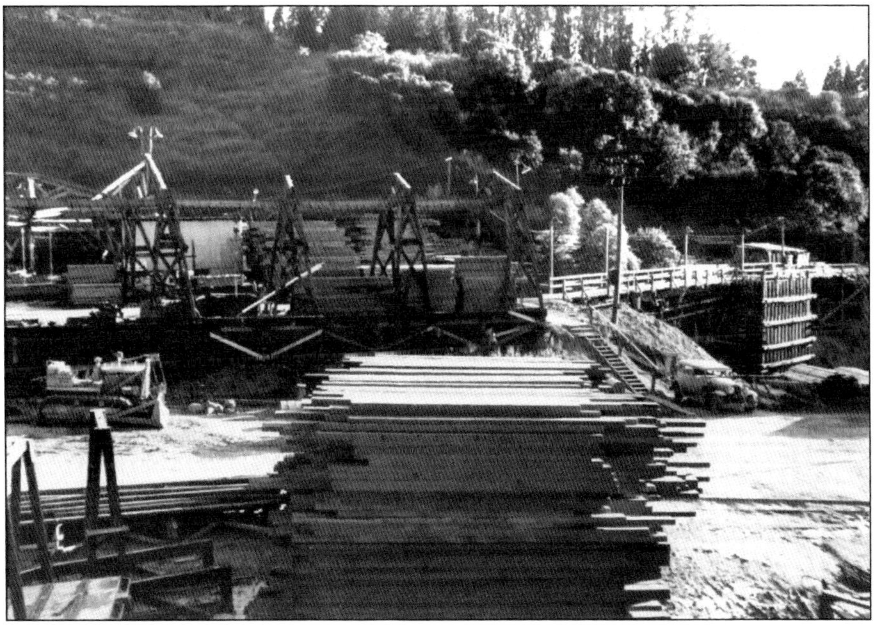

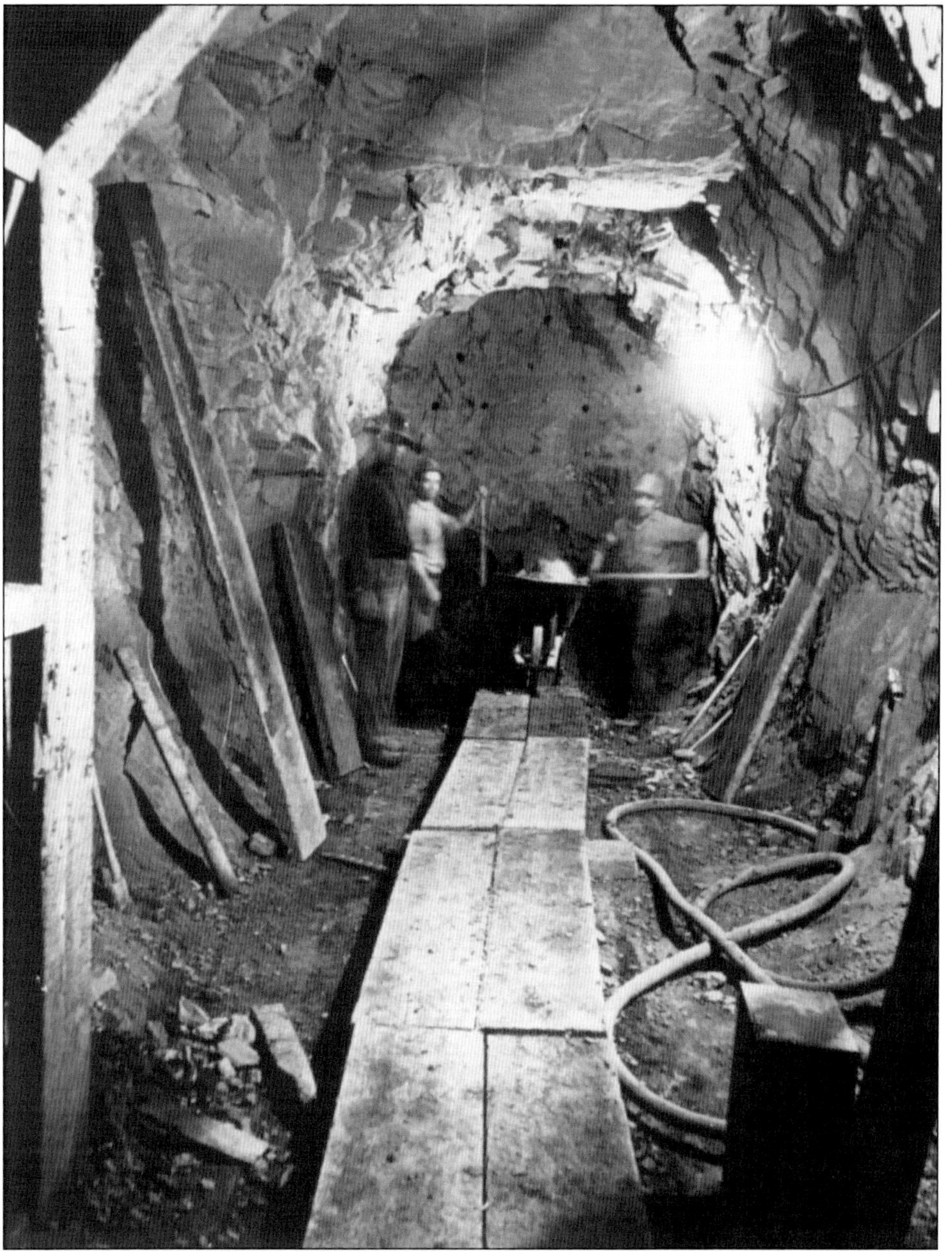

By September 1934, construction of the tunnel was well underway. Over 700 jobs were generated for the project in the first months, although many were less than half-time jobs. Men were eager for any kind of work during the Depression. Miners started at Temescal Canyon to begin the excavation of the east portal. Many of the workers who were employed by Six Companies, Inc., were miners who worked on the Hoover Dam project. One miner, Jim Silva, tried to find employment on the tunnel project only to be repeatedly turned down and told that Irish miners were preferred. After some thought, Silva went to city hall in Oakland, legally changed his name to Sullivan, and was soon hired for the project. Silva is the man at right in this bore excavation photograph. His brother-in-law is on the left, and his brother in the middle. The holes on the back wall were drilled for blasting. (Courtesy Ray Mailhot.)

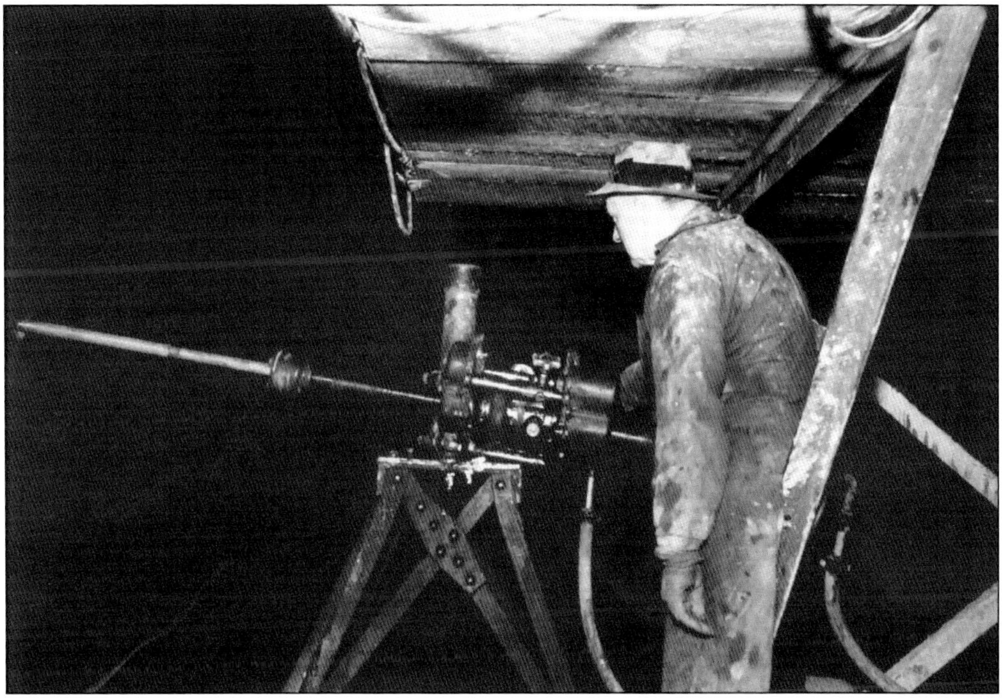

This unidentified tunnel worker is drilling into the right wall of the upgrade (west to east) bores. Pilot holes were drilled, then dynamite was placed into the holes and exploded by using either a plunger or a long fuse. At the height of construction, there were as many as 1,000 people per day working on the project, but progress was slow. (Courtesy Oakland Public Library History Room.)

After the portals were excavated, the retaining walls, drainage systems, and portal masonry were put in place. Tunnel driving and arch excavation followed, then the core was removed using cable shovels and air-powered drills. Geological formations dictated whether excavation started at the top or bottom of the bore. (Courtesy Oakland Library History Room.)

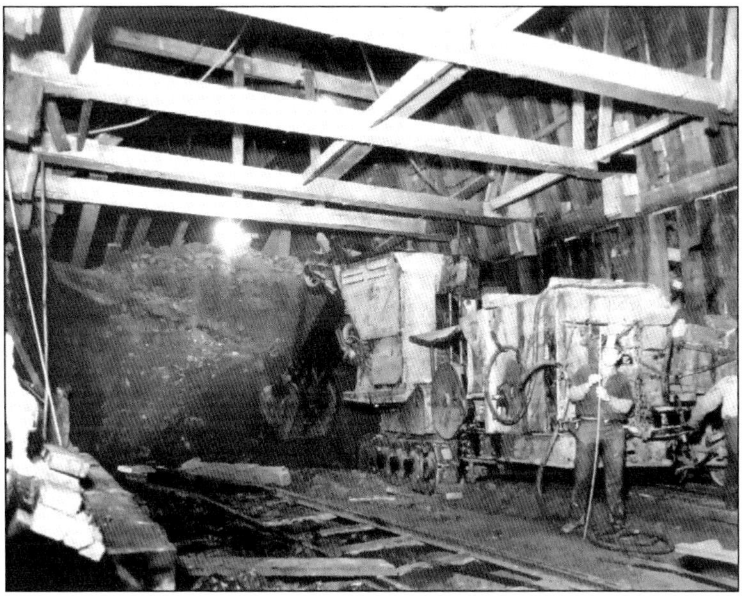

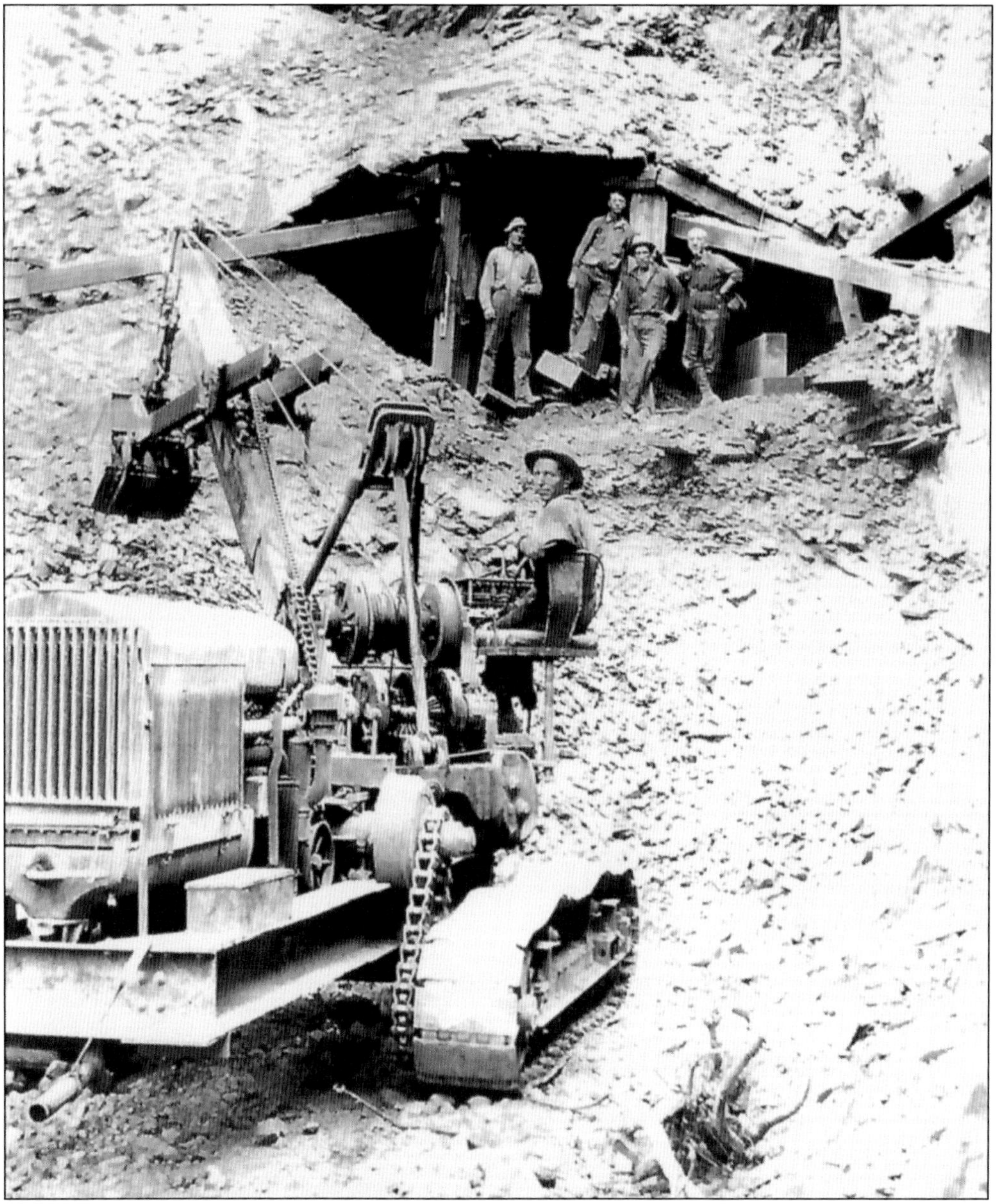

Edgar Baugh was a foreman on the Broadway Low Level Tunnel construction. He is second from the left at the back, near the entrance to a tunnel portal. Baugh had worked on water tunnel construction and nearly been buried alive in a cave-in; it took him more than a month to recover. Cave-ins were common in tunnel construction due to geologic variability and instability of the earth. (Courtesy Richard Reeves.)

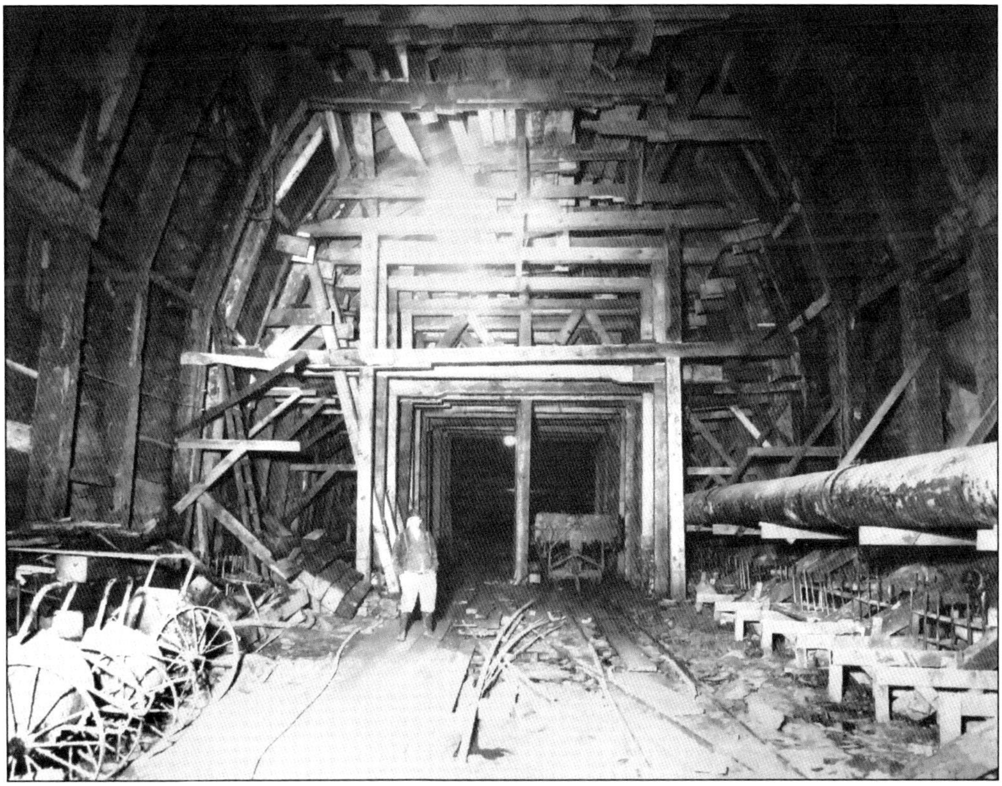

This image looking east in one of the bores shows scaffolding used to support the excavation. Wood timbers, metal ribs, and laggings were used to prepare for the installation of 40-foot steel forms around which the concrete lining of the tunnel was pumped. The pipe at right pushed fresh air into the tunnel for the workers. (Courtesy Oakland Public Library History Room.)

Various kinds of jumbos (work bridges) were used in tunnel construction. They were run on tracks into both tunnel bores. In this photograph of the upgrade tunnel (west to east), a concrete jumbo is finishing the concrete that had been pumped to form the tunnel walls. (Courtesy Oakland Public Library History Room.)

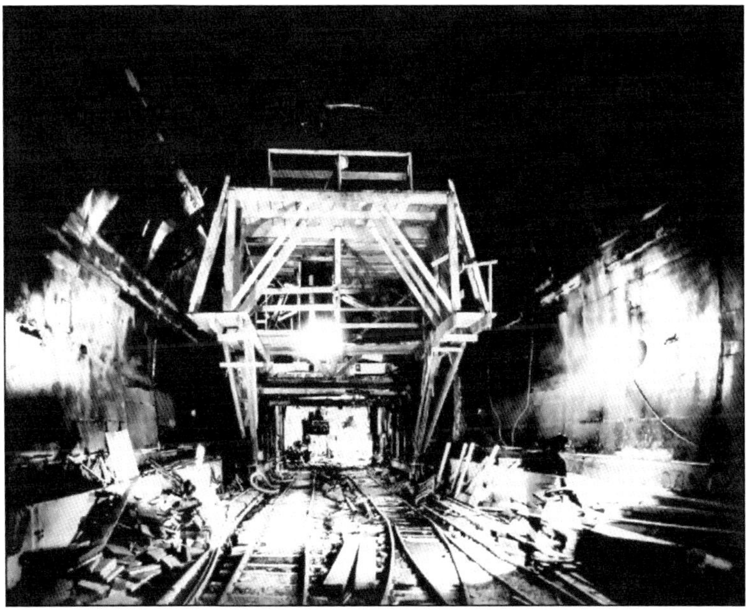

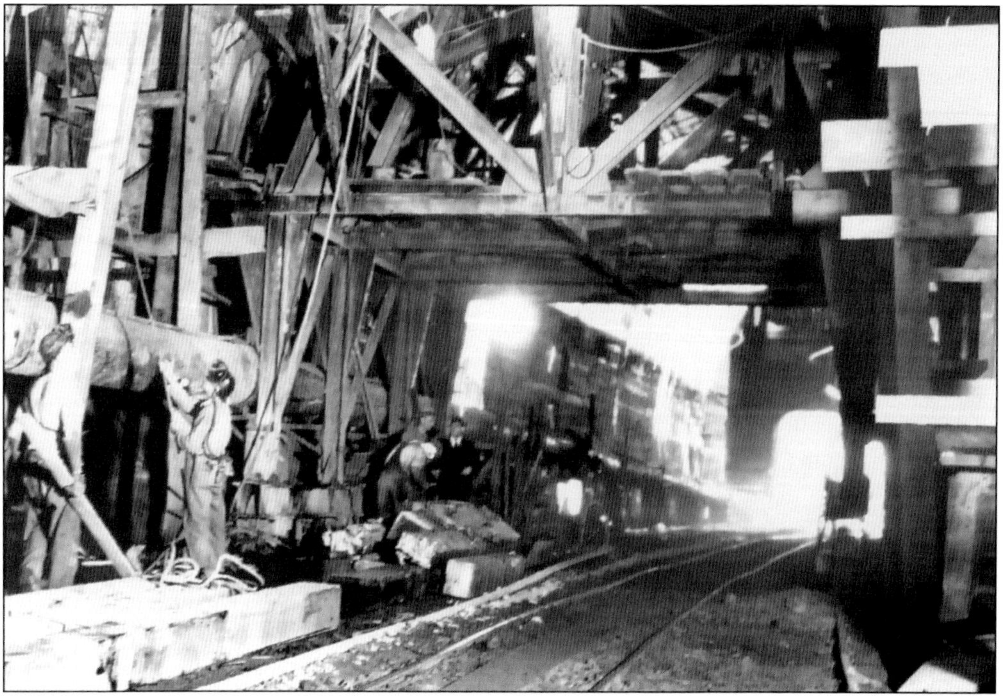

The placing of new timbers and chipping of existing timbers was done by workers to allow for the clearance of the concentric ring of the concrete forms. The forms were in 40-foot sections with one section operating in each bore. Concrete was pumped into the forms to create the tunnel arch. (Courtesy Oakland Public Library History Room.)

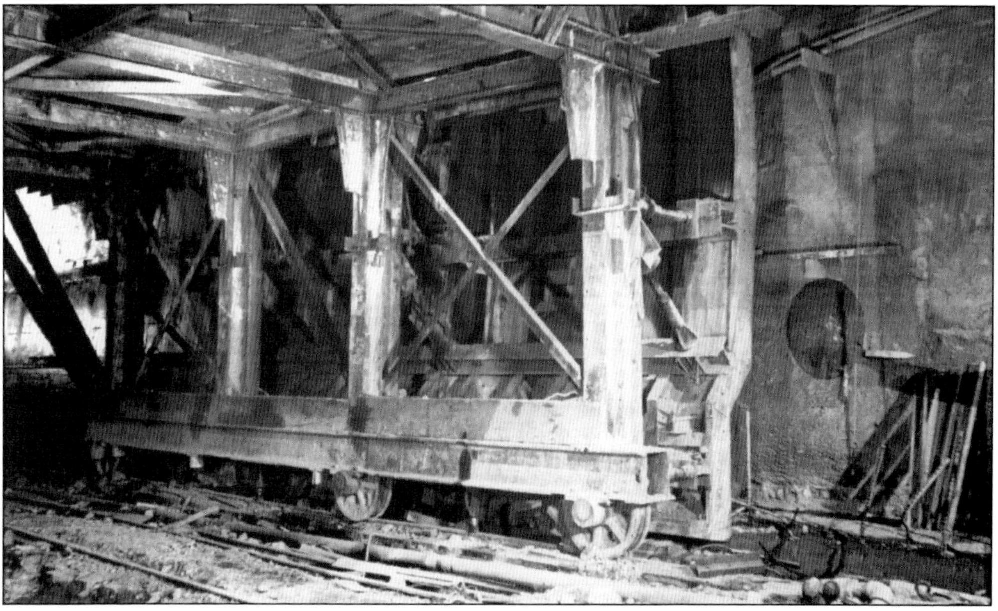

This photograph shows the tracks that the jumbos moved along in the tunnel bores. After the concrete was applied and had hardened, the forms were removed, and the jumbo was rolled forward, then the forms were used again to put the concrete lining on the next part of the tunnel walls. (Courtesy California Department of Transportation.)

Project surveyors Mr. Arnold, Mr. Eitener, and Mr. Brent of the Pollock Construction Company are shown with transit and rod. After Six Companies, Inc., rescinded its contract for the tunnel construction in June 1936, the contract for completion of tunnel excavation and concrete arch ring lining was awarded to the George Pollock Company and R.G. Clifford. Work was started again in December 1936 and was completed in June 1937. (Courtesy Contra Costa County Historical Society.)

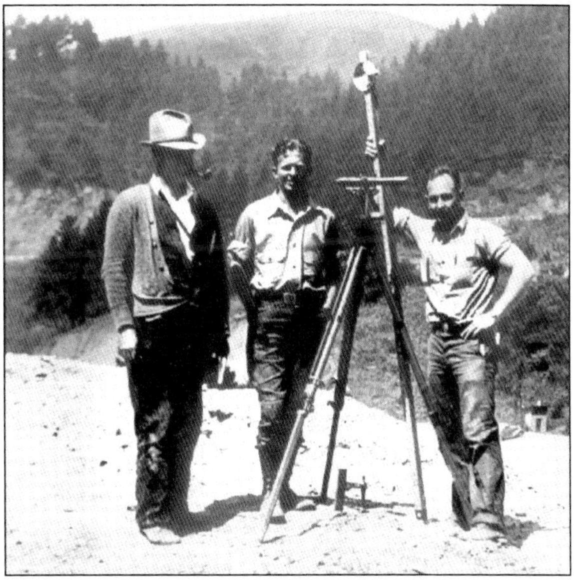

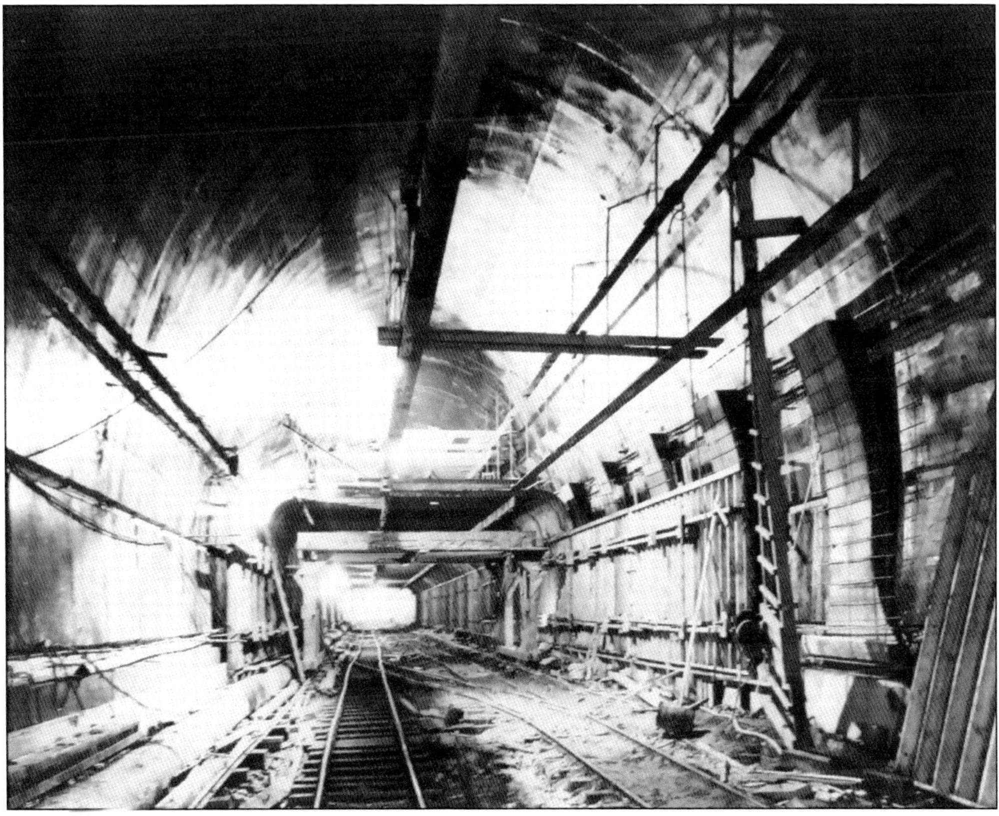

A photograph in the downgrade tunnel (east to west) shows the end of the deck, the floor built across the base of the tunnel, and the side panel that holds up the exhaust and fresh air shafts. The tracks on the deck were used to move the drilling and timber jumbos as well as the muck cars that removed spoil from the excavation site and the forming system for pouring the concrete walls. (Courtesy Oakland Public Library History Room.)

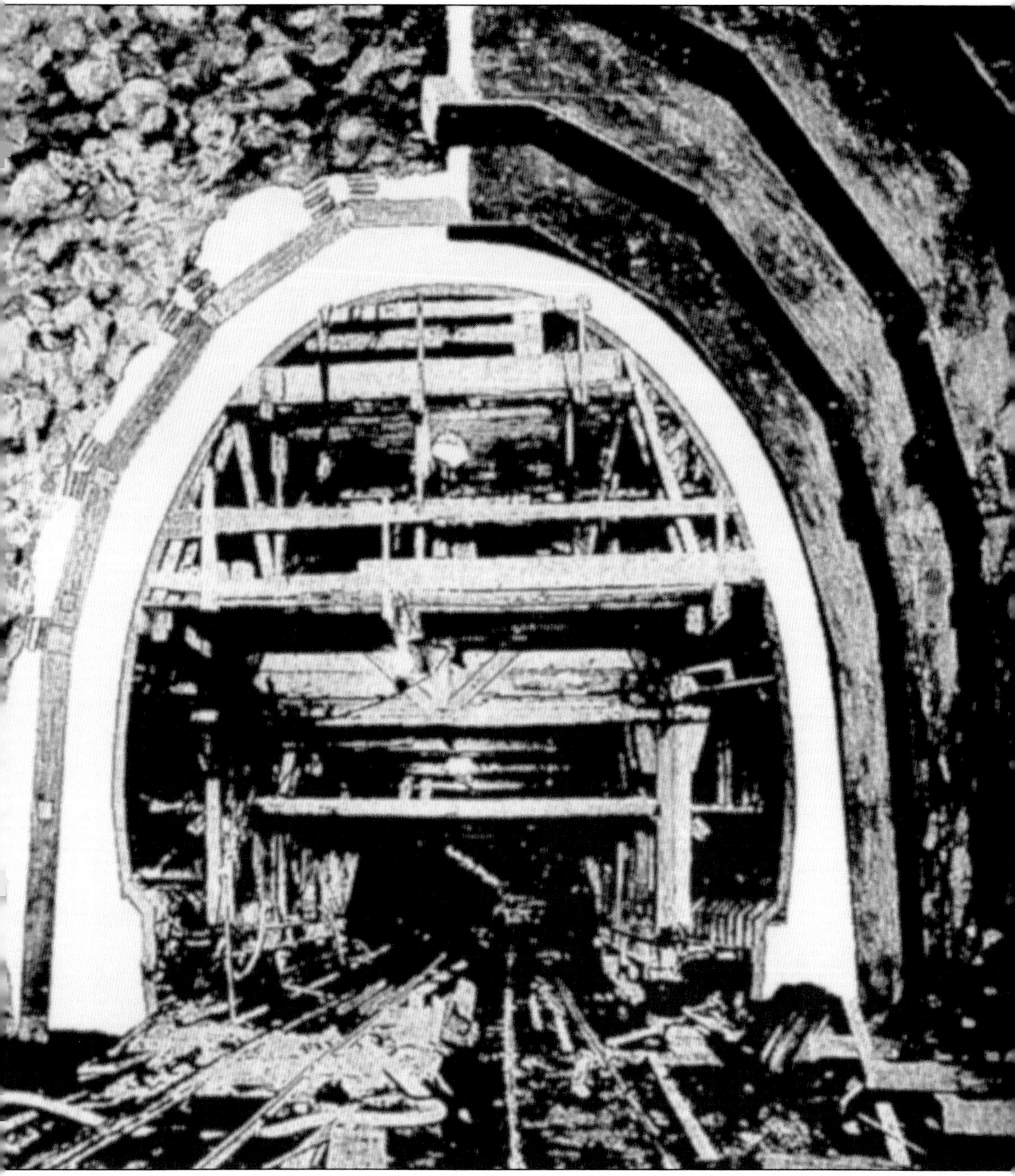

This cross section of the tunnel shows the type of steel form liner used to apply concrete to the tunnel arch and a concrete jumbo structure shown inside. The concrete was pumped on the form and hand-troweled. Some of the concrete walls were as thick as seven feet. After the concrete hardened, a grout jumbo was used to fill cracks and joints in the various segments. (Courtesy Oakland Public Library History Room.)

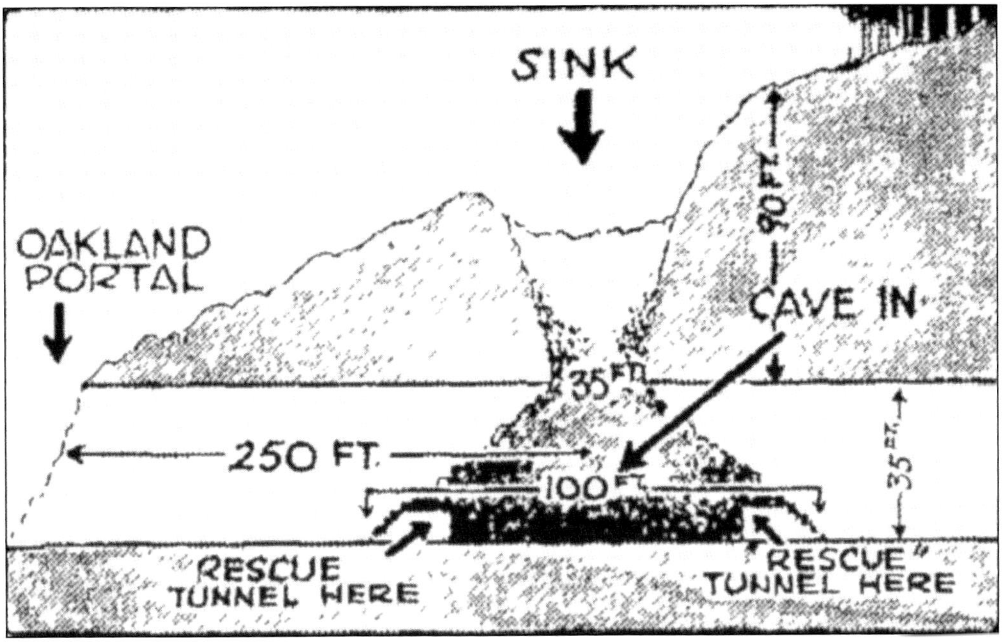

On August 28, 1935, the north bore of the tunnel caved in 250 feet from the western portal, killing three men. A week earlier, Six Companies, Inc., had laid off 600 men because of fears of a cave-in. The contractor had notified the directors of Joint Highway District No. 13 that it thought the tunnel design faulty because of the unknown type and instability of ground being tunneled. (Courtesy *Oakland Tribune.*)

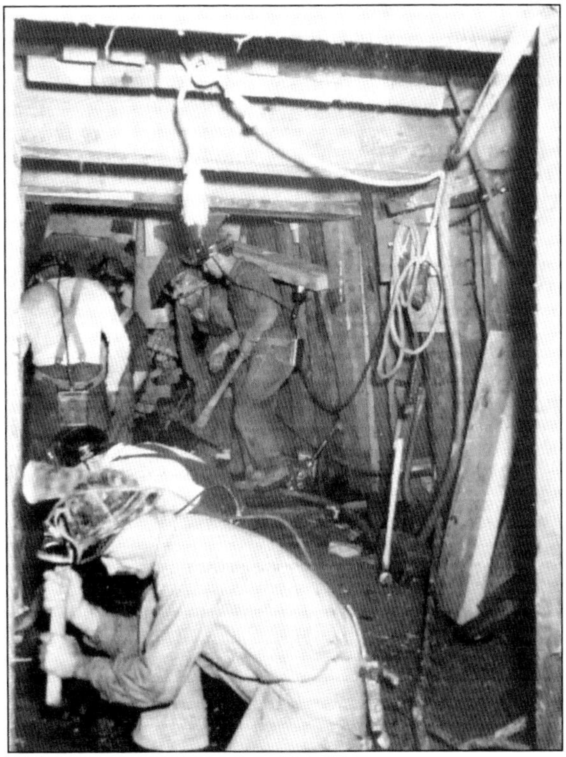

These rescue crews are driving tunnels from both sides in the north bore in an effort to reach the three men trapped in the cave-in. Emergency repairs were being made to the timbering 250 feet from the west portal of the north tunnel shaft when a boulder tore from the roof and plunged through the scaffolding. The three victims were buried beneath tons of earth and rock. (Courtesy Oakland Public Library History Room.)

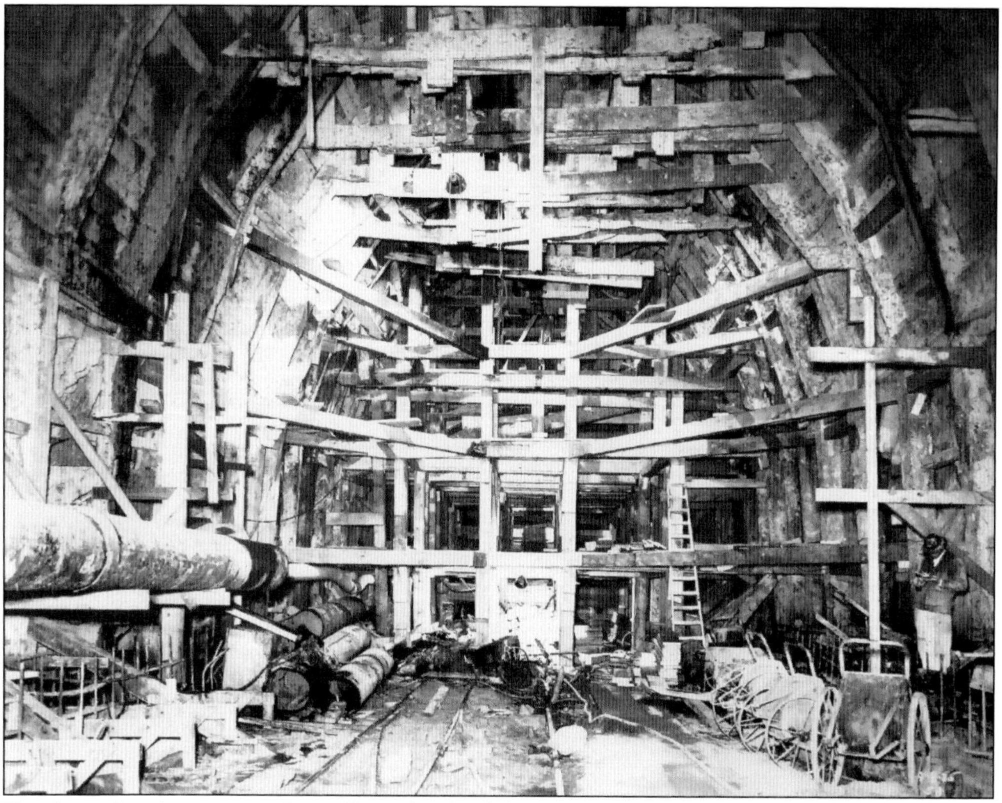

Ten days after the cave-in, the walls and arch of the tunnel bore were being retimbered. A rescue crew of 85 men searched for survivors. The rescue crew would work for an hour and then rest for 20 minutes. A six-foot rescue drift (cross tunnel) was dug from the south bore in an attempt to reach the trapped workers. The bodies of the workers who died were not recovered for five days after the cave-in. (Courtesy Oakland Public Library History Room.)

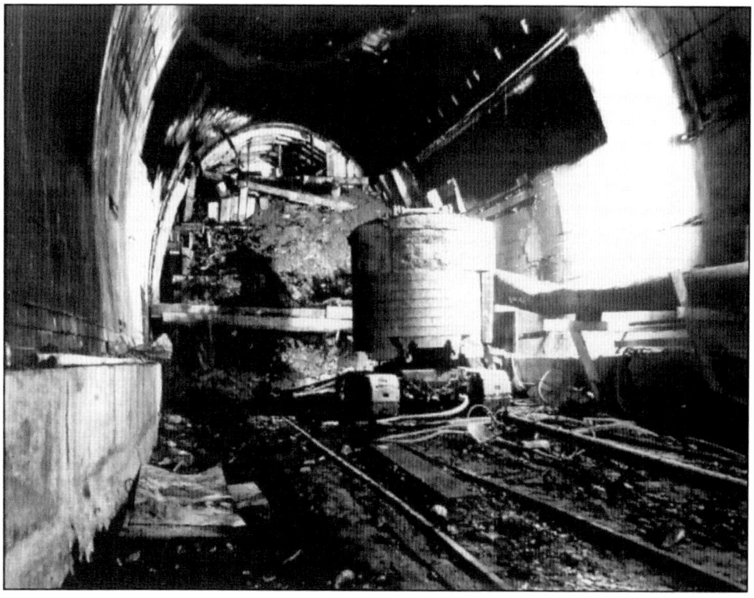

By November 1935, the tunnel was cleared of debris from the cave-in and construction work began again. Manpower was doubled to 1,000 workers, and the speed of work was increased. This cable shovel is working to remove the spoil from the bore. (Courtesy Oakland Public Library History Room.)

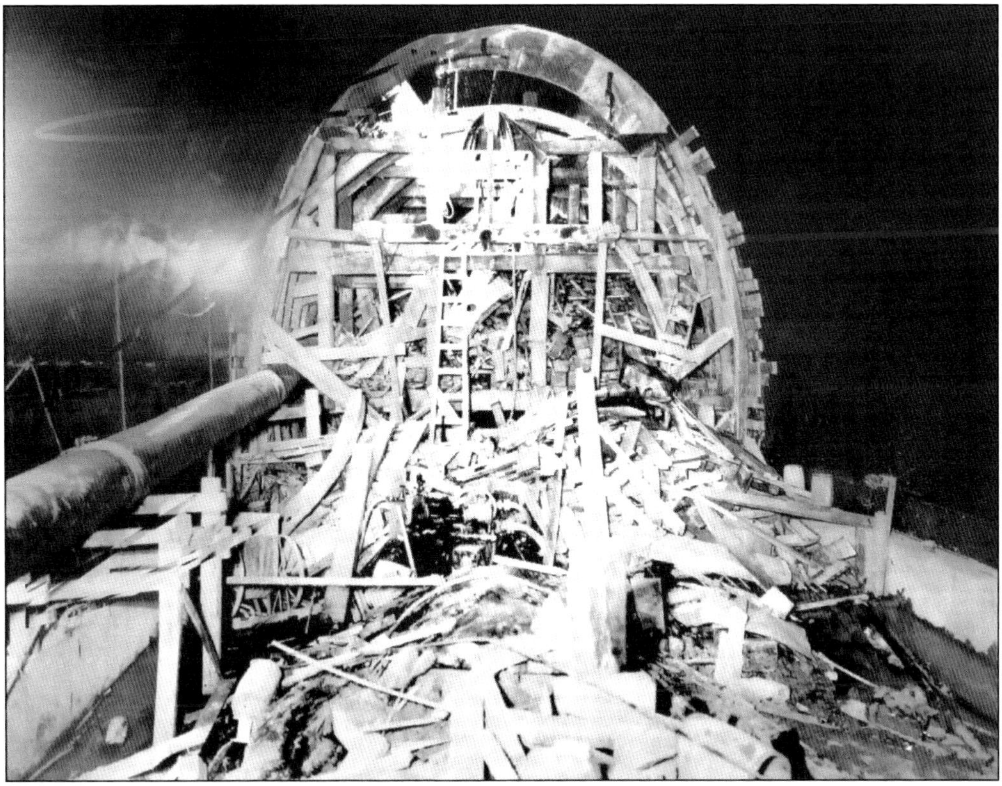

The wood debris from the cave-in is shown at the east end of the downgrade tunnel. The workers killed in the cave-in had been replacing temporary timbering, installed more than six months before, that was splintering. The contractor, Six Companies, Inc., had recently claimed that it would sustain a loss on the job and asserted that Joint Highway District No. 13 was not performing sufficient engineering work on the project. (Courtesy Oakland Public Library History Room.)

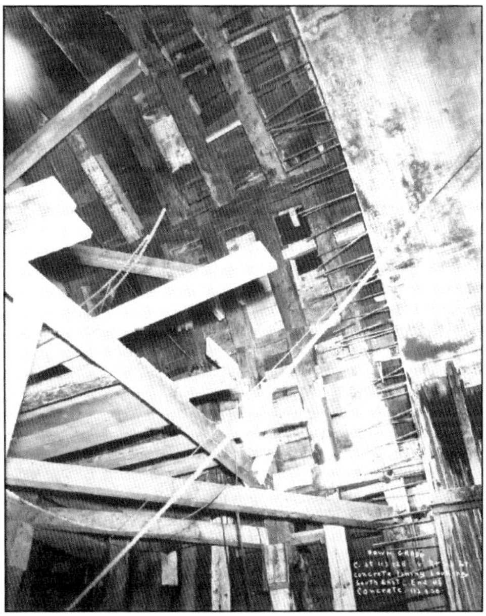

Tunnel officials claimed that the accident would not have occurred if the contractor had followed the excavation work by promptly installing the permanent reinforced concrete lining called for by the plans and specifications. The contractor allegedly excavated 1,000 feet beyond the lining in each bore. The seam between the timbering and the concrete lining is shown in this photograph. (Courtesy Oakland Public Library History Room.)

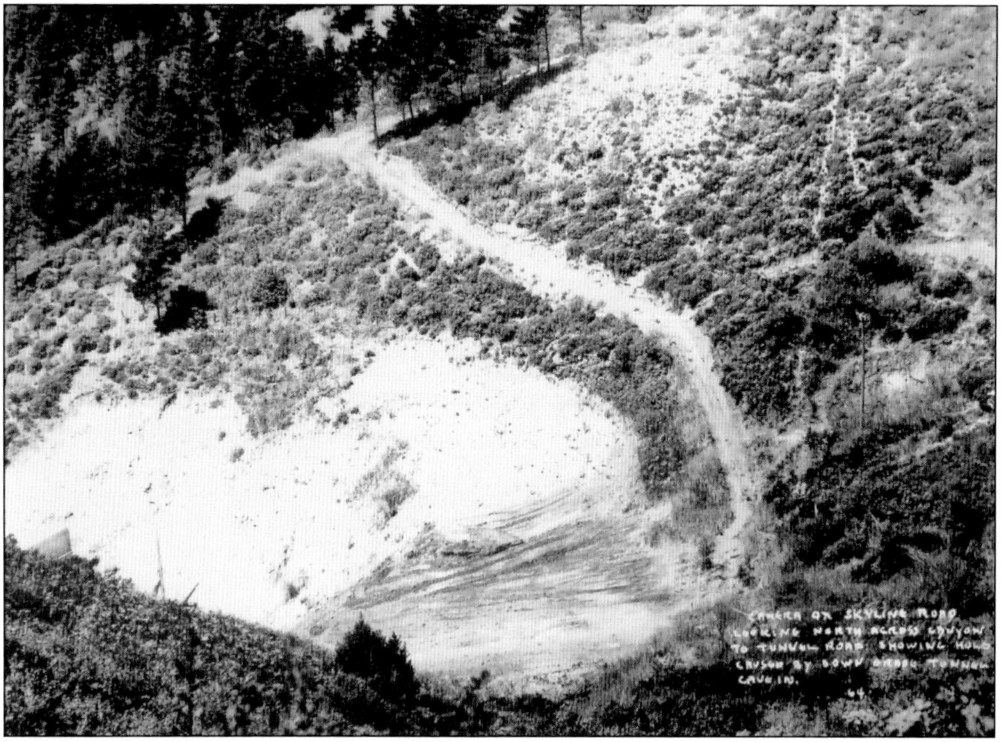

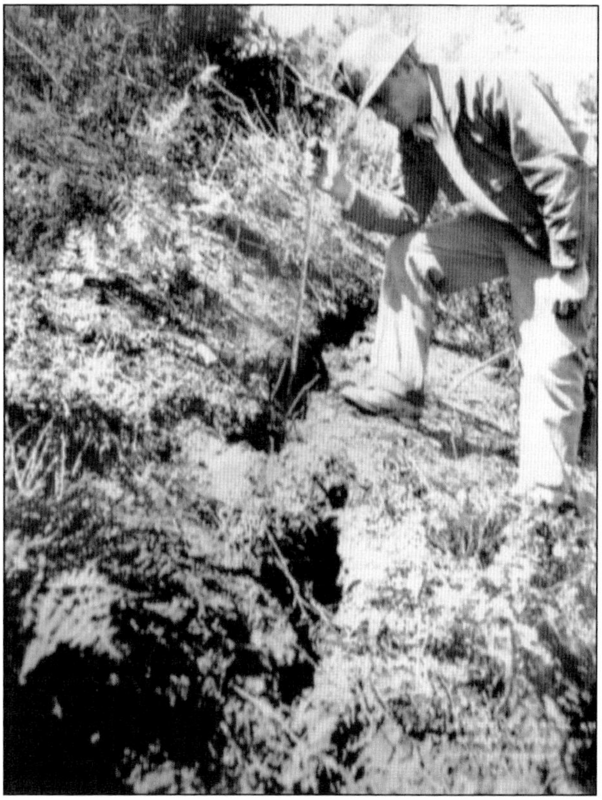

An aerial photograph looking north across the canyon to Tunnel Road shows the hole caused by the downgrade tunnel cave-in. This sink—100 feet in circumference and 15 feet deep on the hillside 90 feet above the cave-in—indicated a complete collapse of the bore. (Courtesy Oakland Public Library History Room.)

W.B. Burger examines the crack in the earth on the top of the tunnel sink. Six months later, another cave-in trapped 60 men. They were rescued, but there was much concern from workers and the State Department of Industrial Relations. In 1936, Six Companies, Inc., withdrew from the project. The job was rebid, and work resumed a month later with eight contractors doing various portions of the job. (Courtesy Oakland Public Library History Room.)

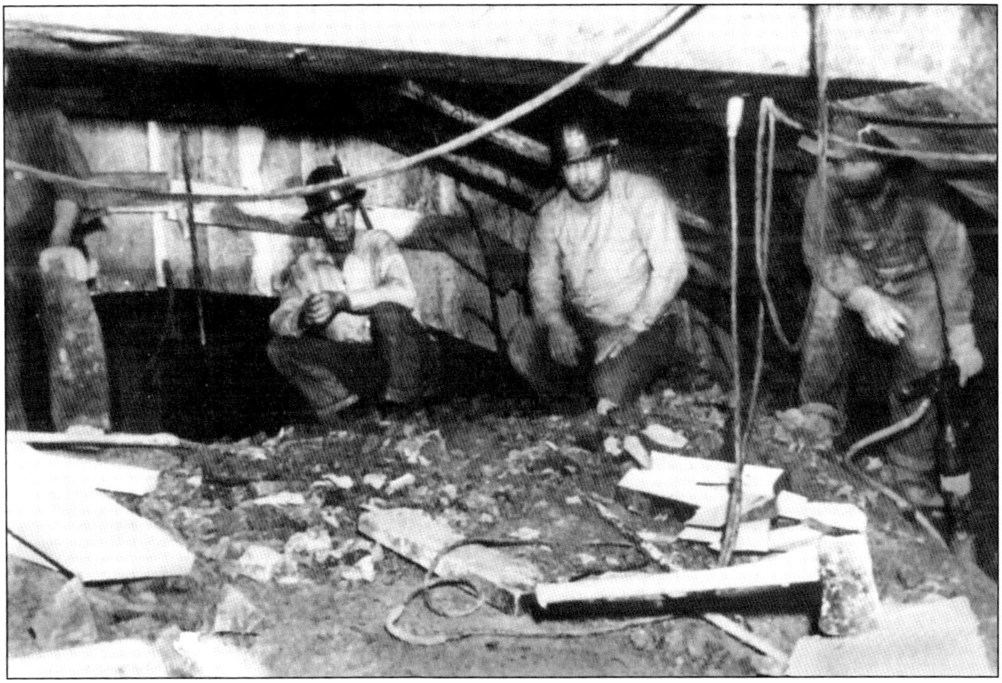

On May 13, 1937, workers finished excavating the second of the two bores through the Oakland hills. The "holing through" of the north (or downgrade) bore took place at a point 900 feet from the Alameda County portal of the tunnel and 400 feet over the Contra Costa County line. As the final barrier was removed, a cold draft swept through the dank tunnel. (Courtesy Contra Costa County Historical Society.)

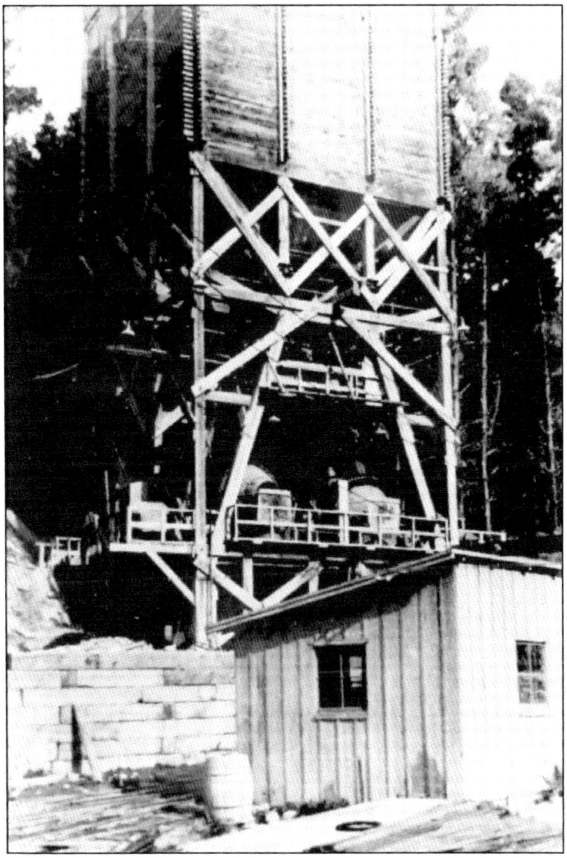

The concrete plant was located at the west approach and provided commercial aggregate and bulk cement. Batches of concrete were fed by gravity to a two-yard mixer that loaded concrete directly into cars on the narrow-gauge railroad. The cars ran up an incline at the tunnel face, dumping their loads into the concrete guns by way of gravity. (Courtesy Contra Costa County Historical Society.)

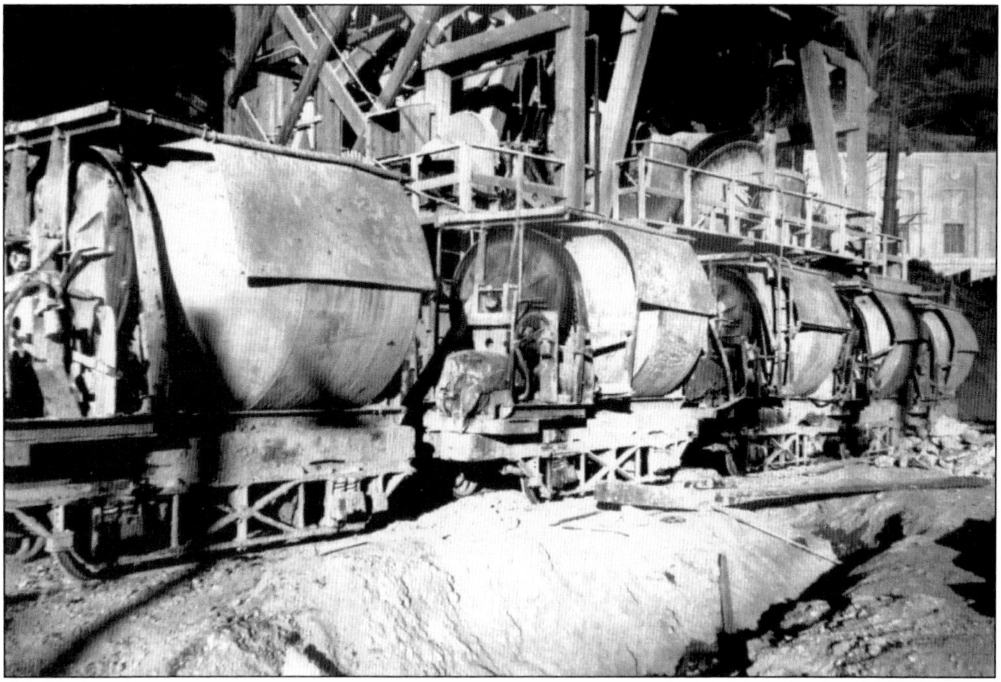

Cars on tracks delivered the concrete from the mixing plant to the inside of the tunnel, where it was sprayed on walls to reinforce the excavation. It was estimated that over 120,000 barrels of concrete, 2,500 tons of reinforcing steel, and 1,000 tons of structural steel frames were used in construction. In addition, more than 700,000 square yards of eight-inch oiled macadam pavement was used to complete the job. (Courtesy Contra Costa County Historical Society.)

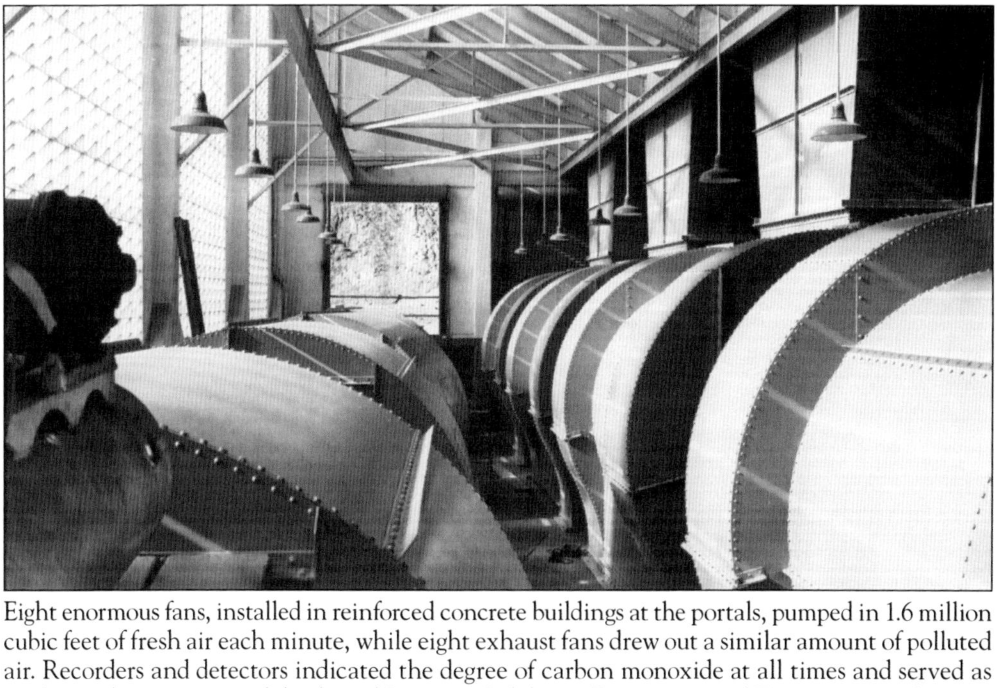

Eight enormous fans, installed in reinforced concrete buildings at the portals, pumped in 1.6 million cubic feet of fresh air each minute, while eight exhaust fans drew out a similar amount of polluted air. Recorders and detectors indicated the degree of carbon monoxide at all times and served as guides to the operation of the fans. (Courtesy California Department of Transportation.)

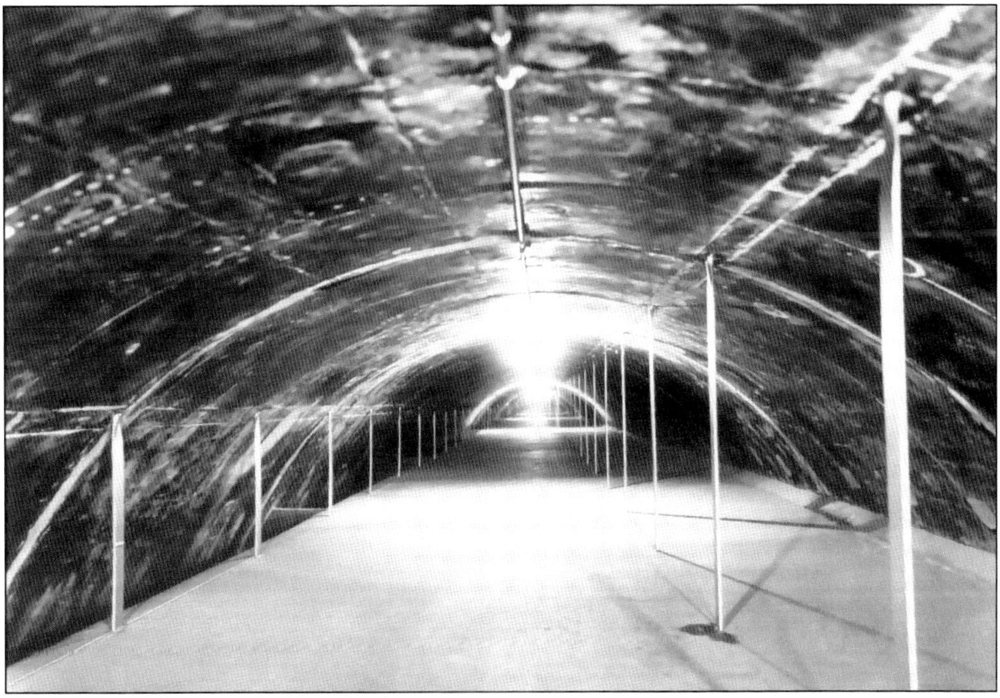

Fresh air ducts were located in the upper portion of the tunnel arches above the exhaust system and admitted air from the outside. The tunnel bores were built to be 15 feet, 8 inches between the roadway and the ventilation duct, allowing ample clearance for vehicles. (Courtesy Oakland Public Library History Room.)

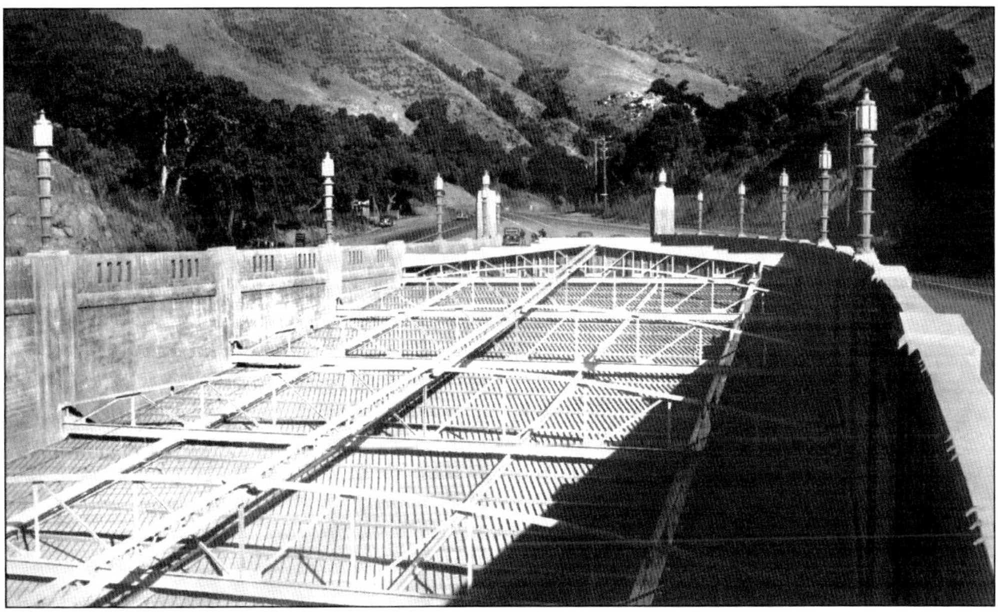

Light transition structures, consisting of overhead louvers that prevent sunlight from falling on the roadway, were constructed at the approaches between the portal walls of the tunnel. The structures allow the human eye to adjust to the transition between the artificial lighting in the tunnels and the direct sunlight outside. (Courtesy California Department of Transportation.)

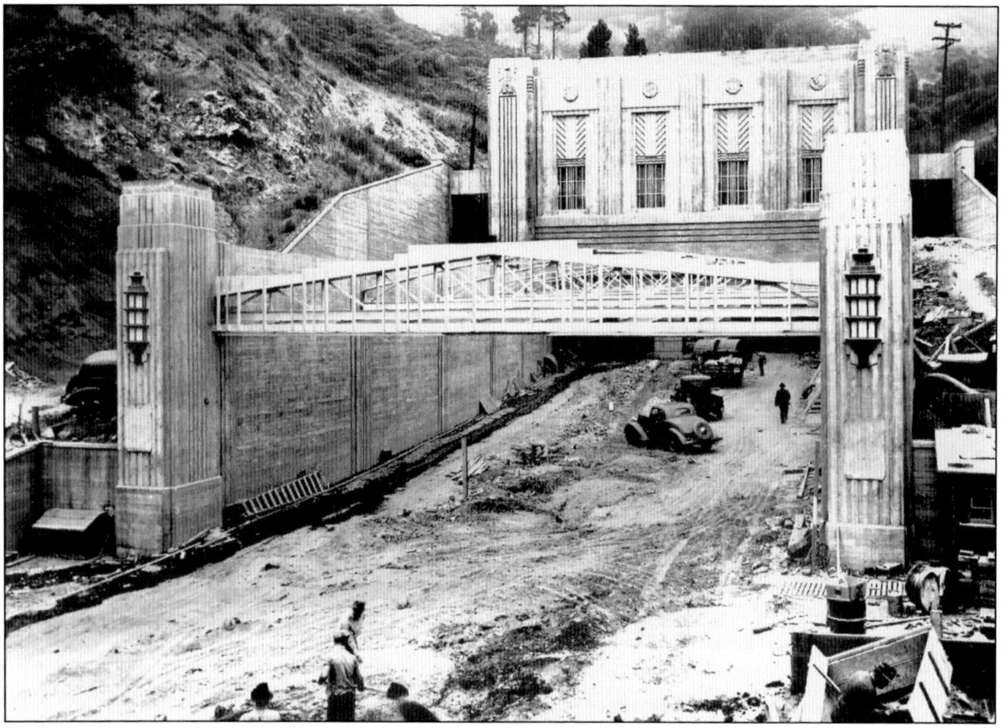

Construction of the west side of the tunnel was nearly complete in this 1936 photograph. The portals and the light transition structures had been installed, and the approach grading and paving were nearly done. The approach roads on both sides consisted of a paved surface 40 feet wide with 10-foot shoulders on each side. The new route would be able to handle 30,000 vehicles per day and would be an important connection with the San Francisco–Oakland Bay Bridge. (Courtesy Contra Costa County Historical Society.)

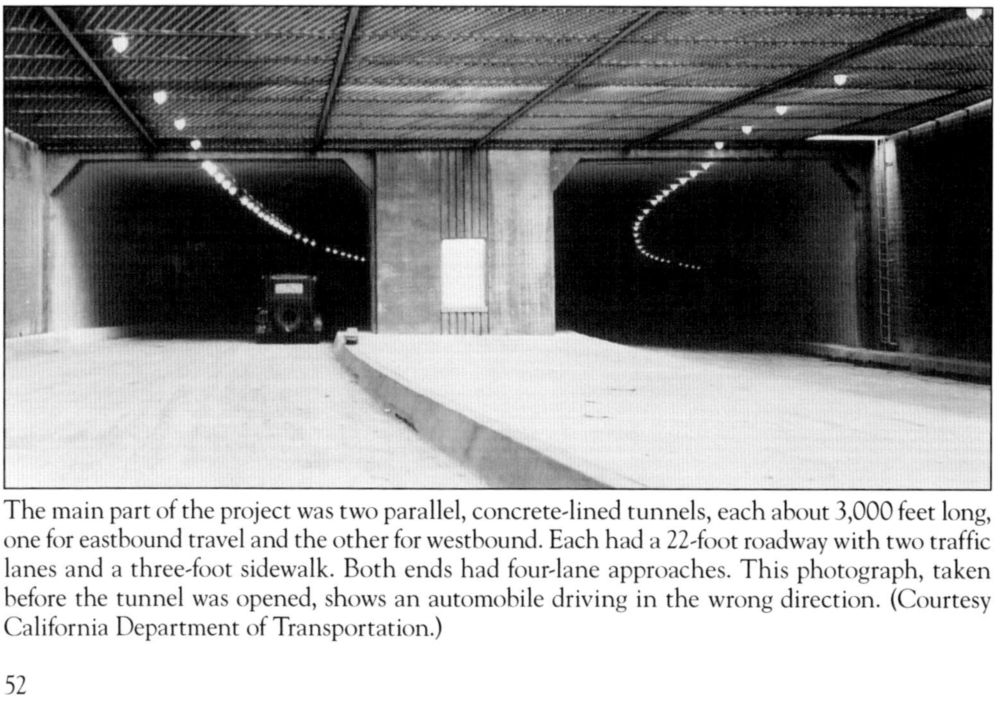

The main part of the project was two parallel, concrete-lined tunnels, each about 3,000 feet long, one for eastbound travel and the other for westbound. Each had a 22-foot roadway with two traffic lanes and a three-foot sidewalk. Both ends had four-lane approaches. This photograph, taken before the tunnel was opened, shows an automobile driving in the wrong direction. (Courtesy California Department of Transportation.)

Broadway Low Level Tunnel Dedication

Sunday, December 5, 1937

Enclosed find check for $________. (Breakfast, $1.00 per plate)

Kindly mail me 1 tickets for the Dedication Breakfast at the Claremont Hotel.

Also mail me 1 (not more than 2) tickets for the speakers' platform.

Name E. B. [illegible]

Address Walnut Creek.

City________

Make check payable to
Broadway Tunnel Committee
313 Financial Center Bldg, Oakland

Breakfast - 10:00 a.m.
Dedication 12:30 p.m.

A community breakfast held at the Claremont Hotel on Sunday morning, December 5, 1937, was attended by federal, state, and county officials, as well as civic leaders from the East Bay area. At the breakfast, Thomas E. Caldecott, president of Joint Highway District No. 13, was honored as the man responsible for the success of the project. He was presented with an engraved copper bucket (see page 125) containing earth dug at the ground-breaking. (Courtesy Contra Costa County Historical Society.)

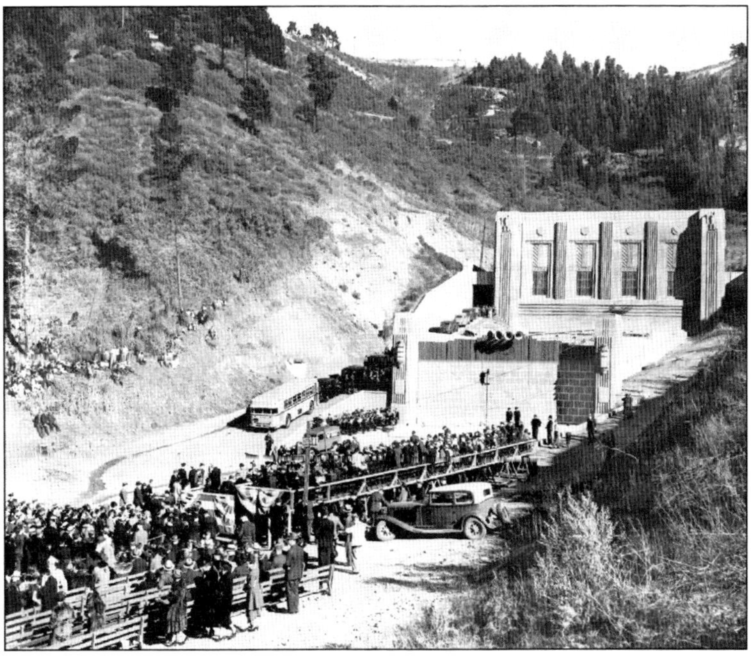

Thousands of people lined the hill at the west portal to witness the dedication ceremony on December 5, 1937. For two hours, more than 10,000 motorists backed up to Broadway and College Avenues to await the signal that opened the new bores linking the two counties. Thousands of spectators in cars viewed the dedication from atop the surrounding hills. (Courtesy Bay Area News Group.)

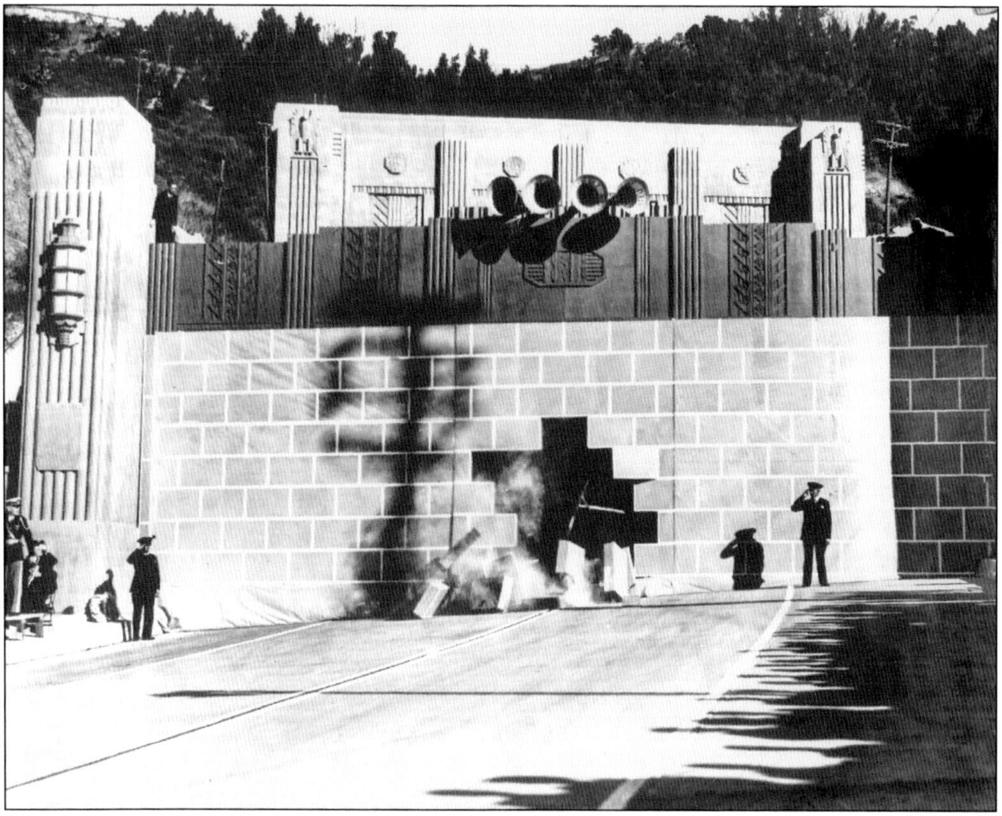

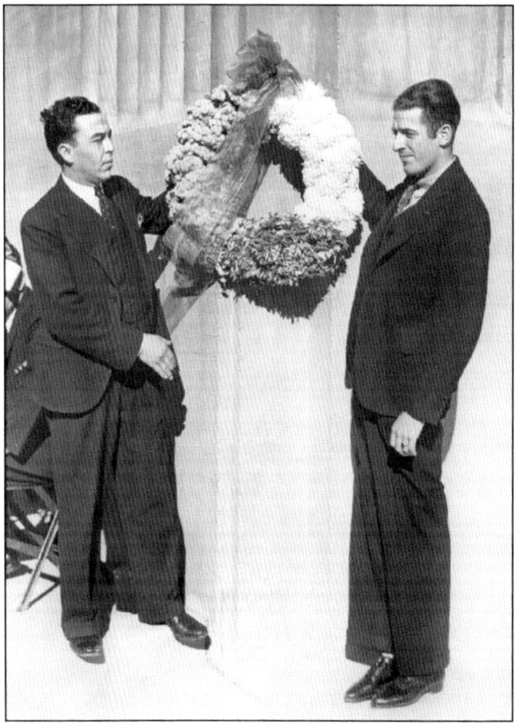

As California governor Frank F. Merriam finished the first part of his speech at the western portal, he touched a switch that set off a charge to break through a barricade concealing the mouth of the tunnel. Artificial chunks of granite fell away, revealing the entrance to the tunnel. (Courtesy Bay Area News Group.)

Fred Maes (shown on the left) and Rupert Bland lay a wreath at the tunnel entrance on behalf of the miners' union for the men killed constructing the Broadway Low Level Tunnel. A moment of silence was observed while a bugler played "Taps" from the opposite hill. (Courtesy Bay Area News Group.)

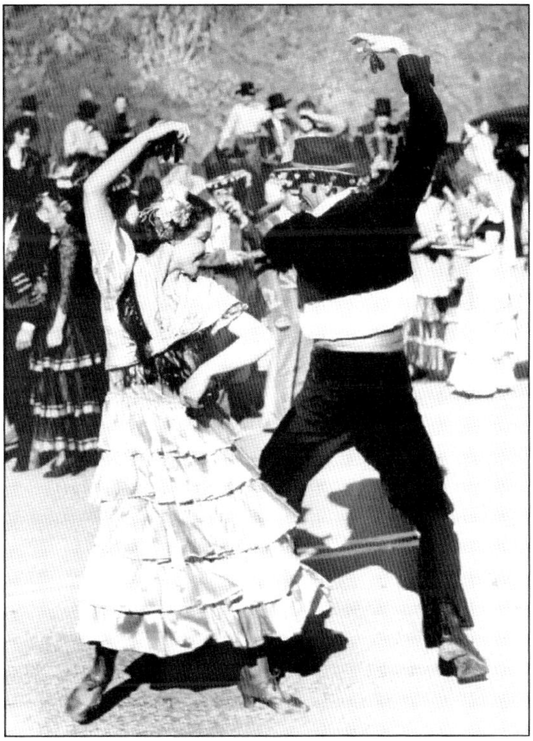

A colorful pageant depicting the Spanish custom of deeding property from father to son was the theme of the ceremony at the west portal. Fifty players in costumes of early Californians reenacted the Peralta family's acquisition of land in Alameda and Contra Costa Counties. (Courtesy Bay Area News Group.)

Dedication ceremonies at the west portal opened at 12:30 p.m. with musical selections played by a band, under the direction of Marshall Craig, that combined students from high schools throughout Alameda and Contra Costa Counties. The band included members from Piedmont High School, Mount Diablo High School, and San Ramon High School. (Courtesy Contra Costa County Historical Society.)

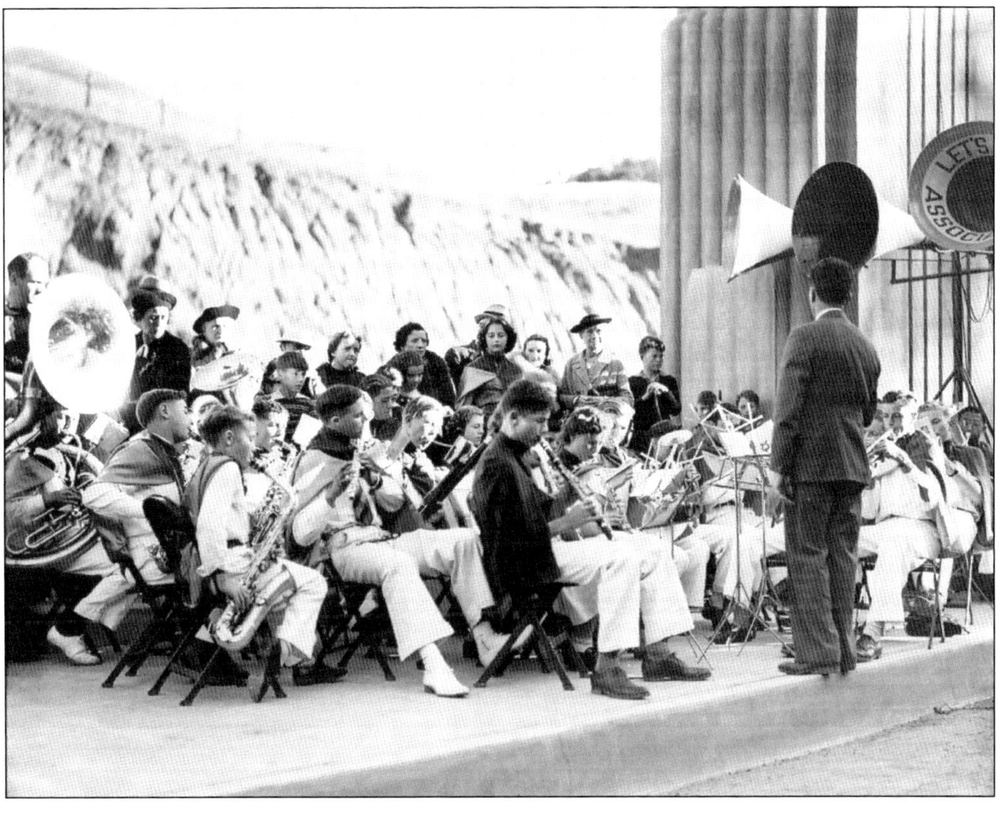

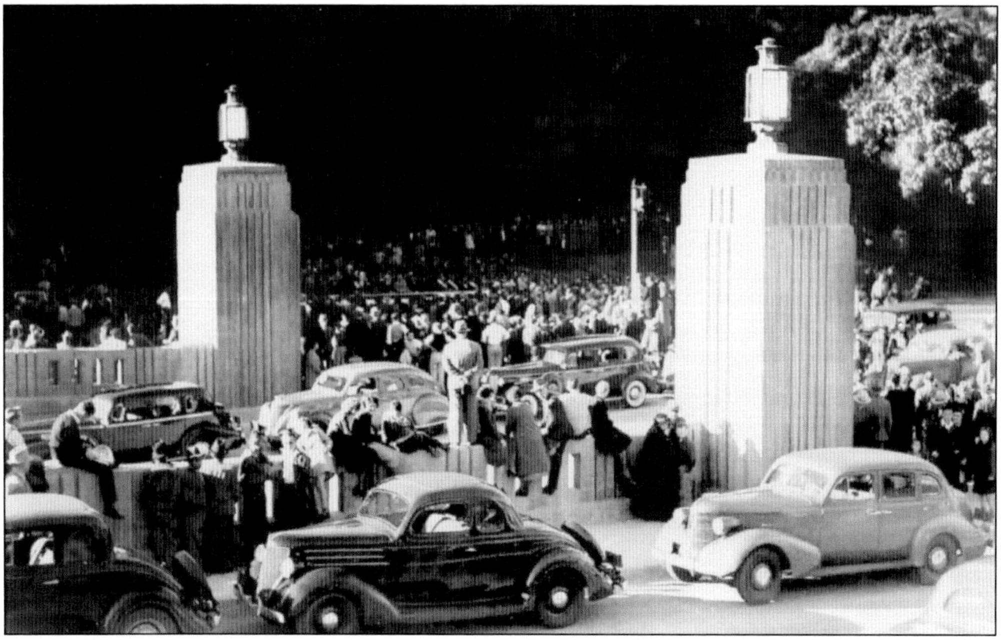

At 2:30 p.m., the official party, led by California governor Frank F. Merriam, traveled by automobile through the tunnel to the Contra Costa side for the final part of the dedication. Governor Merriam completed his speech from the Contra Costa platform, urging that the policies of highway construction be sustained and that gasoline tax money be used for such purposes in the future. (Courtesy Contra Costa County Historical Society.)

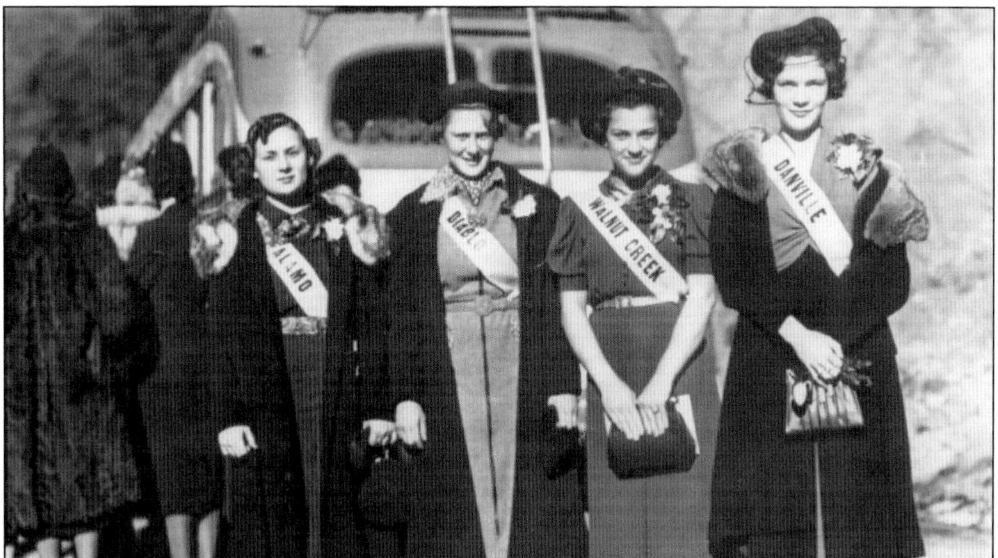

Twenty-four young women from cities in Contra Costa County welcomed the official party of dignitaries to the Contra Costa side of the tunnel. Among the beauties who took part in the dedication were, from left to right, Joan Miles (representing Alamo), Barbara Conklin (representing Diablo), Florence Symmons (representing Walnut Creek), and Mildred Lewis (representing Danville). (Courtesy Museum of the San Ramon Valley.)

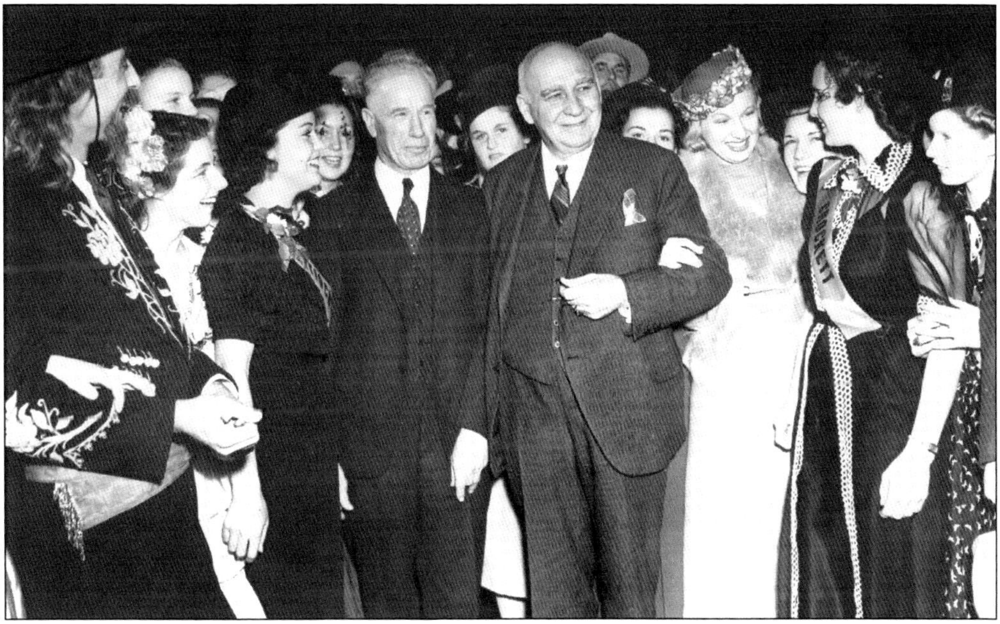

Alameda County supervisor Thomas Caldecott (left) and California governor Frank Merriam (right) were among the dignitaries who attended the tunnel dedication after a breakfast at the Claremont Hotel. Following the speeches at the east portal, more than 4,000 motorists proceeded through the tunnel in the first hour it was open. (Courtesy Contra Costa County Historical Society.)

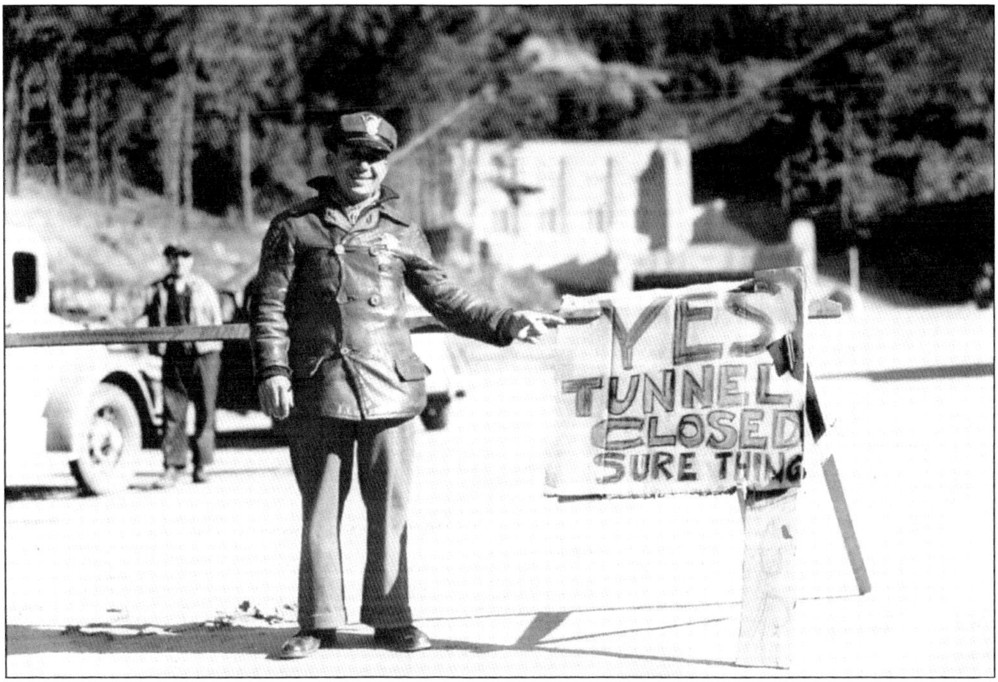

Gus Frates (pictured) was one of the policemen posted at the east and west approaches to the tunnel to keep early arrivals from driving through the tunnel before the dedication ceremonies were completed. The first car to officially pass through the new tunnel contained Gov. Frank F. Merriam and other officials. (Courtesy Contra Costa County Historical Society.)

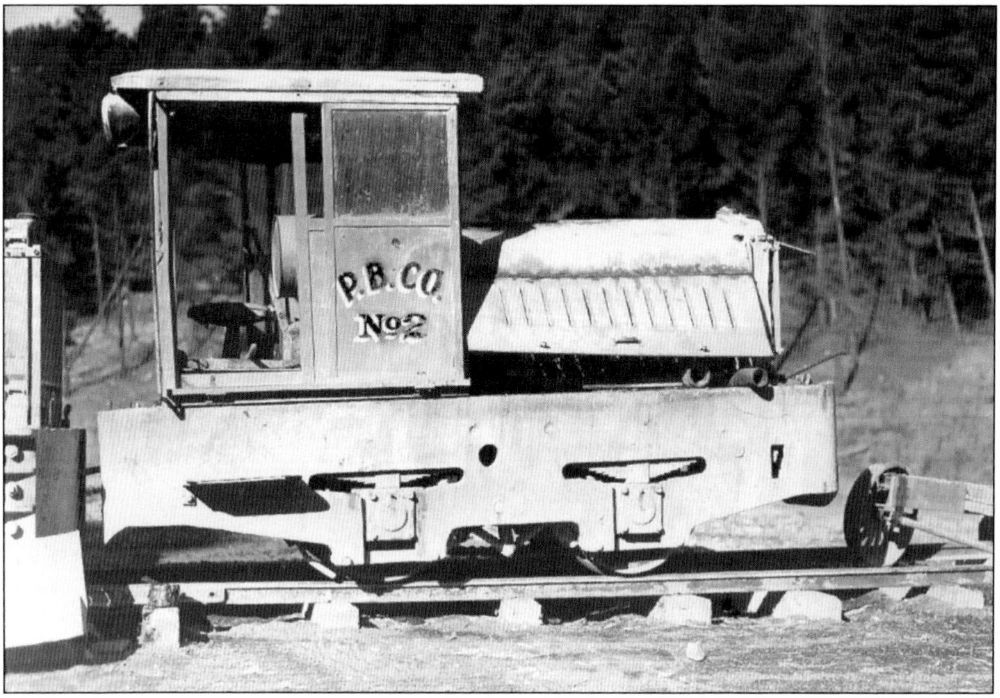

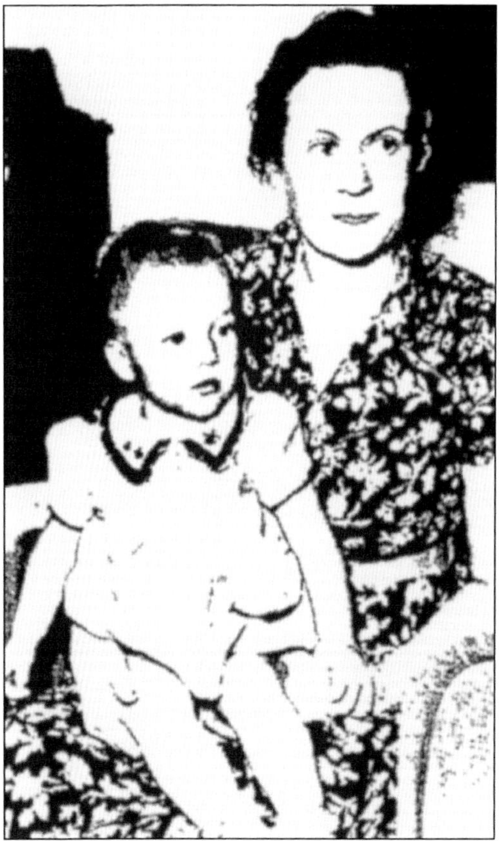

This battery-powered locomotive was displayed at the opening of the tunnel. Within the tunnel limits, five-yard muck cars on 36-inch gauge operated with seven- and eight-ton battery locomotives. Excavated material was loaded into the muck cars and delivered to dump trucks outside the bores. The excess dirt was used as fill on the tunnel approaches. The trains were also used to bring in wood supports used to shore up the excavation. (Courtesy Contra Costa County Historical Society.)

Nancy Borgeson, 15 months old, was the first baby to ride though the Broadway Low Level Tunnel. In 1903, her grandmother Gertrude McNeil was the first woman to drive through the Kennedy Tunnel. Nancy and her parents received special permission from Harry M. Stow, secretary of Joint Highway District No. 13. Thirty years earlier, Stow's father had granted permission to Nancy's grandmother to be the first woman to travel through the Kennedy Tunnel in a horse and surrey. Nancy rode through in a car. She is shown with her mother, Bertha Borgeson, youngest daughter of Gertude and Robert McNeil. (Courtesy *Oakland Tribune*.)

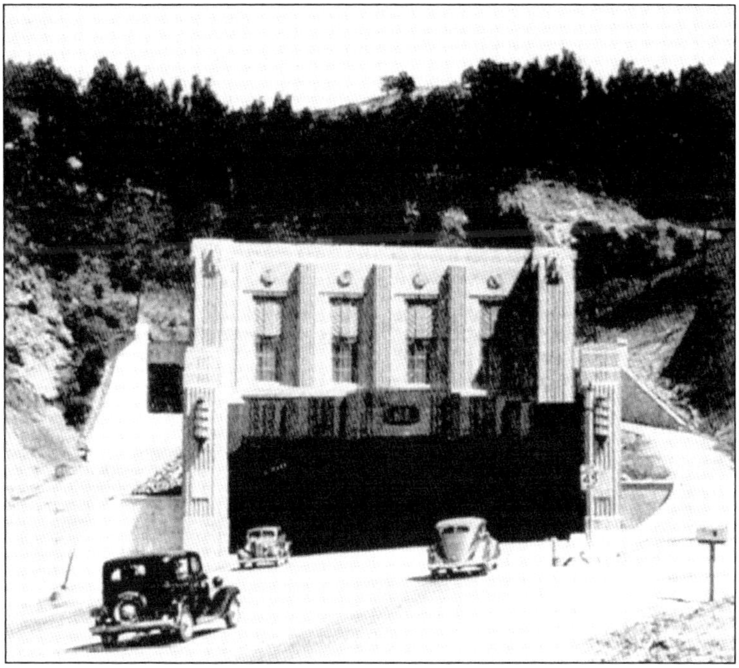

The west portal of the Broadway Low Level Tunnel is shown in this 1939 photograph. Cars travelled east and west through the two bores (and past the mailbox, visible at lower right in the image, of a home located near the tunnel on the west side). Travel from Fourteenth Street and Broadway in Oakland through the hills and into the sunshine of Orinda took just 17 minutes via the newly opened tunnel. (Courtesy Chris Treadway.)

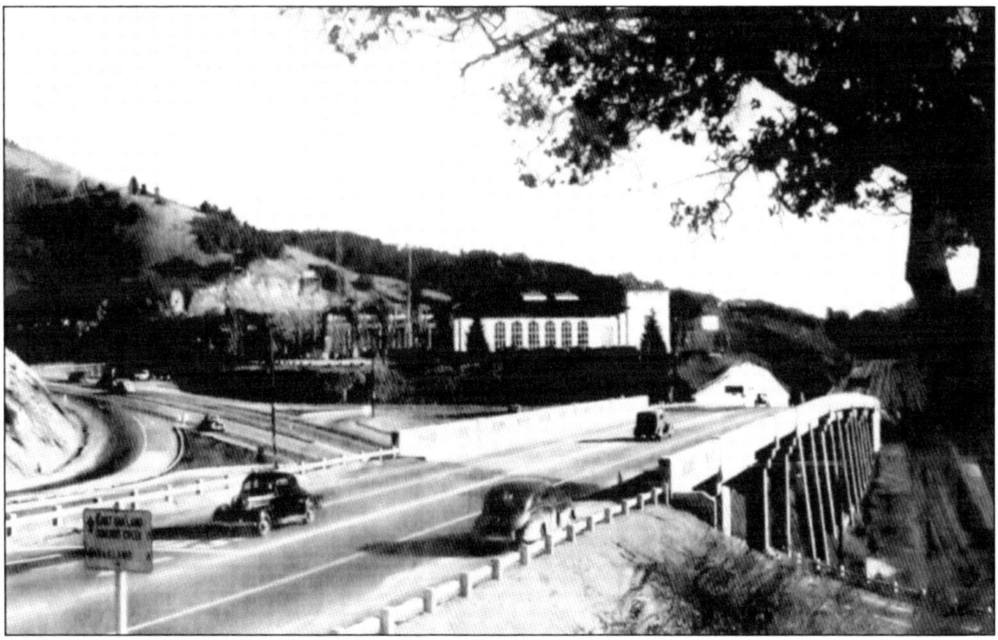

The highway to and from the west portal of the tunnel is shown in this photograph taken shortly after the tunnel opened in 1937. A Pacific Gas and Electric Company substation is visible in the background. The intersection of Highways 24 and 13 is now at this location. (Courtesy Chris Treadway.)

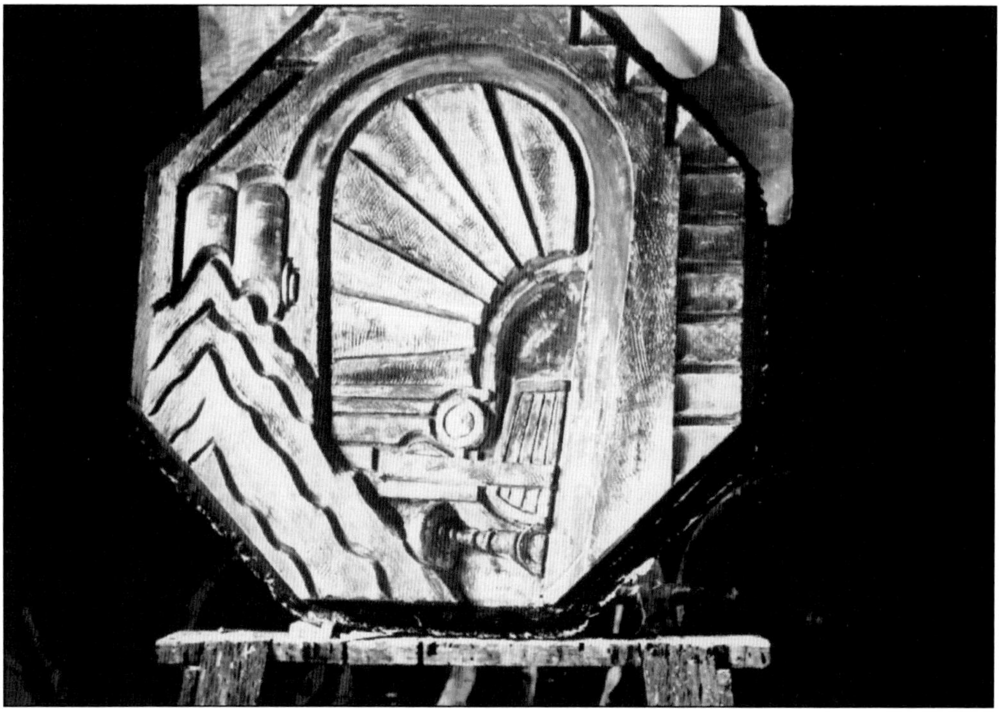

Henry H. Meyers was the architect for Joint Highway District No. 13, and he designed both the portal buildings and the approaches. Meyers had worked with George Posey on the Posey Tube, where he first used Art Deco ornamentation on the tube's portal buildings. Decorative detailing on the Broadway Low Level Tunnel is shown on the reinforced concrete medallions and other parts of the tunnel. The same four medallions appear on the faces of the two tunnel portals. The medallion above shows a car exiting a tunnel, and the eagle below was visible on the face of the eastern tunnel portals. (Above, courtesy California Department of Transportation; below, courtesy Lafayette Historical Society.)

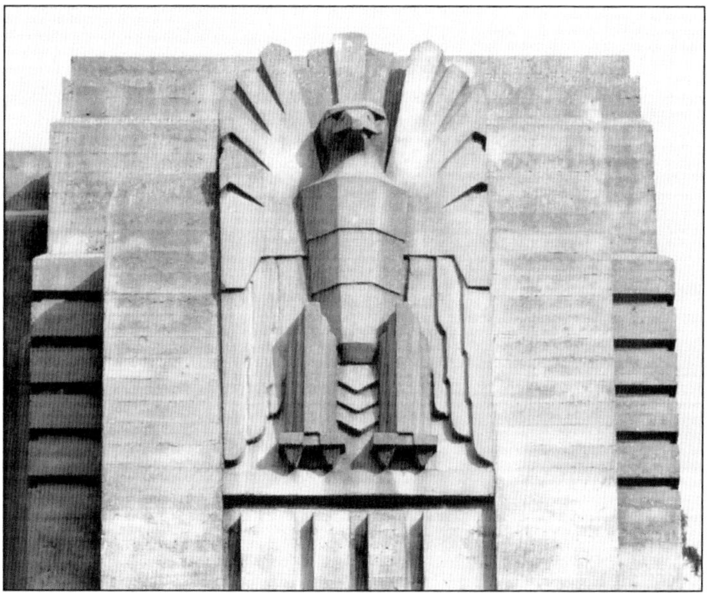

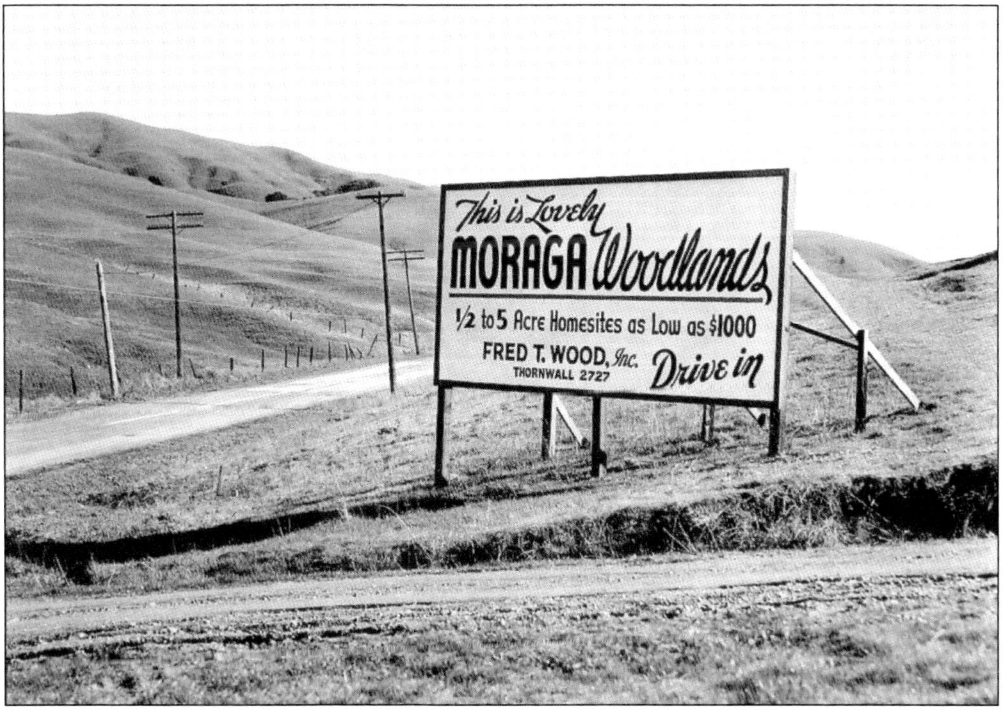

With the opening of the Broadway Low Level Tunnel, hundreds of East Bay residents purchased property in Contra Costa County. Oakland realtor Fred Wood had never seen such a demand for real estate as he did following the construction of the tunnel. He reported that he sold seven homesites in his Moraga Woodlands development in one day. Wood advertised at the homesites and in the *Oakland Tribune*. In 1938, half-acre to five-acre lots were available for purchase at a beginning price of $1,000. (Above, courtesy Contra Costa Historical Society; below, courtesy *Oakland Tribune*.)

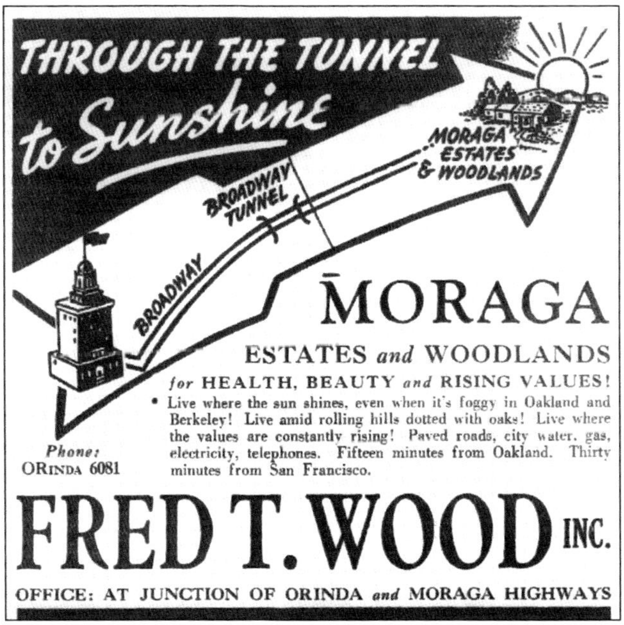

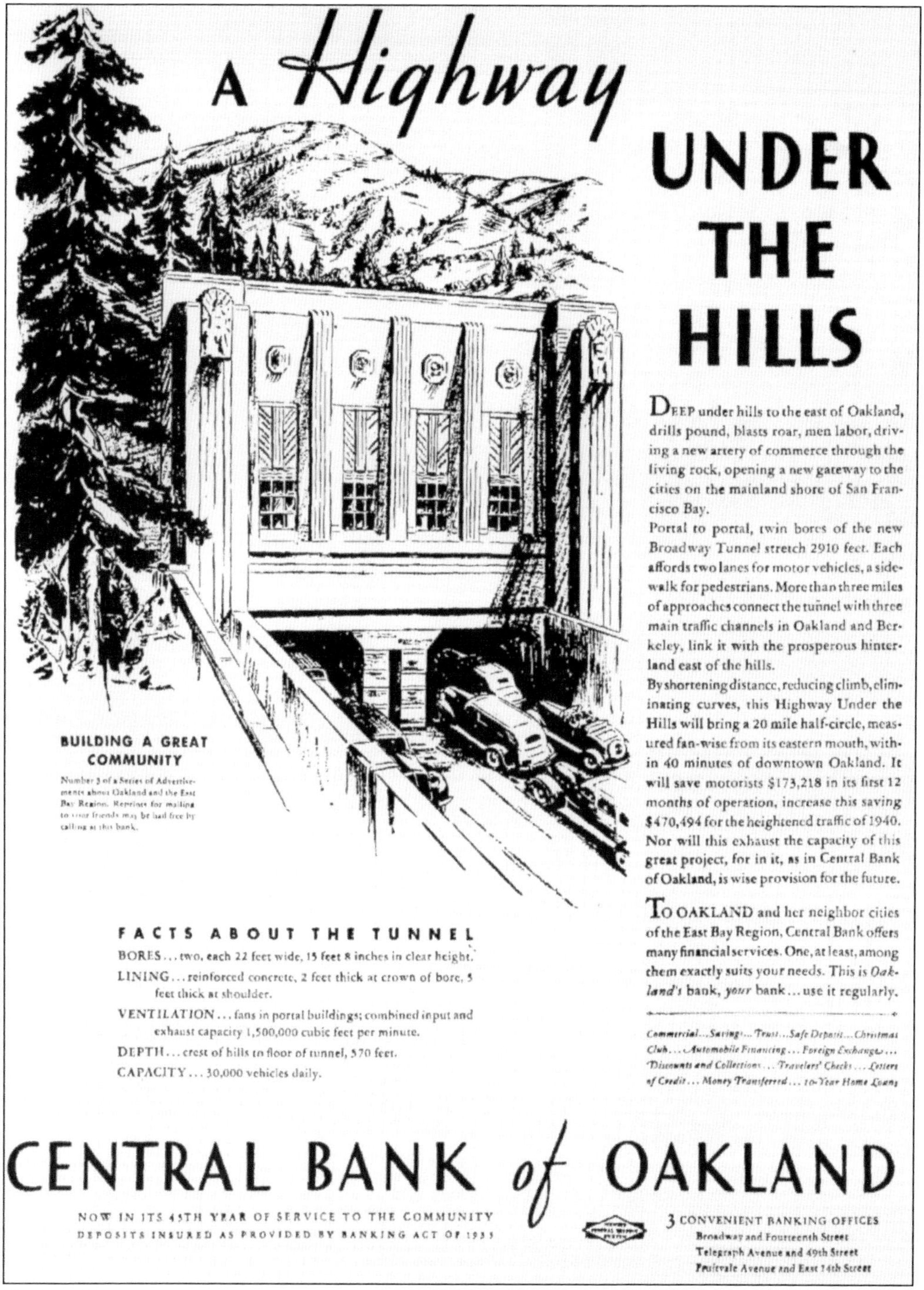

Oakland businesses were excited about the new tunnel and included it in their advertising. The Central Bank of Oakland touted that the tunnel played a role in "building a great community." According to this advertisement in the *Oakland Tribune*, this was "Number 3 of a Series of Advertisements about Oakland and the East Bay Region. Reprints for mailing to your friends may be had free by calling at this bank." (Courtesy *Oakland Tribune*.)

Four

The Third Bore

In the postwar era of the 1950s, the state had made improvements to Highway 75 (later Highway 24) at the approach to the Broadway Low Level Tunnel that changed it from a two-lane road to a four-lane freeway. As the population of cities east of the tunnel increased, so did the number of automobiles using the tunnel.

At its 1960 session, the California Legislature officially designated the Broadway Low Level Tunnel as the Caldecott Tunnel in honor of the late Thomas E. Caldecott, who had been an Alameda County supervisor and president of Joint Highway District No. 13 when the original tunnel was built in the mid-1930s.

Construction on the third bore began in November 1961 about 150 feet north of the second bore of the original tunnel; this bore was designed to be larger than the two preceding tunnels. The state made sure there was ample land available should a fourth bore need to be constructed in the future. Scientific advances and information from the construction of the original bores were available to aid in construction of the third bore.

The third bore was completed in October 1964. It was approximately 300 feet lower than the existing Kennedy Tunnel and built on a four-percent grade descending from the Orinda end toward Oakland. Both ends were built on curves in order to provide a smooth transition into the approaches at each end. The new tunnel had a 28-foot roadway with a four-foot sidewalk to the right of traffic and a two-and-a-half-foot curb on the left with 17 feet of vertical clearance.

The third bore cost nearly $25 million—more than twice the cost of the original two tunnels. After the third bore opened in 1964, the two original bores were each separately closed for needed maintenance, which included installing fluorescent overhead lighting. The middle bore was then used to accommodate commute-direction traffic in mornings and evenings. Pop-up barriers were added when the center bore's direction was changed.

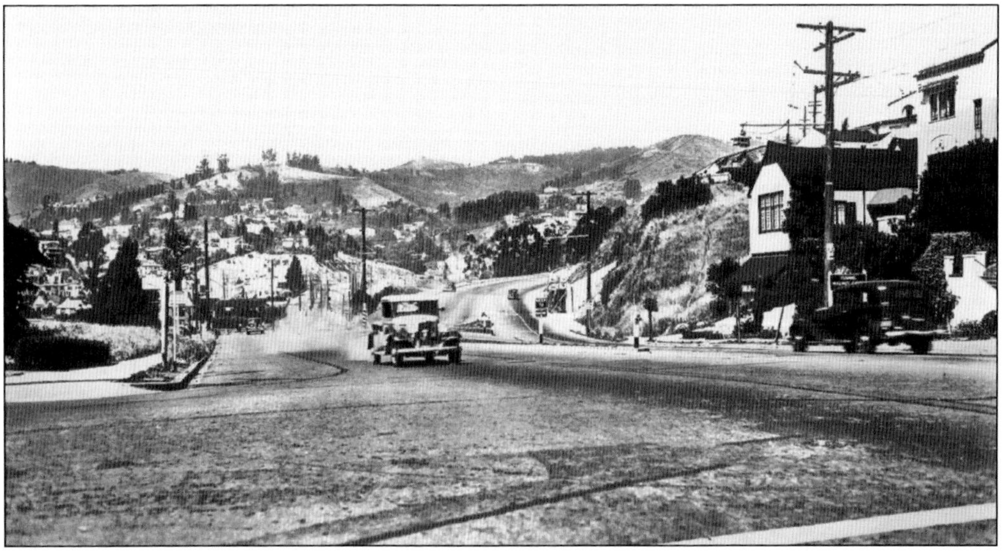

The intersection of Broadway and Patton Street is shown in this 1940s photograph. Patton Street connected to the approach to the newly built Highway 24 and the Broadway Low Level Tunnel. Today, this intersection is part of the Broadway exit from Highway 24 and leads to an on-ramp to the eastbound lanes of Highway 24 going to the Caldecott Tunnel. (Courtesy California Department of Transportation.)

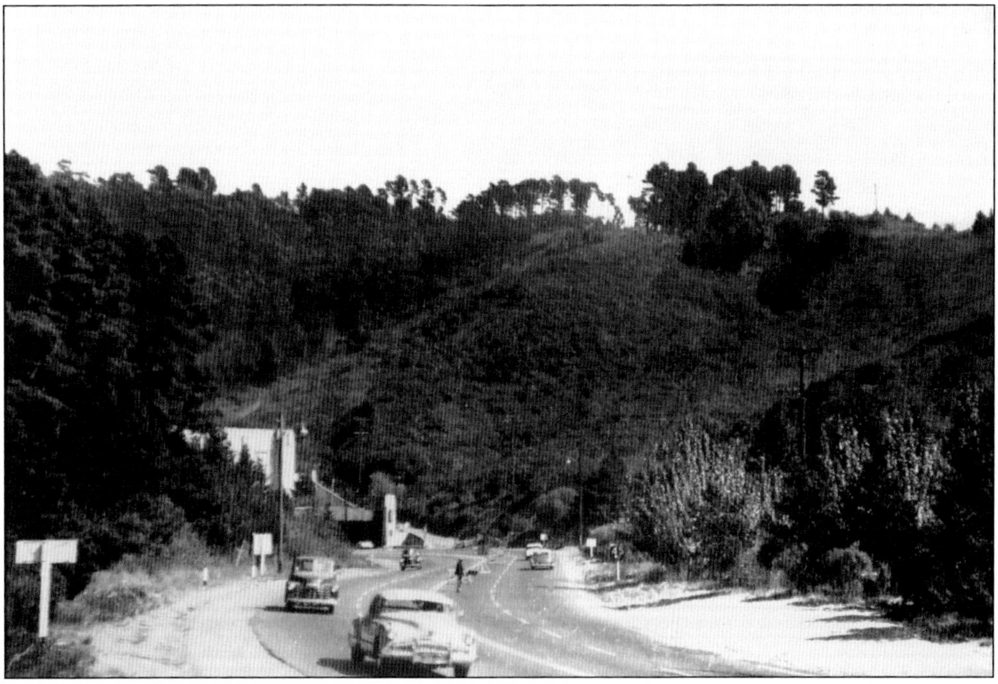

In this September 1953 image, a flagman provides traffic control on Highway 24 at the approach to the west portal of the Broadway Low Level Tunnel. In the 1950s, the state made improvements to the tunnel approaches that expanded the two-lane roads to four lanes. (Courtesy California Department of Transportation.)

In December 1950, a million tons of rain-soaked earth came down on Tunnel Road near the Orinda Crossroads and blocked all four lanes of Highway 24. The immensity of the slide can be seen in the lower photograph that shows three men standing in front of the debris. A four-lane bypass was built on the shoulder of the highway. In April 1951, workers were able to begin clearing away the dried earth, transporting it to a nearby site to be used as fill. Slides were common along the highway, especially during the heavy rains of the winter season. A sinkhole in April 1958 was caused when a five-foot water drainage pipe traversing the highway broke 25 feet underground. It closed three lanes of traffic and left only one lane open on both sides. (Both, courtesy Contra Costa County Historical Society.)

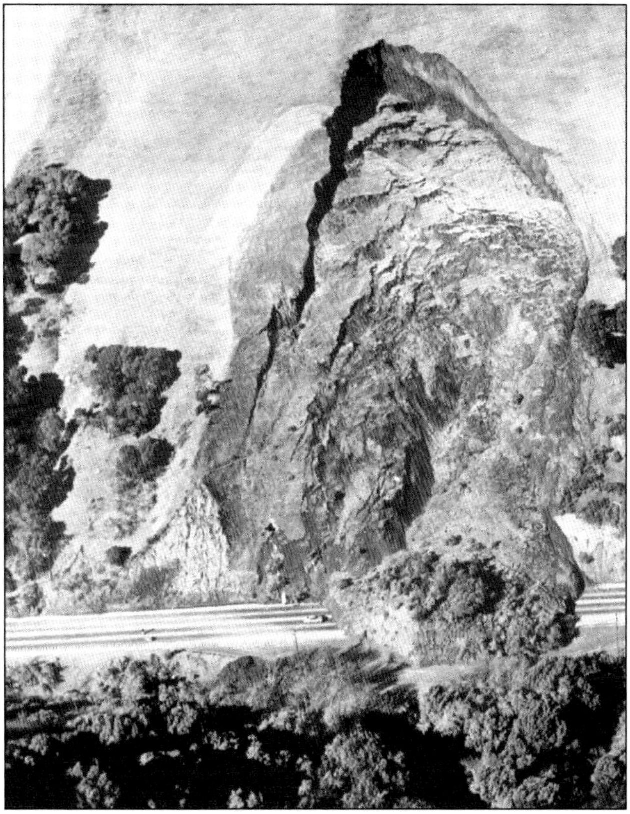

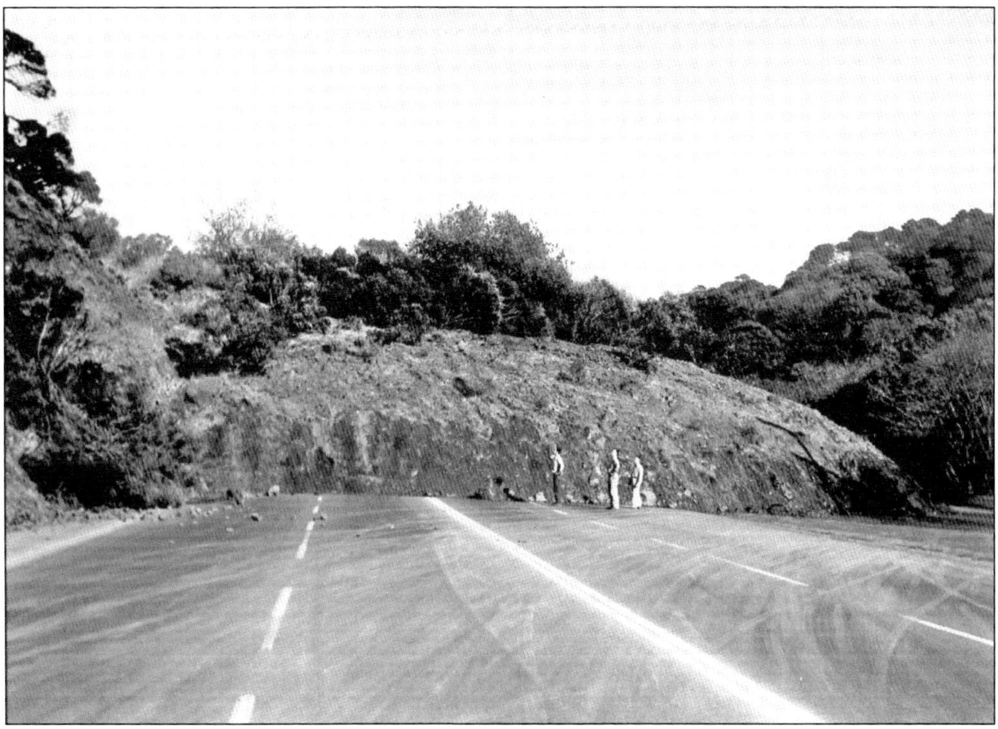

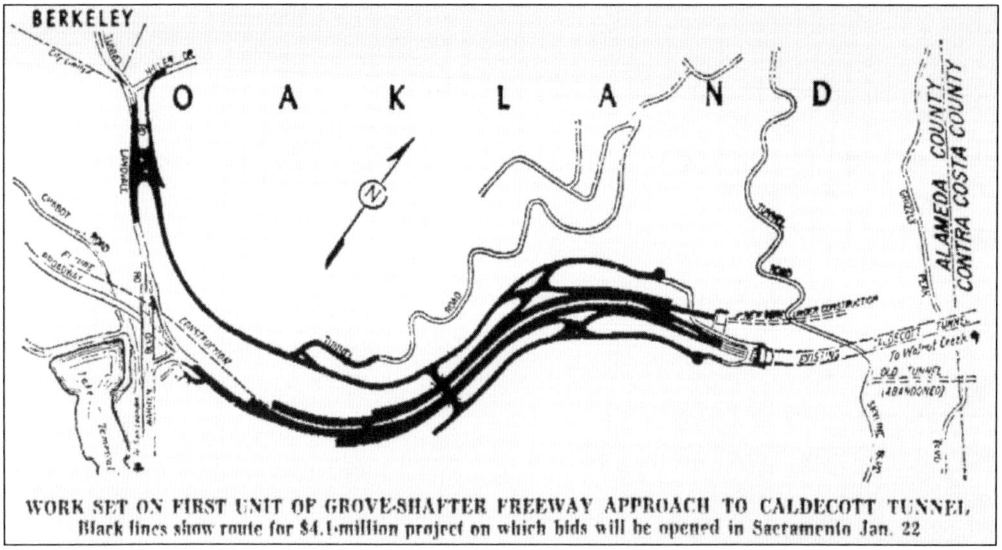

By 1958, the State of California had approved an eight-lane freeway from the Eastshore Freeway to the Broadway Low Level Tunnel. The Grove-Shafter Freeway was to be six miles in length and would help to accommodate the traffic loads, which were estimated to increase to more than 54,000 vehicles per day by the 1960s. In the late 1950s, local city streets were jammed at peak periods by the movement of about 83,000 vehicles per day, some going to the western approach to the Broadway Low Level Tunnel. (Courtesy *Oakland Tribune*.)

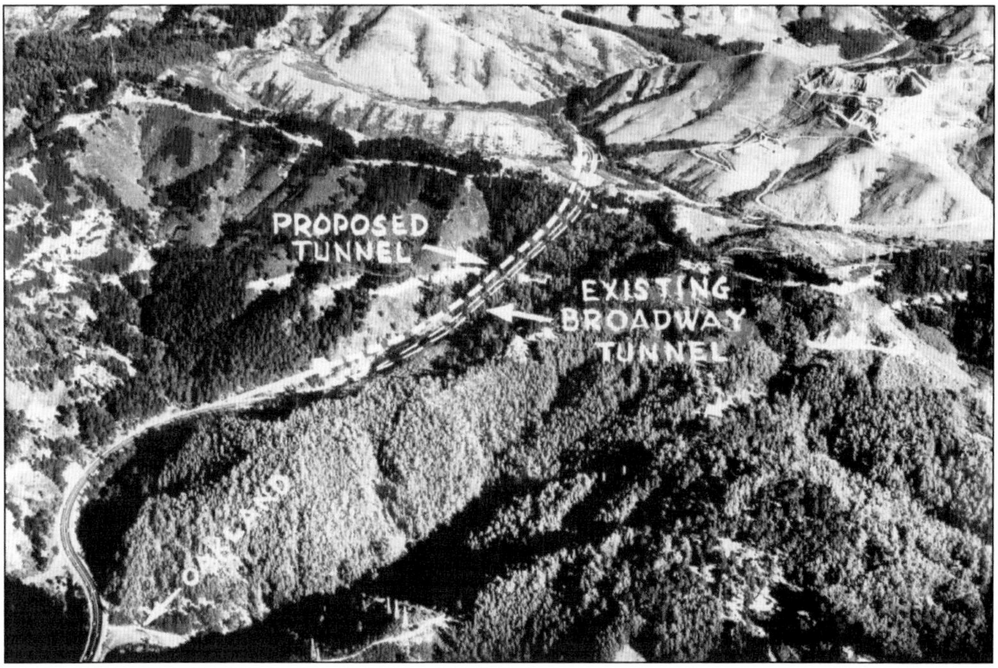

The construction of the Broadway Low Level Tunnel changed Contra Costa County from farming communities to major suburbs of Oakland and San Francisco, and during the 1950s, the population of cities east of the tunnel exploded. Fortunately, the California Division of Highways had purchased additional land north of the existing bores on which to build an additional tunnel. This 1959 image shows the site of the new bore. (Courtesy California Department of Transportation.)

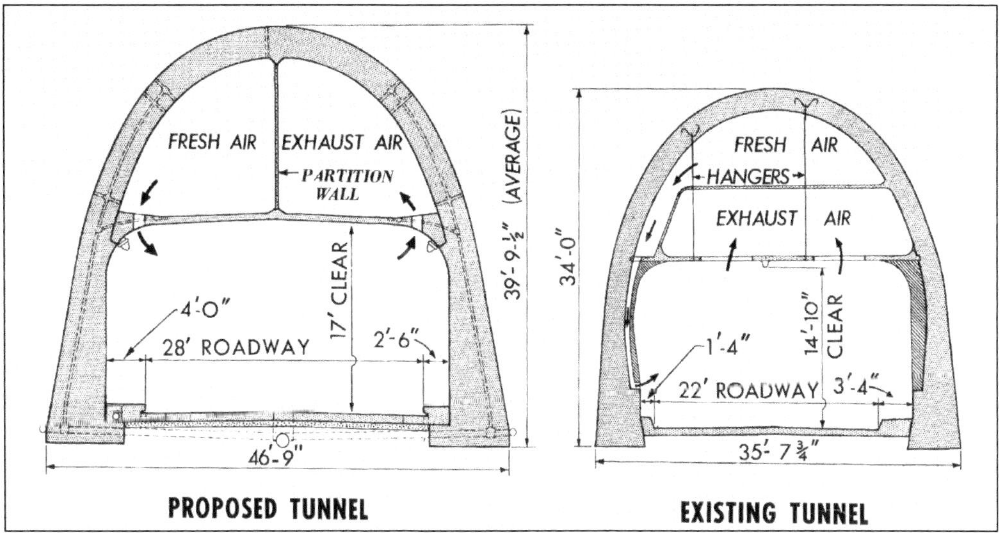

This 1959 image shows a cross-section of the proposed third bore that reveals the changes made since the construction of the initial two bores of the tunnel: the roadway is wider, with additional space on the sides of the lanes; the height of the bore itself, as well as the ceiling height, is bigger to accommodate taller vehicles; and the ventilation system has been improved. (Courtesy California Department of Transportation.)

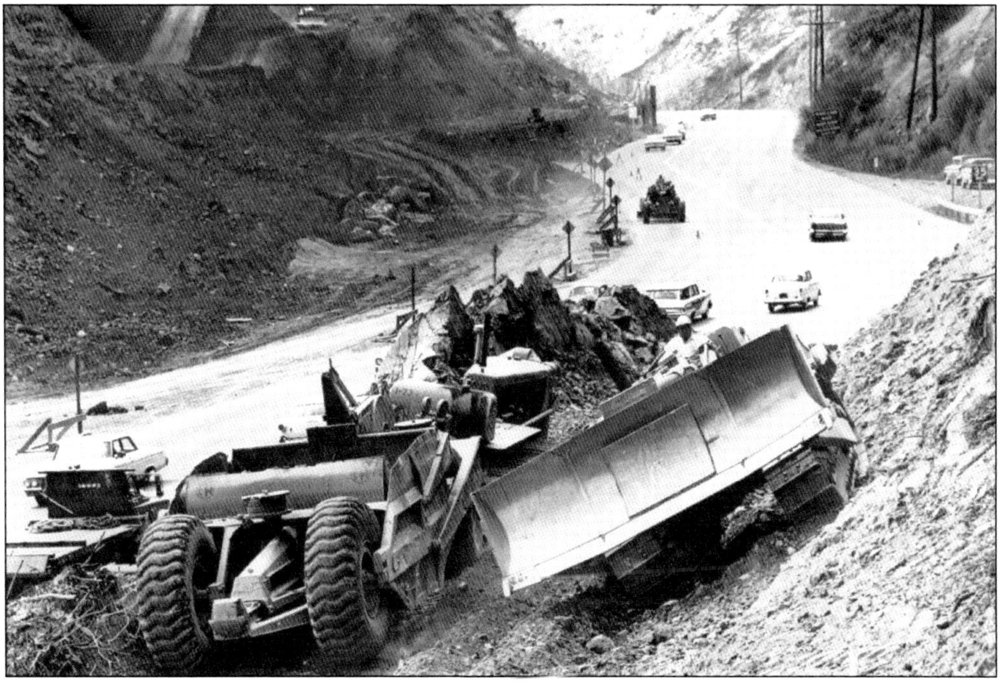

Before work could begin on the new bore, a first phase—which included extensive drainage work and excavation for the approaches—started in December 1960 and involved moving more than 400,000 cubic yards of material. Excavated material at the east end went into the detour, which was constructed prior to driving into the tunnel. With the completion of the excavation and detour, space was available for the contractor to install necessary facilities and begin work on the west portal service road, bridges, and the tunnel. (Courtesy Oakland Museum of California.)

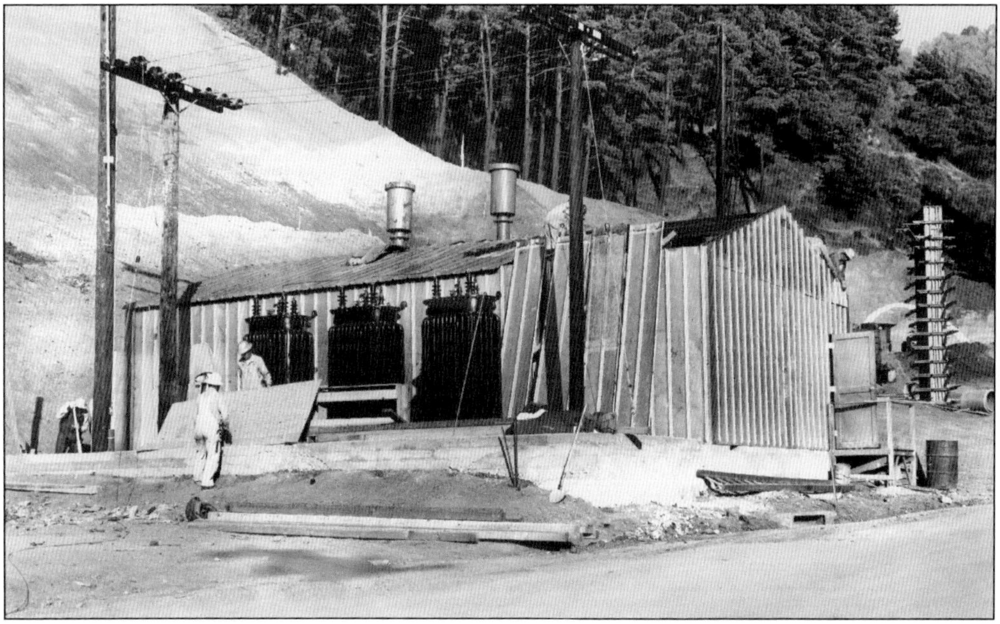

The power plant that supplied the electricity for the construction of the third bore was located near the western portal. Electricity, supplied by Pacific Gas and Electric Company, ran compressors to furnish air to pneumatic drills, huge shovels, concrete mixers, and saws and charged batteries for the cars that hauled equipment. (Courtesy Oakland Museum of California.)

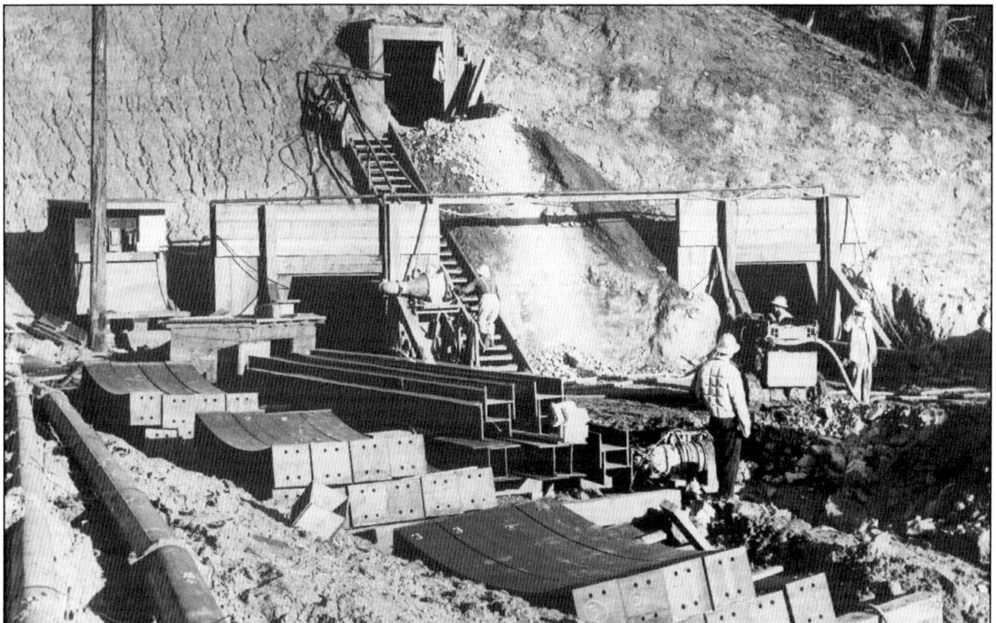

The first phase of the tunneling operation consisted of placing three small shafts (drifts) in the mountain. One of the drifts was at the crown, and the others (one at each side) were at the lower limit of the steel tunnel supports, about 14 feet above the roadway grade. At a distance of 117 feet into the hill, a sandstone material was discovered by excavation workers. (Courtesy Oakland Museum of California.)

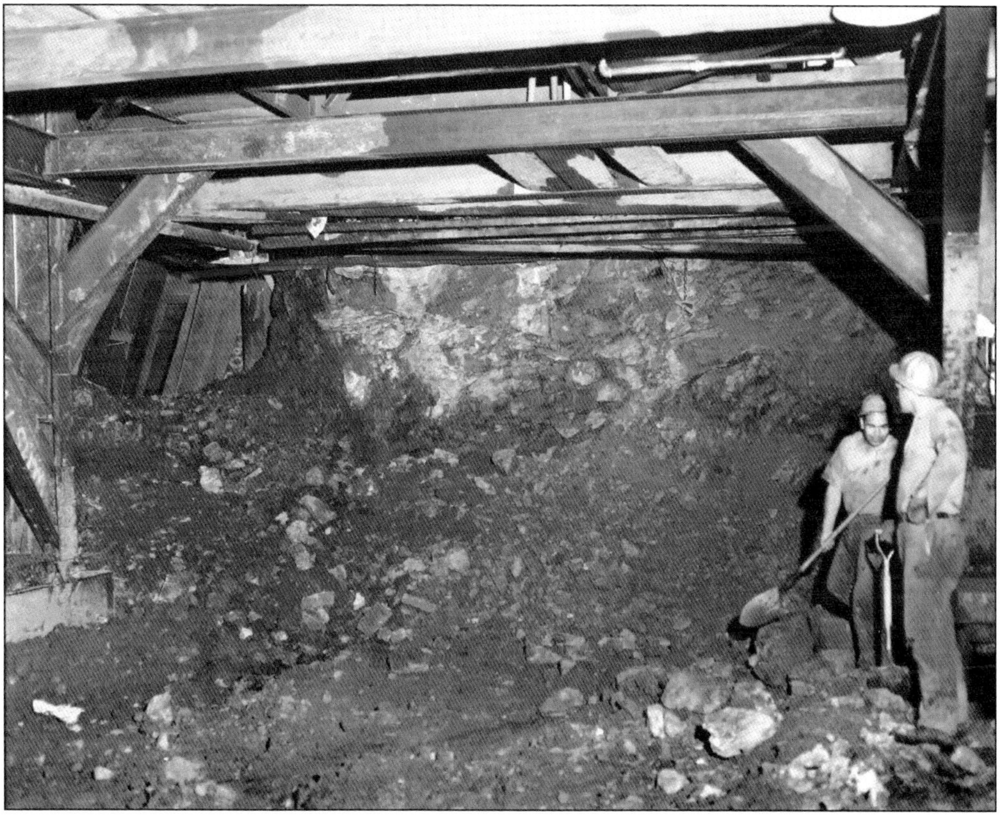

These workers are shown digging a smaller tunnel known as a heading. Once the top heading had moved some distance into the rock, workers began excavating immediately below the floor of the top heading. This is a called a bench. One advantage of using this method was that engineers coud use the heading tunnel to gauge the stability of the rock before moving forward with the project. (Courtesy Contra Costa County Historical Society.)

The third bore was dug from the inside out. The three small minor drifts were joined to form one big opening at the arch of the tunnel. Once the drifts were connected and the steel arch ribs (pictured) were set in place, workers joined the drifts from the inside out. This "portaling" technique was safer for workers, as it reduced the chances of a cave-in. (Courtesy California Department of Transportation.)

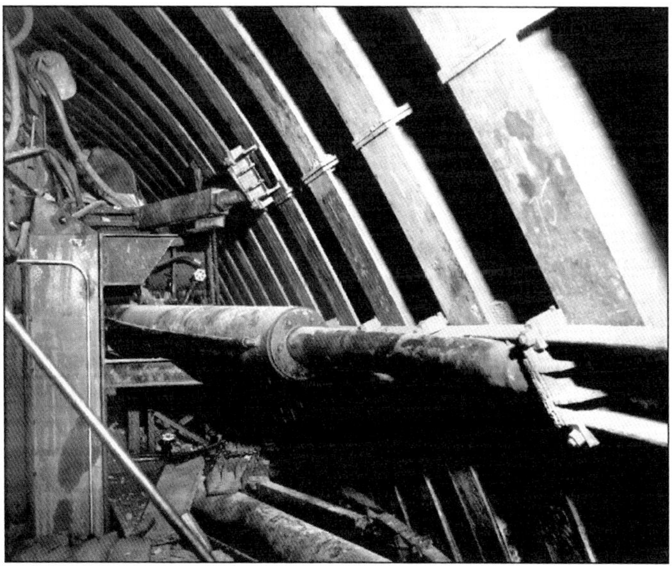

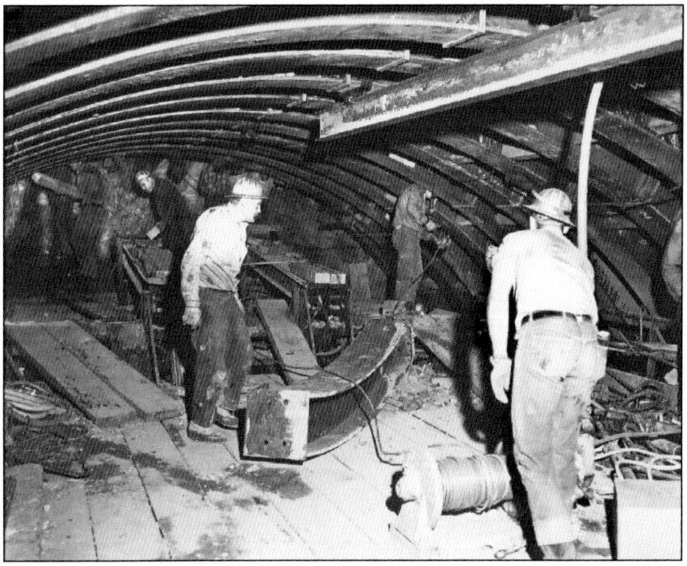

The large steel ribs (tunnel supports) were erected in four sections—one lower section on each side was handled from below, and two crown sections were set up from atop the jumbo. Workers then performed blocking and installed lagging behind the steel supports to retain the unstable material. These tunnel workers are installing the steel arches that support the roof of the tunnel. (Courtesy California Department of Transportation.)

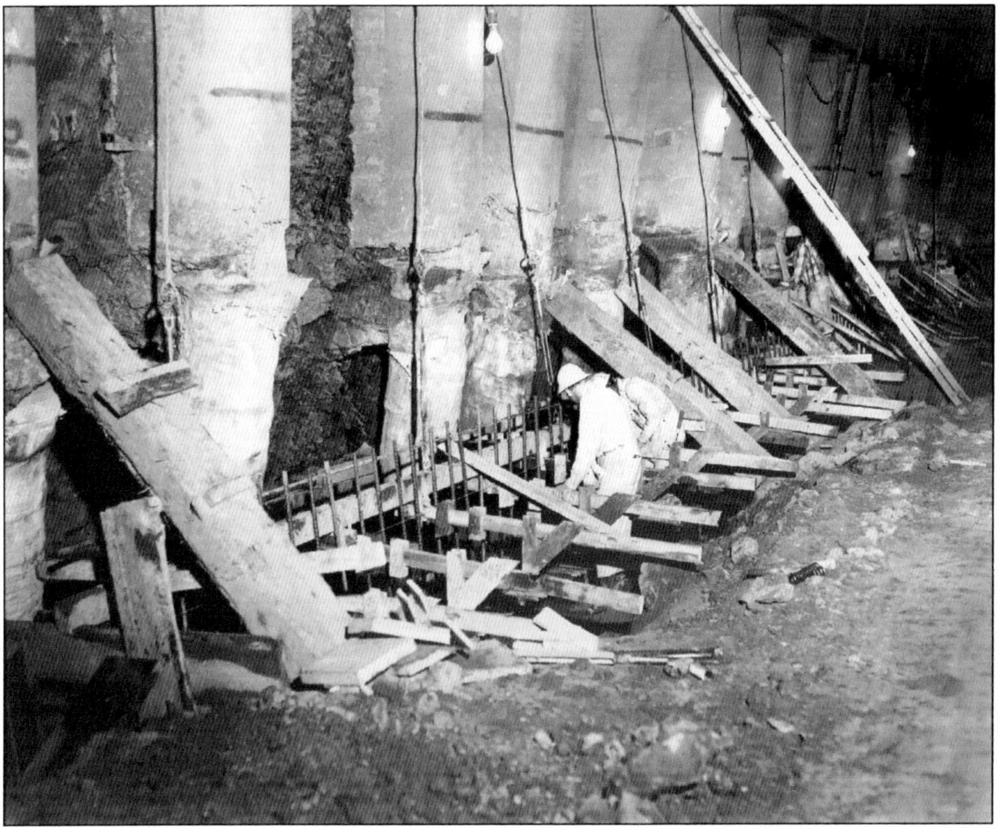

This image shows workers performing underpinning (supporting the wall plates) in the west end of the tunnel in 1962. Underpinning was accomplished by mining or drilling holes at intervals in the foundation level, forming pilasters, and placing concrete up to the wall plates. After the pilasters became the supports, the rest of the excavation was finished to roadway level, and the footings were poured. (Courtesy California Department of Transportation.)

The jumbo was a two-level piece of moveable equipment that was placed in front of the digging face of the tunnel. Pipes and steel on its second level controlled 18 hydraulic jacks that pushed against the digging face to prevent cave-ins while workmen excavated tons of earth around the jacks with air-driven tools. The jumbo's platforms allowed workers to dig at various levels on the face without fear of a cave-in. (Courtesy Oakland Museum of California.)

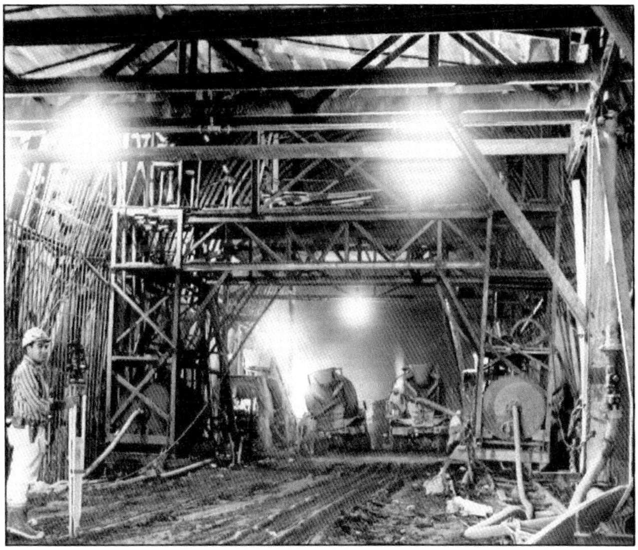

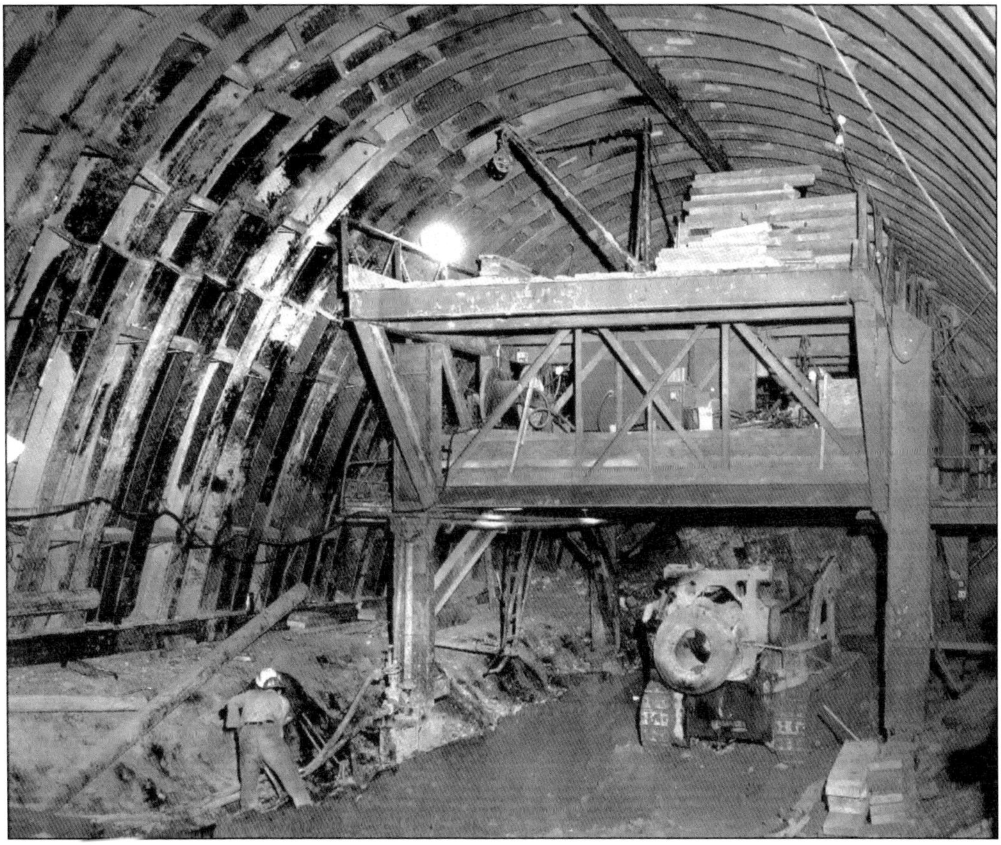

The material in the bore, which was mined by spading (or blasting, if needed), fell to the tunnel floor under the Breastboard jumbo and was picked up by front-end loaders called muckers, dumped into a dumpster, and hauled to a canyon west of the job to be used as fill for part of the freeway. The jumbo provided workers with extra protection from cave-ins. (Courtesy California Department of Transportation.)

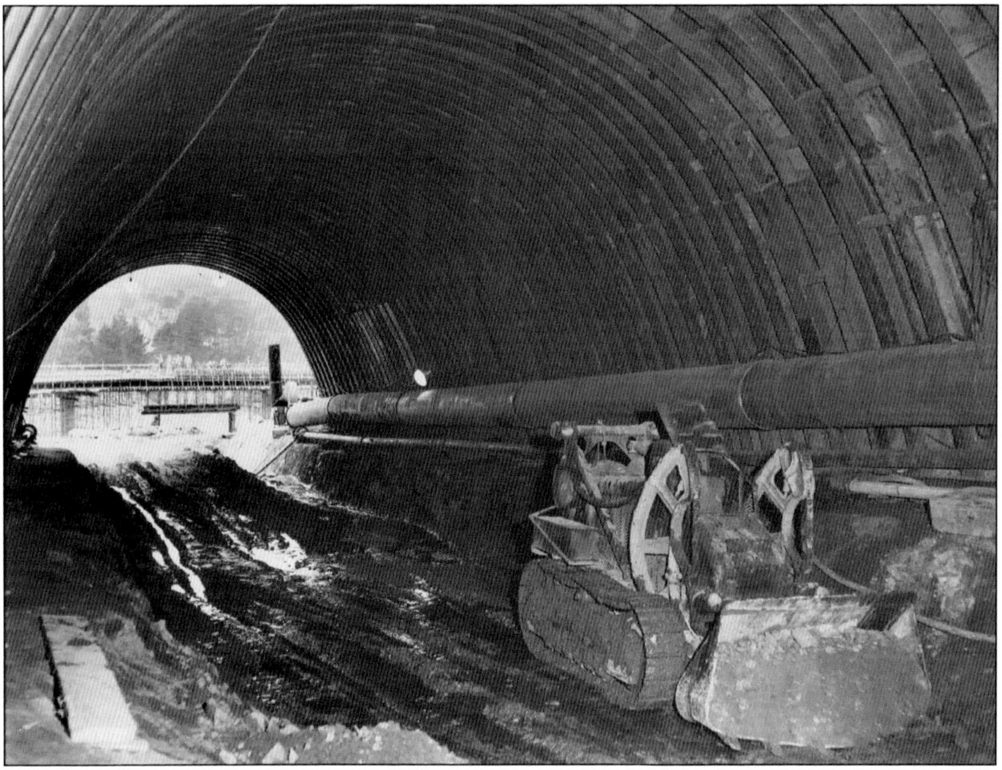

The workers went from drift to drift to install the steel ribs from wall plates to crown. Each rib consisted of six sections. Excavation carefully proceeded from the inside ribs out toward the portal. Workers excavated just enough material to give sufficient working room. With this method, workers always had steel overhead to protect them. (Courtesy California Department of Transportation.)

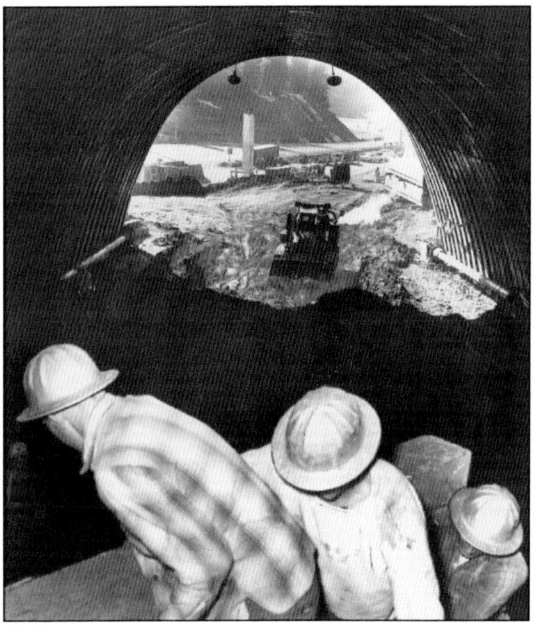

Workers carry a support beam into the bore while excavation of the roadway goes on outside the east portal. The miners were a tough, hardy lot, and the working conditions were difficult. The work was noisy, dirty, frequently wet and muddy, always hazardous, and usually done in cramped space from precarious perches. (Courtesy Oakland Museum of California.)

Miners digging the new bore of the tunnel holed through on January 9, 1963, shortly before midnight—nearly 12 hours ahead of schedule. Two charges of dynamite blasted out nine inches of sandstone inside the pilot drift alongside the main bore of the tunnel. Ronald Payne, one of the miners who had bored 3,300 feet from opposite sides of the tunnel, barely had room to shake the hands of the men opposite him. (Courtesy Oakland Museum of California.)

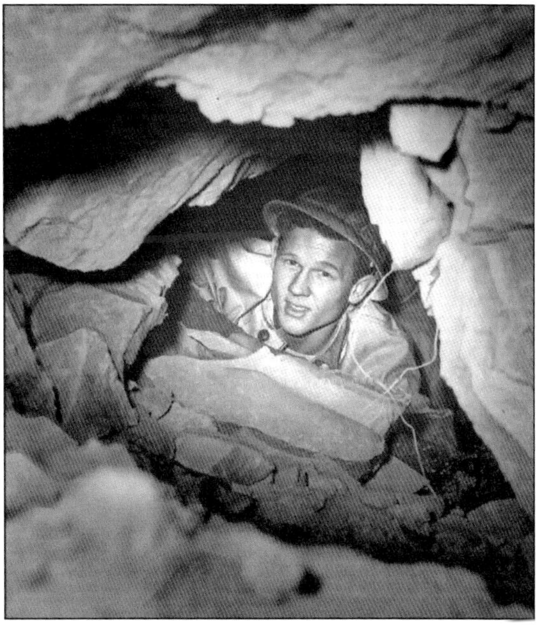

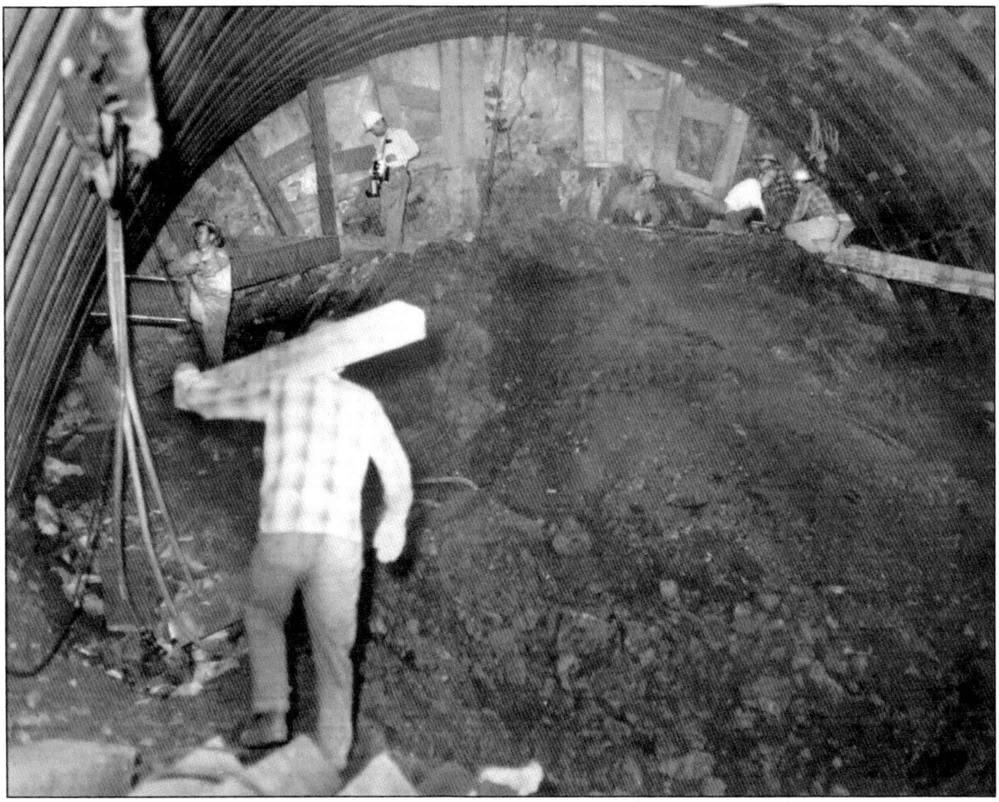

This image shows excavation in the third bore. Tools used to portal out the bore included air compressors, hand spades, jackhammers, and air-propelled mucking machines that removed the excavated material. Once the portaling was complete, work continued around the clock on the actual tunnel. (Courtesy Oakland Museum of California.)

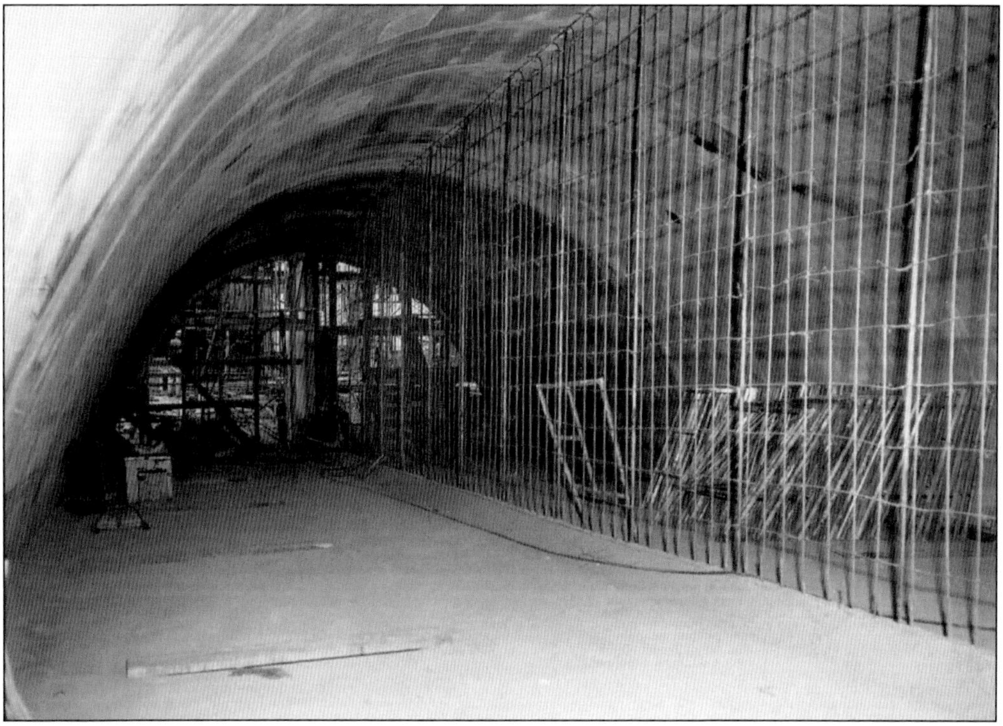

Workers installed a new transverse system of ventilation in the third bore. Fresh air was taken in at the westerly portal building and carried along a duct above the roadway. It was discharged into the roadway section through openings at one side of the ceiling. The fresh air mixed with exhaust fumes from vehicles and was drawn out through exhaust ports on the opposite side of the ceiling, then carried to the westerly portal building and discharged into the atmosphere. The two fresh-air and two exhaust blowers have a capacity of 500,000 cubic feet of air per minute. The construction of the partition between the two ducts is shown above; the unfinished roadbed is shown below. The exhaust air is automatically and continuously tested for carbon monoxide content; if needed, ventilation machinery will automatically speed up until the concentration is lowered to a desired level. (Both, courtesy California Department of Transportation.)

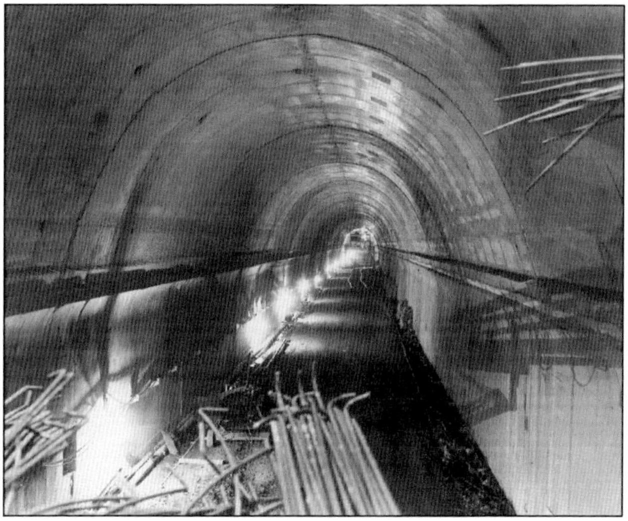

Ventilation was needed to provide fresh air and to remove explosive gases such as methane and other noxious gases, including blast fumes. An exterior ventilating plant used a forced draft through large lightweight pipes, with booster fans at intervals, to accomplish this. This image shows the steel and timber laggings that supported excavation of the upper portion of the tunnel. (Courtesy California Department of Transportation.)

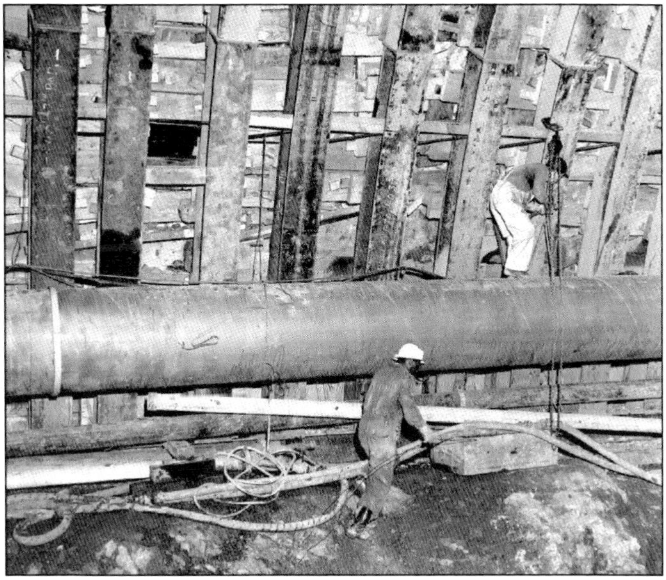

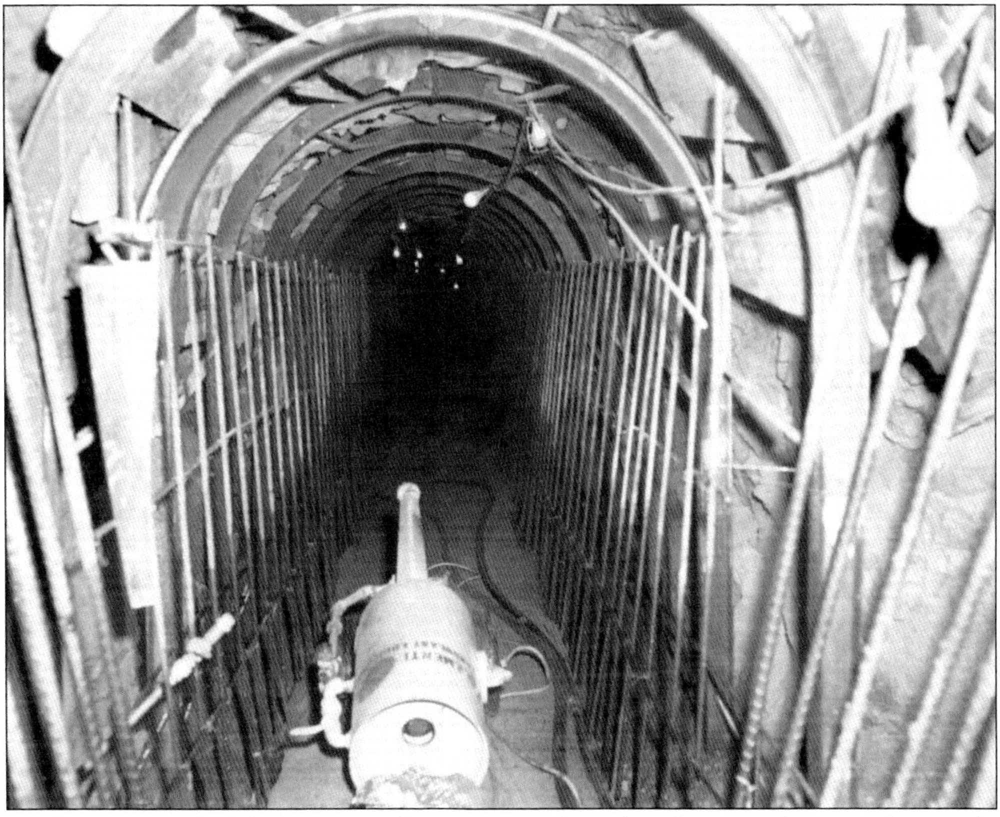

Small cross tunnels (adits) connect the main tunnels at three locations between the portals. These were intended to be used for additional safety during construction and are useful for tunnel maintenance and emergency operations. Three adits, each four feet wide by seven feet high, were constructed to connect the third bore to the second bore. (Courtesy California Department of Transportation.)

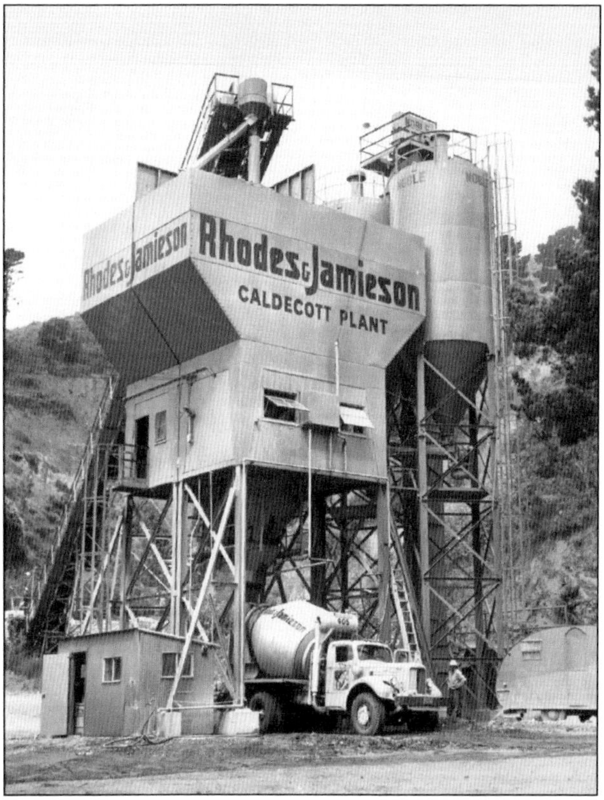

More than 100,000 tons of concrete were poured into the third bore of the tunnel. It took about nine months to pour the arched roof, the sides, the roadway, and the ceiling of the 3,300-foot-long bore. Contractors leased special concrete holding equipment (shown below) and guns to pour the arched roof and walls of the tunnel. The guns pumped a high-pressure blast of air behind a two-and-a-half-ton batch of concrete, pushing the mixture up through pipes leading to the arched top. At the top, it was pushed along by air through 200 feet of additional pipe and then dropped into the wood and steel forms. Concrete trucks loaded the mixture at the concrete plant outside the western portal. It was estimated that about 125 cubic yards of concrete were poured each day, with each cubic yard weighing about two tons. (Both, courtesy Oakland Museum of California.)

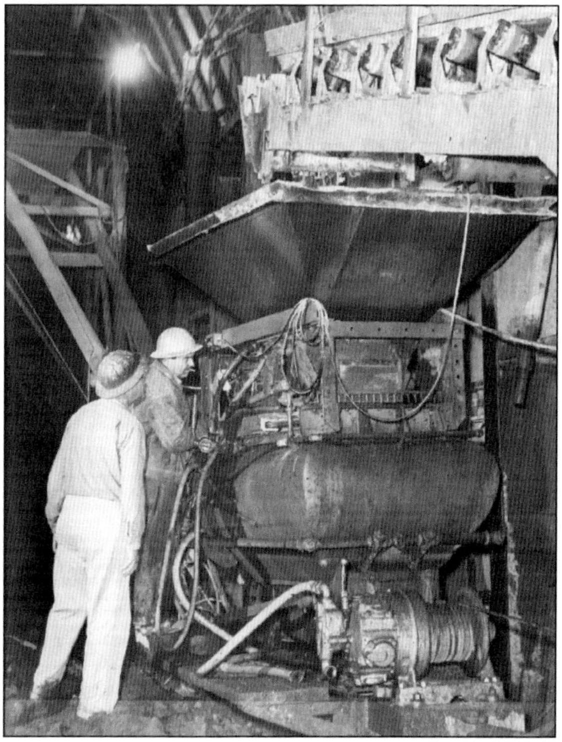

This image shows the seam between the sections of the bore that have been concreted and those that are awaiting concrete. For many years, steel rib sets served as the first-stage support for rock tunnels, with workers' close spacing of the wood blocking against the rock being important to reduce bending stress in the rib. The rib system served only as a first-stage, temporary support and required the application of a concrete lining for corrosion protection. (Courtesy Oakland Museum of California.)

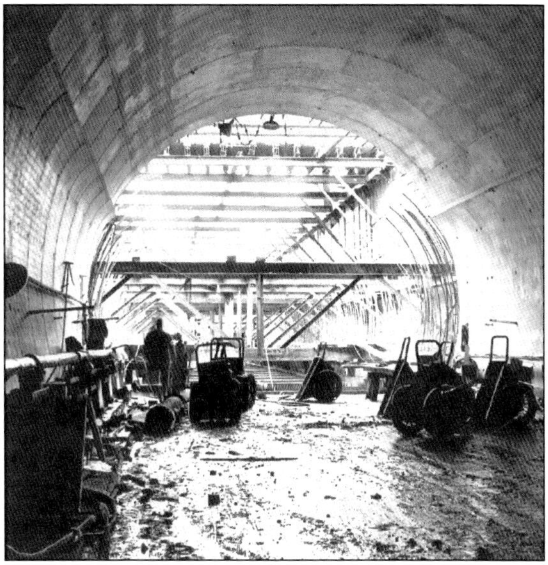

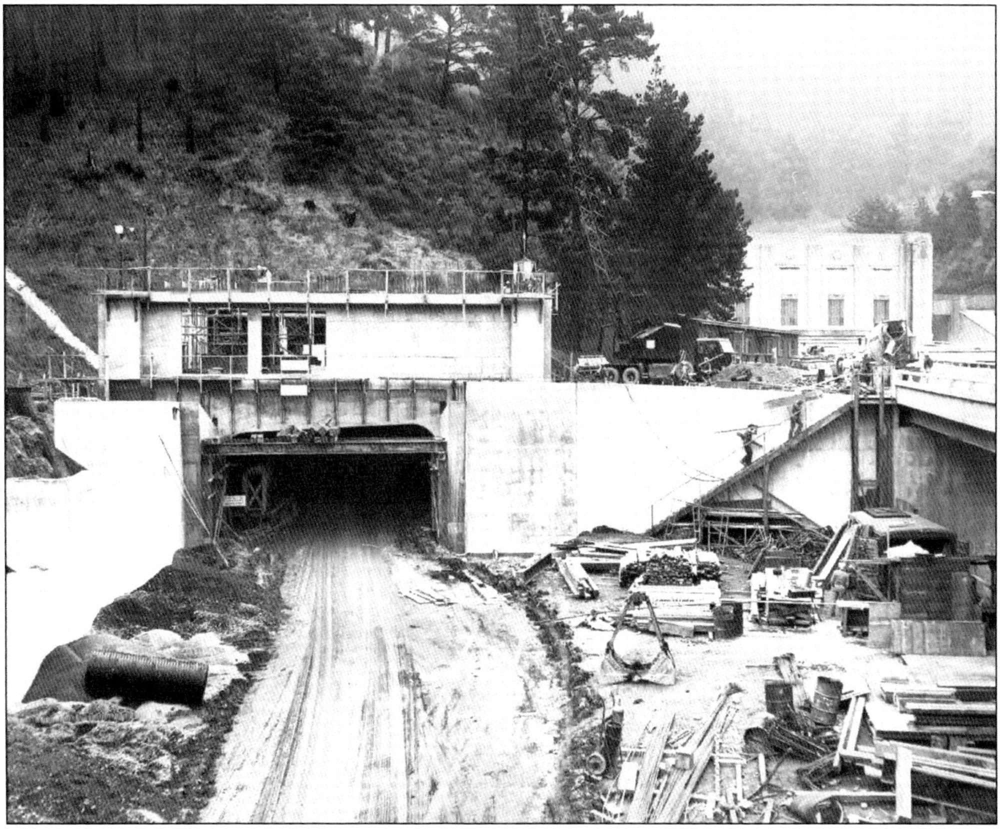

Work continues at the western portal of the third bore in this 1963 photograph. The building being constructed above the bore was to house the controls for all three bores. Service road bridges were built over the roadways at the western portal so that maintenance and service vehicles could access any one of the tunnels without having to contend with traffic. (Courtesy California Department of Transportation.)

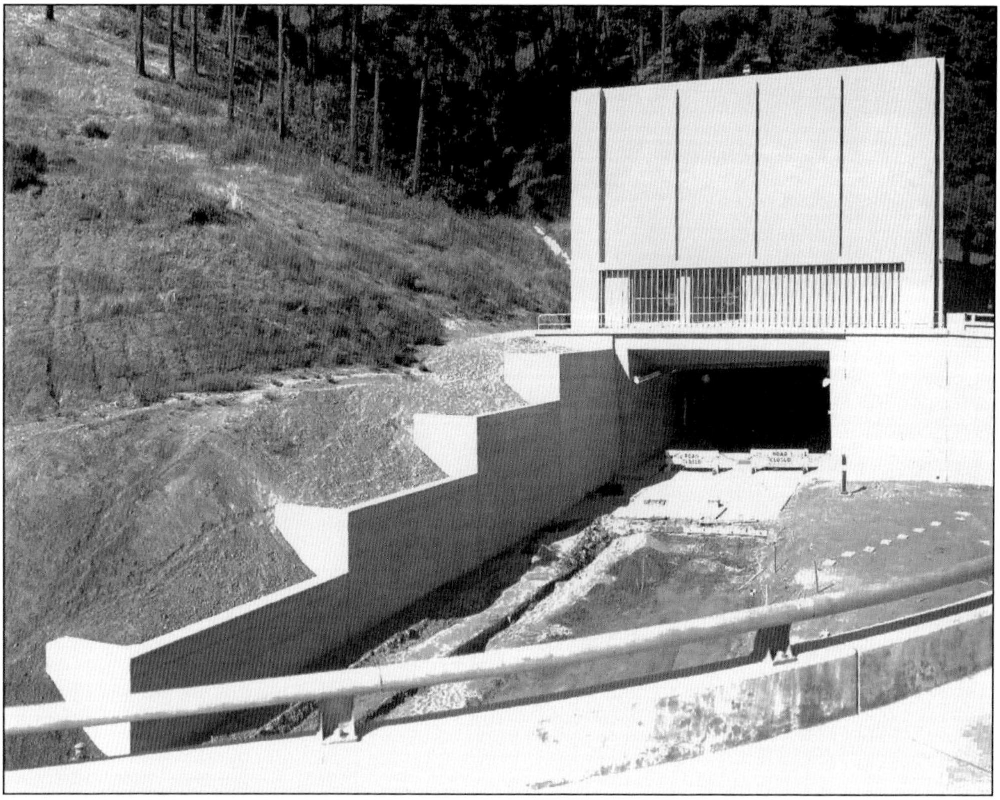

The nearly complete western portal of the third bore is shown in these 1964 photographs. The five-story portal building has been finished, as has the service road bridge. The approach is ready to be paved. The new bore was built on a four-percent grade descending from the eastern end toward Oakland. Both ends of the tunnel were built on curves in order to provide a smooth alignment into the canyons at each end. When all three tunnels were completed, the southernmost existing bore was to be used for traffic from Oakland to Orinda, and the third bore was to carry traffic from Orinda to Oakland. The traffic in the center bore would be one-way, but the direction could be changed to accommodate traffic at peak hours. The tunnel utilized a daily crew of 17 people, including a console operator, a tunnel foreman, and three tunnel operators; each day's operations included three working shifts. (Both, courtesy California Department of Transportation.)

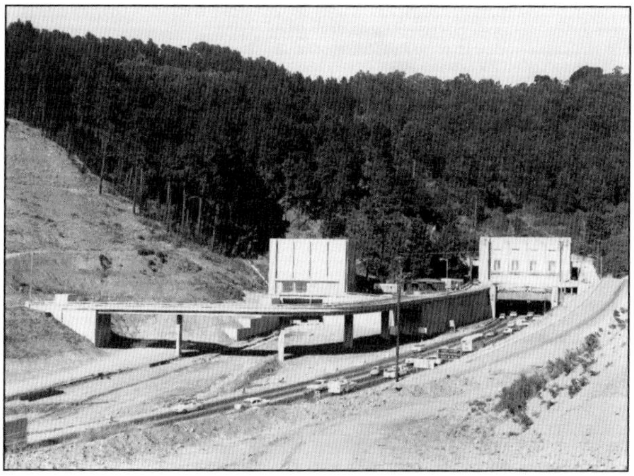

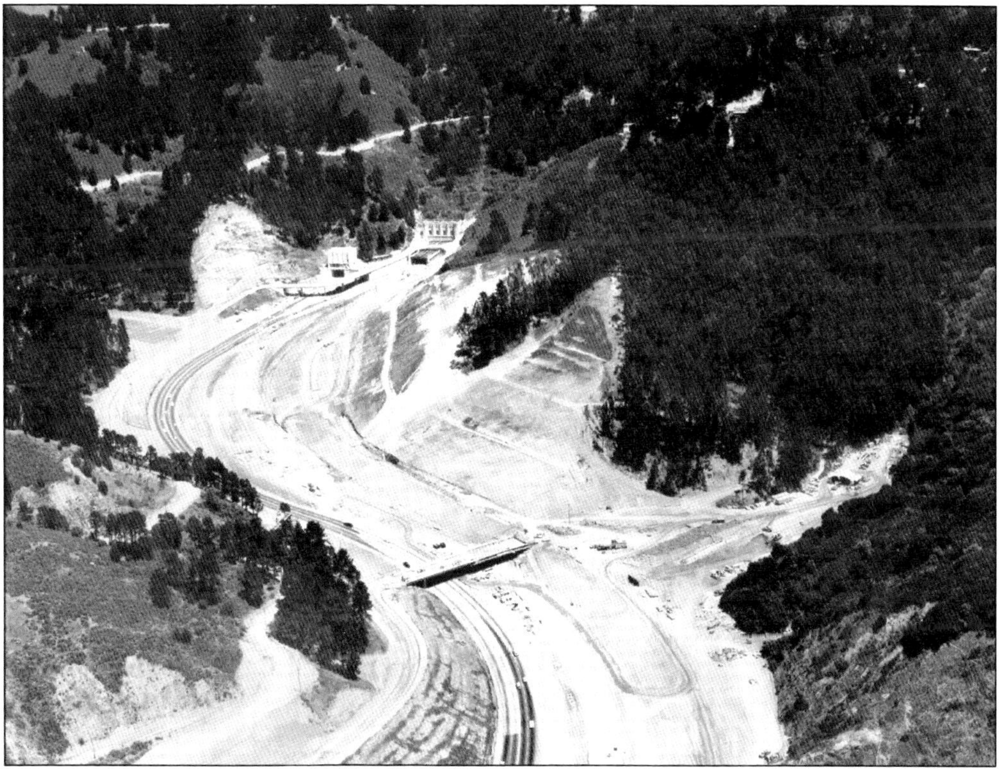

The approaches to the Caldecott Tunnel are shown in these aerial photographs from 1964. The third bore is visible at right in the photograph below. In the photograph above, the exit from the third bore is shown from the west and is shown on the left. After the third bore was completed and opened to traffic, the first two bores were closed, one at a time, and renovated. Damaged pavement was removed and replaced, the roadway area surfaces were cleaned and painted, drainage facilities were repaired, ventilation equipment was overhauled, emergency facilities were added, lighting was modernized, and controls were changed so that all three of the tunnels could be operated from the new portal building. (Both, courtesy California Department of Transportation.)

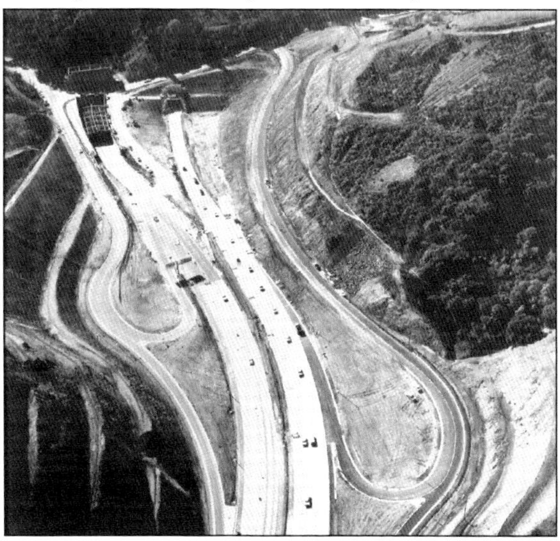

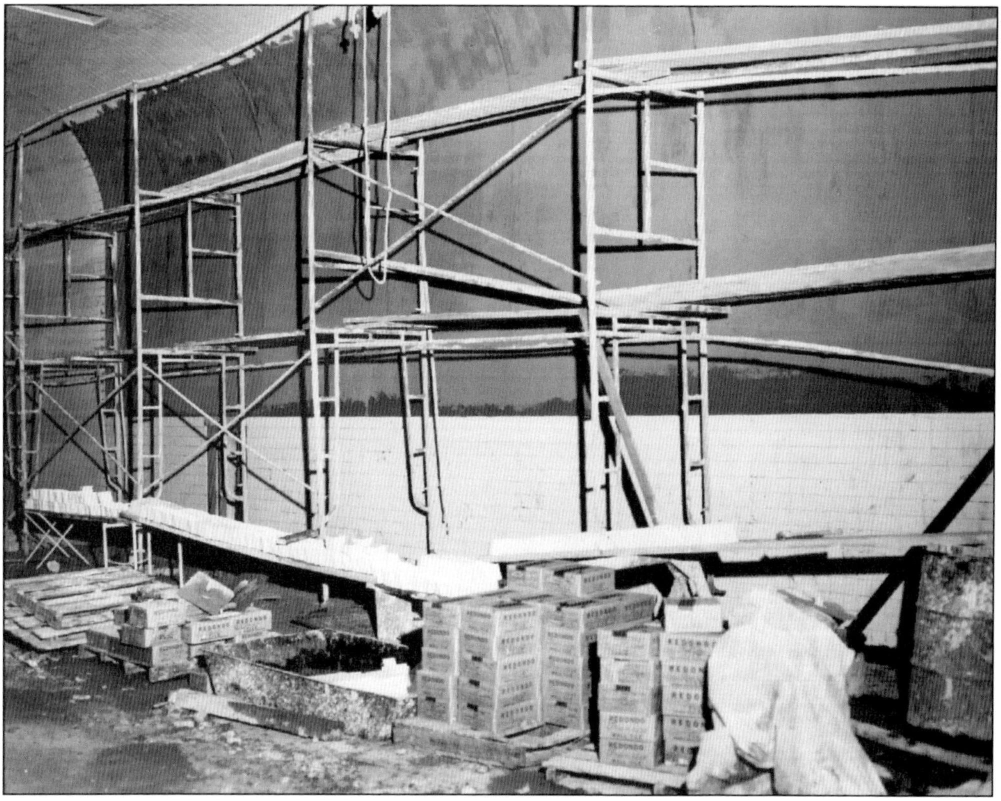

After the construction of the tunnel was complete, the walls and ceiling of the third bore were tiled with five acres of "sea foam" green tiles. The previous two bores of the tunnel had not been tiled because of prohibitive costs. Ceramic tile is easy to clean because particles of dirt, grime, and exhaust fumes do not get embedded in the material, and tile is resistant to moisture. Tiles also work well in tunnels because they can be easily arranged to cover almost any shape. Tiles are also easy and inexpensive to replace should they become worn or damaged, and they provide a reflective surface for safer driving conditions using less artificial light. (Both, courtesy California Department of Transportation.)

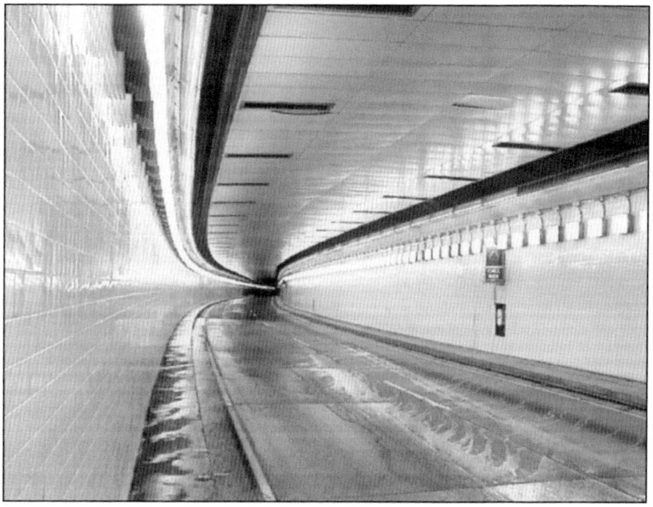

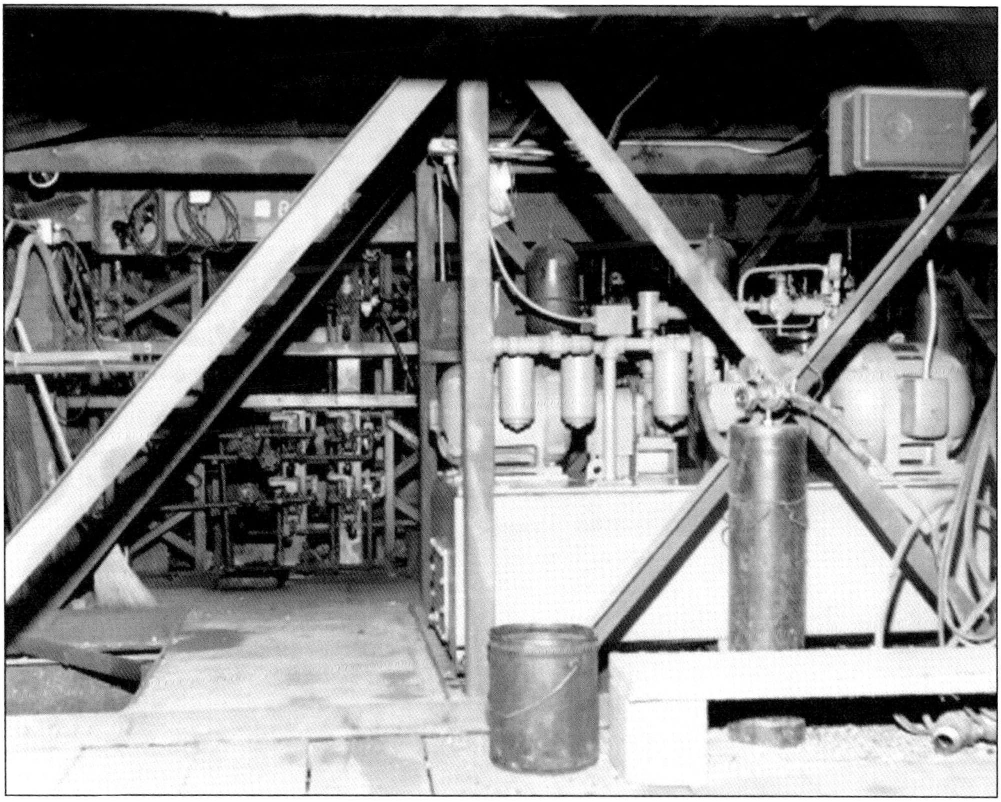

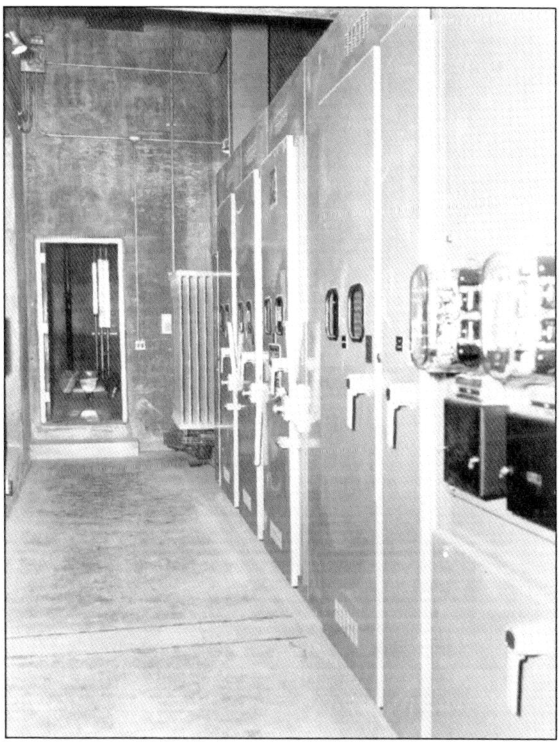

Power for the new bore was provided by a 12-kilovolt-ampere generator (pictured above) located on the Oakland side of the tunnel. The power was used for lighting, signage, and all of the safety systems (ventilation, carbon monoxide analyzer, intercom, telephone, public address system, and the closed circuit television monitoring system). Continuous non-glare lighting is provided by fluorescent lights on each side of the tunnel ceiling. The intensity of the light increases near tunnel entrances to provide a smooth transition for drivers' eyes during the daytime. The photograph at right shows equipment in the electrical switch gear room. (Both, courtesy California Department of Transportation.)

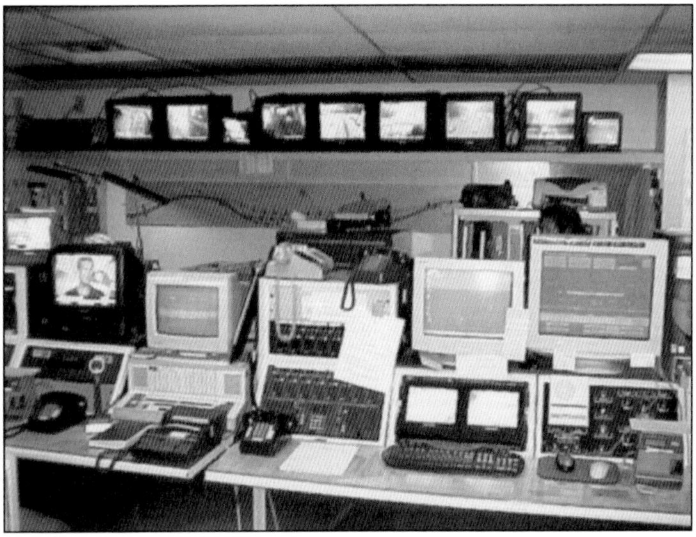

Television cameras placed above each portal are remotely controlled so that tunnel operators can monitor traffic. By viewing the transmissions, operators can detect accidents, emergencies, or the need for lane control. The operators for the Caldecott Tunnels also monitor traffic conditions in the Posey Tube, which connects Oakland and Alameda. (Courtesy California Department of Transportation.)

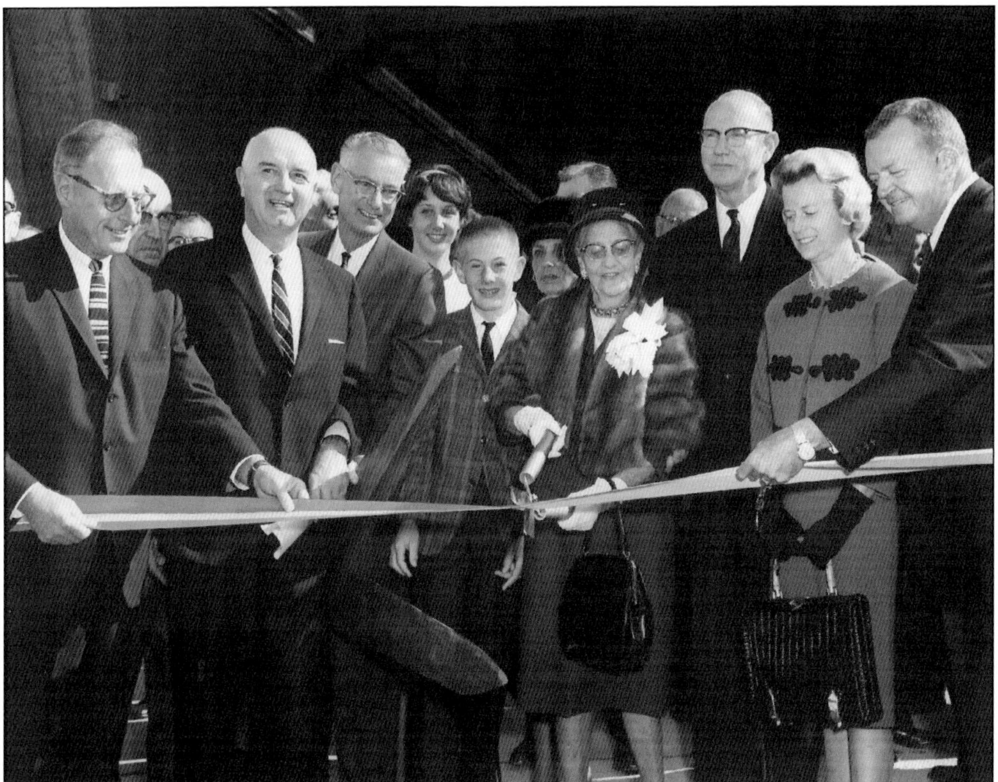

On August 18, 1960, the tunnel was renamed the Caldecott Tunnel, honoring Alameda County supervisor Thomas E. Caldecott, who played a major role in the planning and implementation of the Broadway Low Level Tunnel. His widow, Eveline Caldecott, shown cutting the tape, and his family were present at the dedication. (Courtesy Thomas P. Caldecott.)

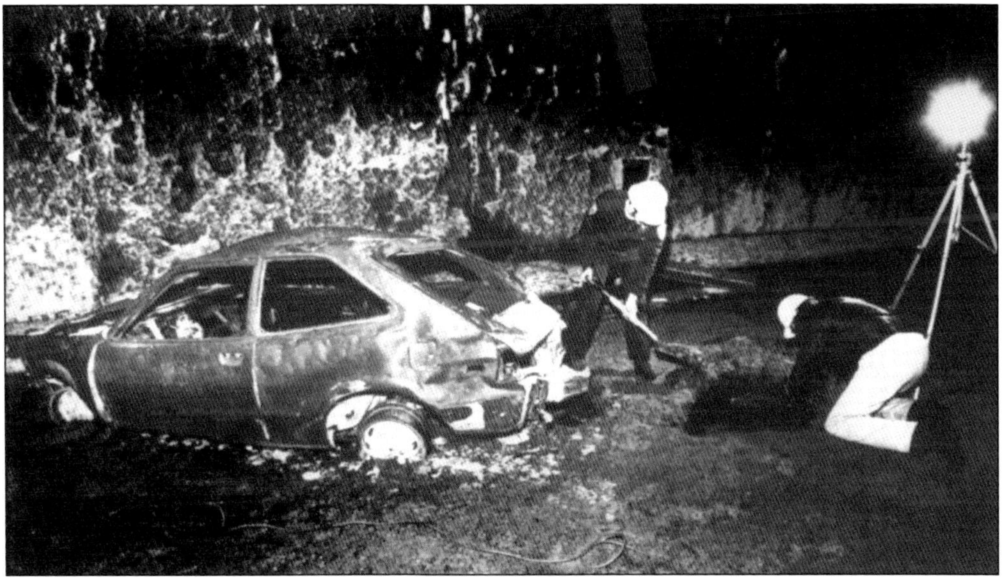

Just after midnight on April 7, 1982, a westbound driver lost control of her car and struck the tunnel wall in the third bore. When she got out to inspect the damage, traffic in the bore slowed. A tanker truck, carrying gasoline and traveling at a high speed, struck the car. An empty bus following the truck hit the car and the tanker. The bus driver was ejected from his vehicle and killed, and the bus continued along in the tunnel and crashed near the exit portal. (Courtesy Contra Costa County Historical Society.)

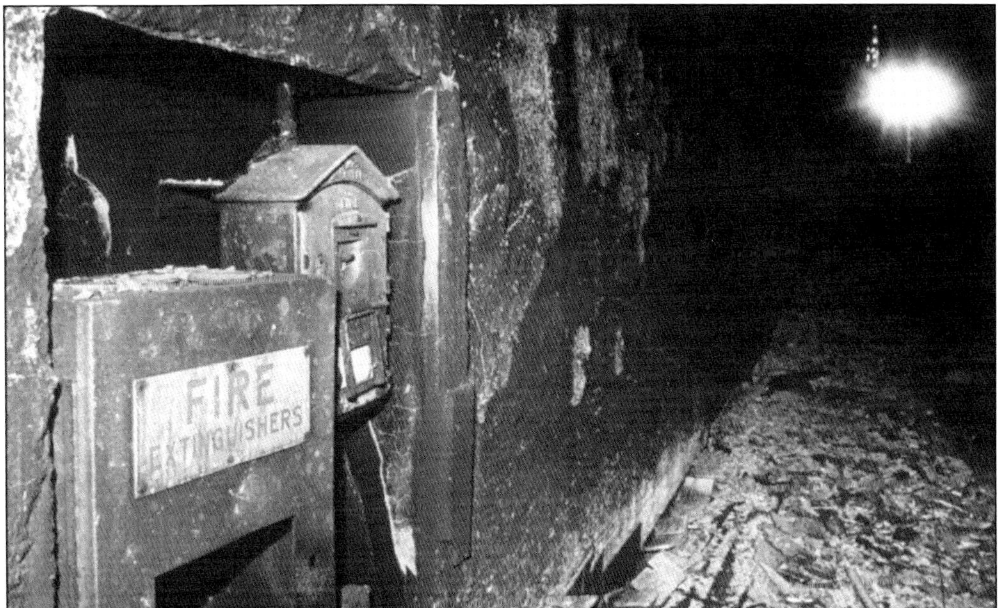

During the 1982 accident, the tanker was leaking gasoline and unable to move. Small fires had started around the leaks. The driver was able to escape the tunnel, but gasoline continued to escape into the drainage system. The downgrade of the tunnel caused the smoke to flow uphill toward oncoming vehicles. About 20 vehicles were able to get out of the bore, but four vehicles were left trapped behind the burning tanker. (Courtesy Contra Costa County Historical Society.)

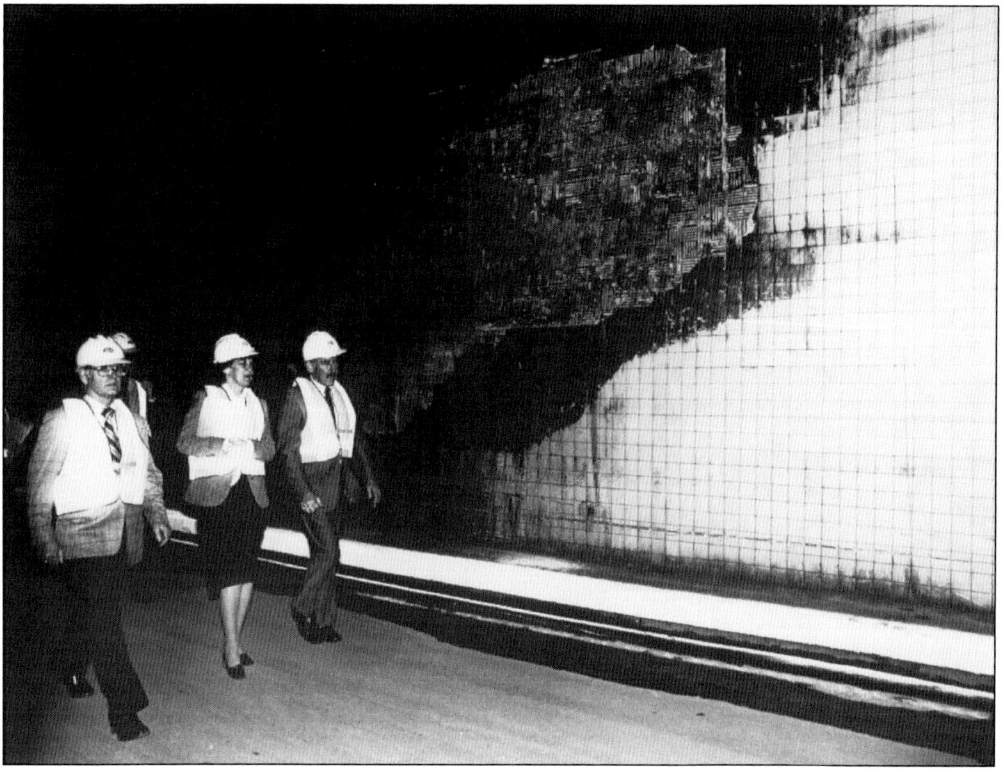

Two people died in the initial crashes, five were killed by smoke and fire, and two suffered from smoke inhalation. The fire raged for 28 to 40 minutes, burning about 8,700 gallons of gasoline. The temperature in the tunnel was estimated to reach over 1,800 degrees Fahrenheit. The tiles and grout in the tunnel were damaged by the intense heat, and other equipment in the tunnel was destroyed by the fire. The tunnel was closed for repairs for several months. (Courtesy Contra Costa County Historical Society.)

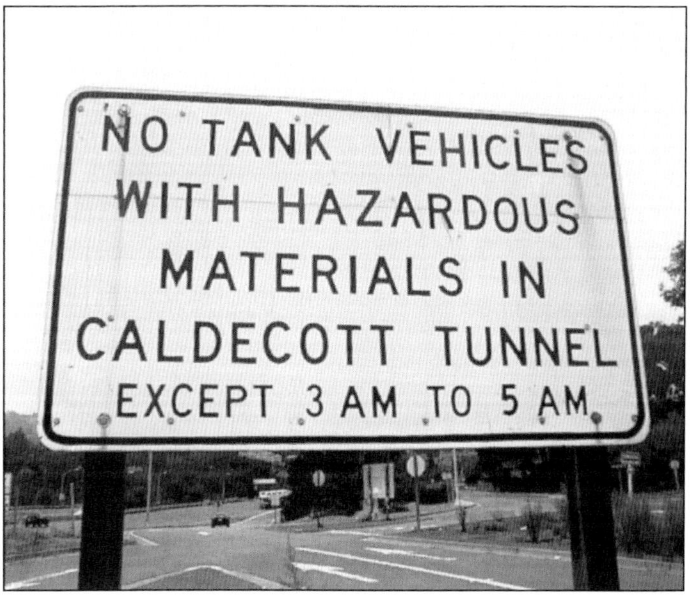

As a result of the fire in the third bore, the Federal Highway Administration established the Fire Memorial Tunnel Test Fire Program, which studied the speed at which the 1980s fire spread, evaluated alternative ventilation approaches, and reviewed emergency egress standards. This led to travel restrictions for tanker vehicles carrying hazardous materials through the bores of the Caldecott Tunnel. (Courtesy Ray Mailhot.)

Five

The Fourth Bore

In 1998, the Metropolitan Transportation Commission—in cooperation with the Alameda County Congestion Management Agency, the Contra Costa Transportation Authority, and Caltrans—decided to study what could be done to alleviate the traffic congestion that had continued to increase on Highway 24 since the opening of the third bore in 1964. One option would be to build another tunnel bore through the hills. Other options were also investigated and evaluated in terms of cost and traffic-mitigating potential. Meetings included representatives from both Alameda and Contra Costa Counties, as well as from transit agencies from both counties.

The commission eventually decided that adding a fourth bore would help existing and future reverse-commute (eastbound in the morning, westbound in the evening) and weekend traffic congestion at the tunnel.

Funding for the project came from a number of sources. The initial cost for the Caldecott Fourth Bore Project was estimated at $420 million, which included the construction of the Caldecott Fourth Bore, realignment of westbound Highway 24 to the northbound Highway 13 ramp, Kay Street improvements, and landscaping. The funding sources included $1.4 million from SAFETEA-LU (Safe, Accountable, Flexible Transportation Equality Act: A Legacy for Users), federal funds from a 2005 surface transportation congressional bill; $11.3 million from CMIA (Corridor Mobility Improvement Account), proceeds of general obligation bonds approved by California voters in 2006; $19.3 million from STIP (State Transportation Improvement Program), state funds used to finance state, regional, and local transportation projects; $20 million from TCRP (Traffic Congestion Relief Program), state funds for congestion relief projects; $50 million from Regional Measure 2, which raised bridge tolls and was passed by voters in 2004; $120.6 million from Contra Costa County Measure J, passed by voters in 2004; and $194.3 million from ARRA (American Recovery and Reinvestment Act of 2009) federal stimulus funds. After some revisions, the project was funded for $417 million.

Construction contracts were awarded by Caltrans, and excavation on the fourth bore began in August 2010 on the westbound side. About three-quarters of the tunnel were excavated from the Orinda side because geological formations were more stable on that side. Excavations on the eastbound (Oakland) side began in March 2011. The breakthrough of the top heading excavations took place on November 29, 2011, about 200 meters in from the Oakland side. The completed bore opened on November 15, 2013.

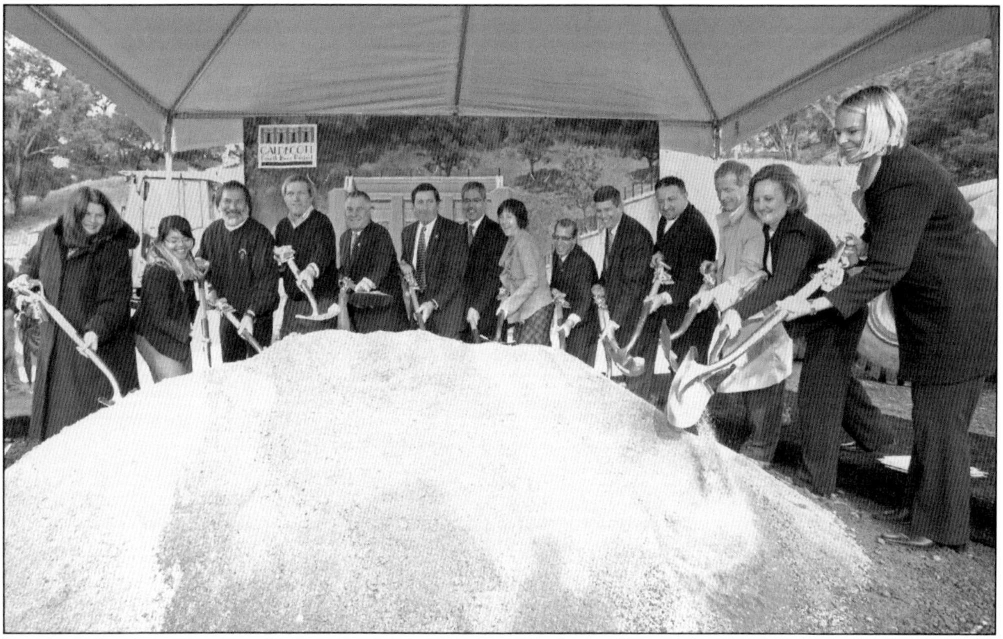

State and local officials participated in the ground-breaking ceremonies for the fourth bore project on January 22, 2010. The project was expected to cost $420 million and take four years to complete while employing more than 5,000 workers. The project would dramatically reduce commute congestion in both Alameda and Contra Costa Counties. In the below photograph, Caltrans District 4 director Bijan Sartipi (fifth from left), Cristina Ferraz, project manager for the Caldecott Tunnel (seventh from left), the executive staff, and fourth bore project managers celebrate the breaking of ground. (Both, courtesy California Department of Transportation.)

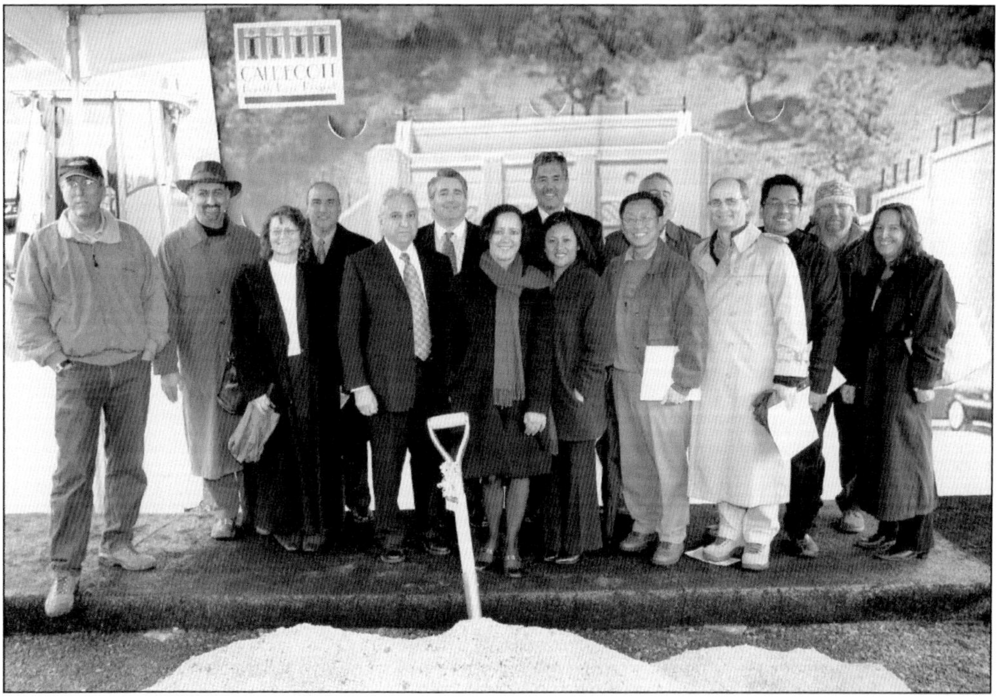

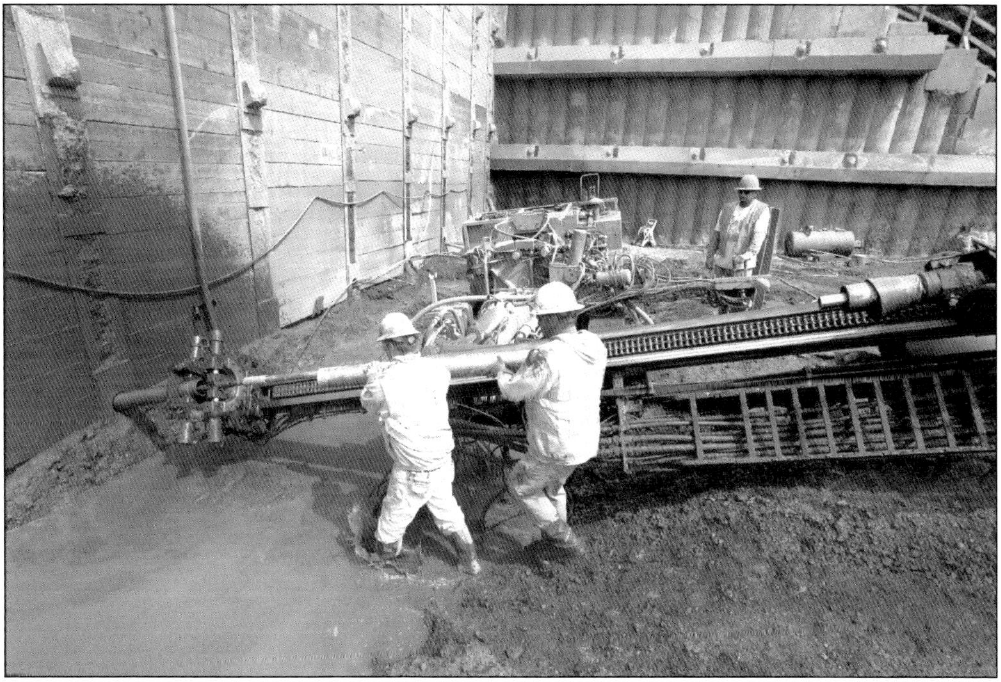

Tieback construction is an earth-retention technique that uses grouted tension-resisting steel strands designed for permanent or temporary support. Three to six feet of soil were taken from the top of the excavation. Inclined holes were drilled into the exposed face. Tension-resisting steel strands were inserted into the holes, grouted, and tensioned. A drainage system was installed on the exposed face, followed by the application of reinforced shotcrete (fiber-reinforced concrete) facing. Bearing plates were fixed to the heads of the tieback strands. The installation process was repeated until the designed wall depth was reached. The finished tieback walls provided an area of reinforced ground. The eastern approach to the tunnel was constructed in June 2010. (Both, courtesy California Department of Transportation.)

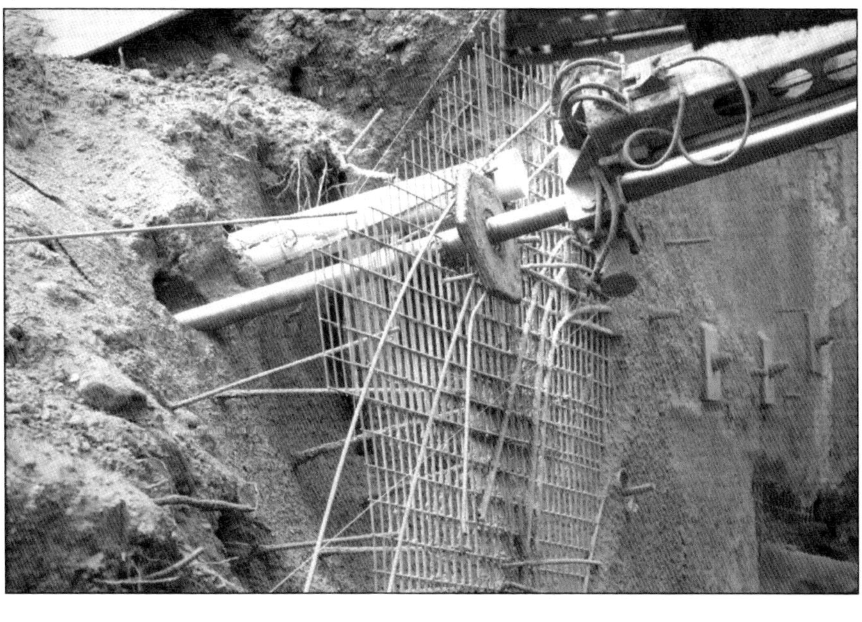

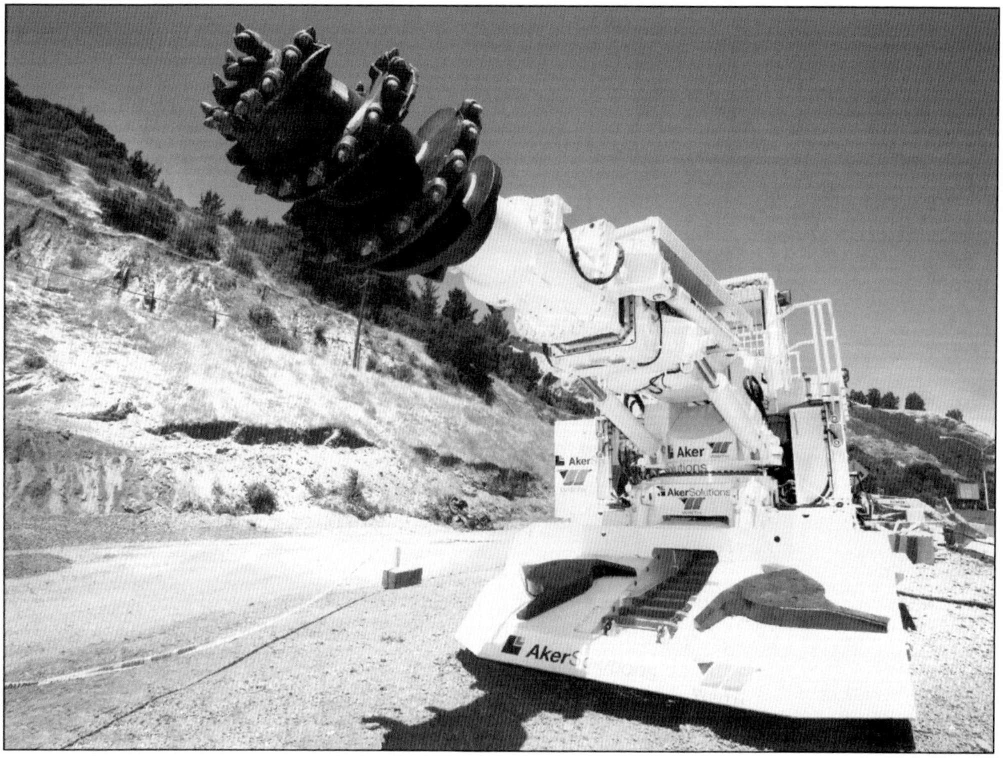

The German-built Wirth roadheader was shipped from Europe to the Port of Oakland via the Panama Canal. It was able to excavate faster and more safely than many miners working by hand. The roadheader excavated from the Orinda side, and a smaller roadheader worked from the Oakland side. Excavation progressed about six feet per day with workers reinforcing the excavation before moving forward. The length of the excavated section was based on the surrounding geology. The harder the rock, the farther excavation could progress before support was needed. (Both, courtesy California Department of Transportation.)

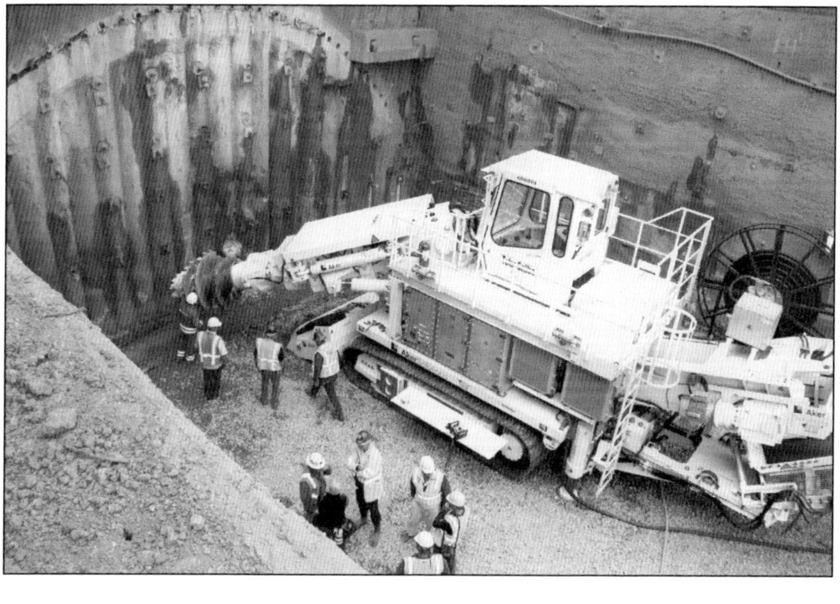

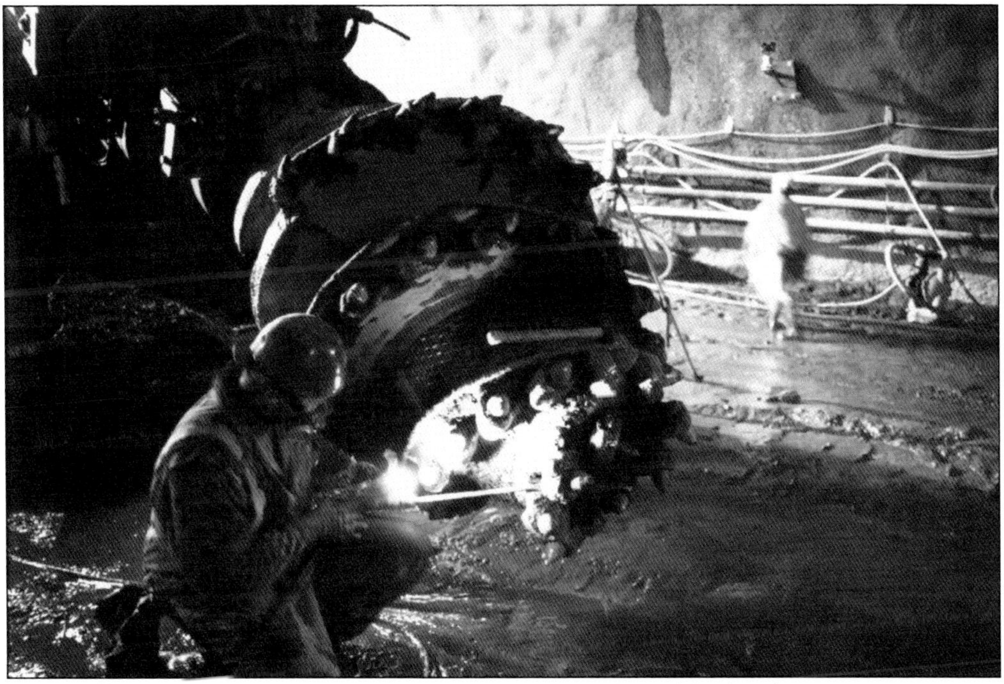

The roadheader had a long, extendable arm and a barrel-shaped, high-velocity rotating cutting head with hardened steel teeth that ground into the rock. On-site mechanics frequently inspected and replaced the roadheader's 48 teeth, or "picks," which wore down from the grinding, as well as the tunneling machine's electric cable and other equipment. (Courtesy California Department of Transportation.)

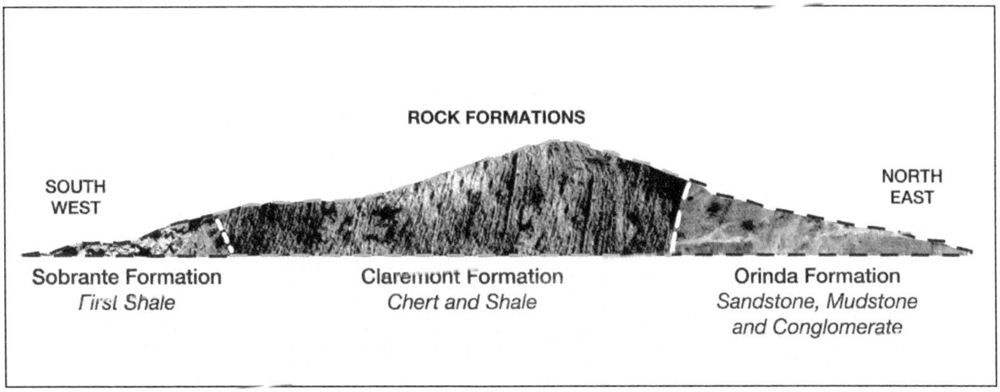

The fourth bore was excavated from both the Orinda and Oakland sides, with the excavation on the westbound side beginning in August 2010. About three-quarters of the tunnel were excavated from the Orinda side, because the Orinda and Claremont geologic formations were more stable than the Sobrante. The eastbound Oakland side excavation began in March 2011. (Courtesy California Department of Transportation.)

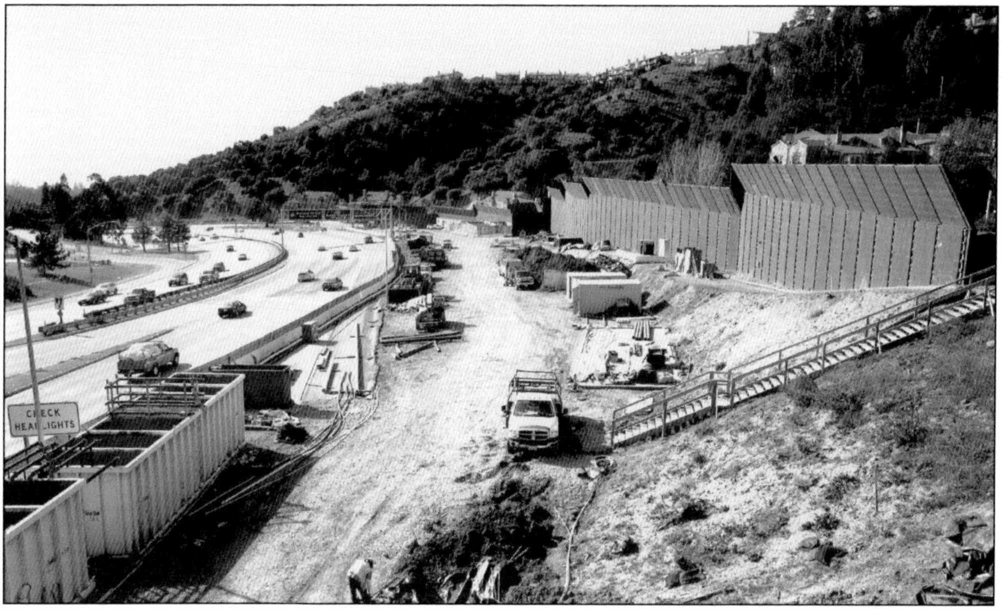

Before excavation began, construction on the fourth bore was already underway in early 2010 as contractors cleared brush and prepared to erect retaining walls on both sides of the tunnel and a sound wall on the west end. This photograph shows work on the west-side approach to the new bore, including the construction of a temporary sound wall. (Courtesy California Department of Transportation.)

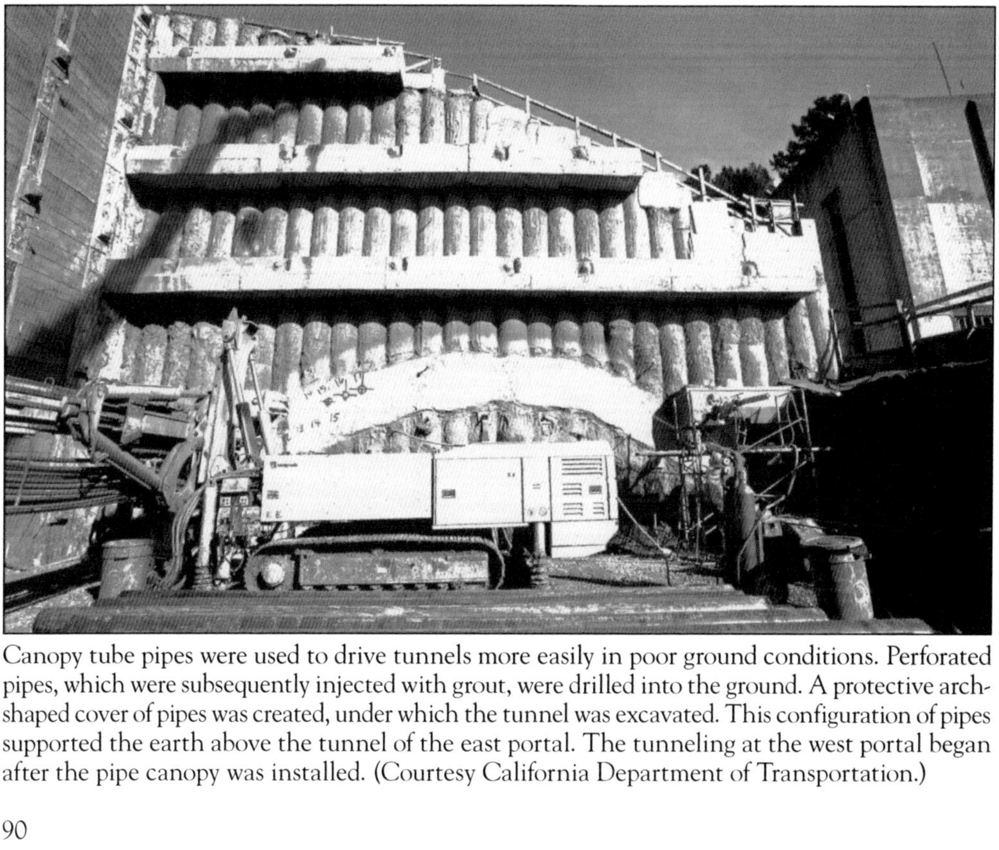

Canopy tube pipes were used to drive tunnels more easily in poor ground conditions. Perforated pipes, which were subsequently injected with grout, were drilled into the ground. A protective arch-shaped cover of pipes was created, under which the tunnel was excavated. This configuration of pipes supported the earth above the tunnel of the east portal. The tunneling at the west portal began after the pipe canopy was installed. (Courtesy California Department of Transportation.)

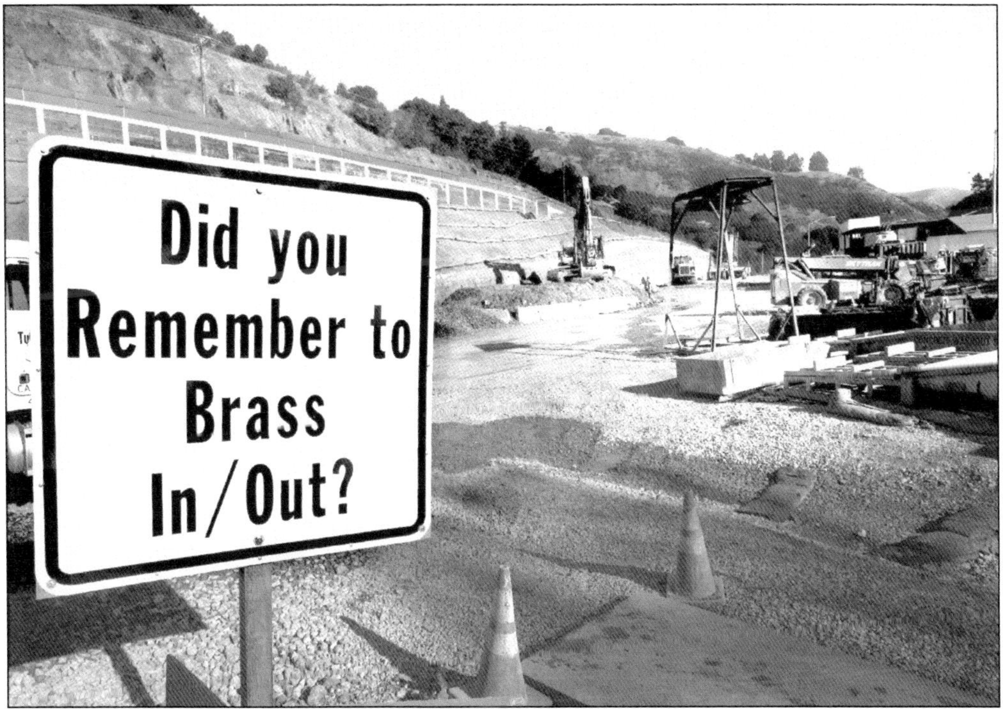

Workers from Tutor-Saliba, Caltrans, and all subcontractors were required to use the brass board, a vestige of the mining industry, shown here at the eastern portal. A "tag board" at the entrance to the tunnel was used to indicate who was in the bore. Every time a worker went into the tunnel, he had to "tag in" or "brass in" by placing a brass tag with his name stamped on it on the "in" side of the tag board. When leaving the mine he "tagged out" or "brassed out" by moving his "brass" to the "out" side of the board. Brass tags were used because brass has a very high melting point. In the event of a catastrophic fire inside the tunnel during construction, the brass tags would identify which workers were inside the tunnel. (Both, courtesy California Department of Transportation.)

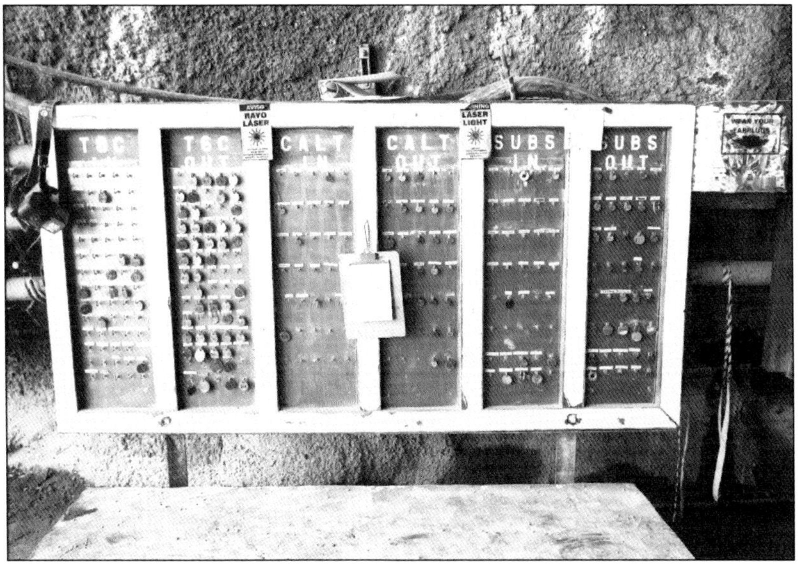

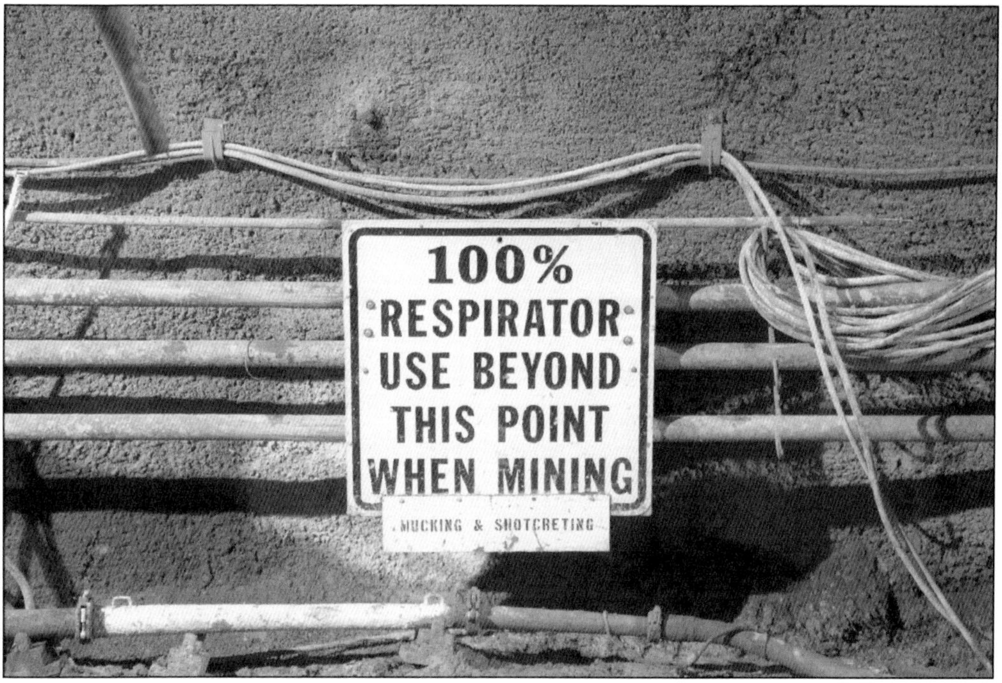

Safety was a priority while on the job site. Appropriate training, equipment, and clothing were required for all employees. Respirators were used by workers who were mucking or shotcreting to protect them from inhaling dust and silica. Dust-control measures required crews to allow for dust particles in the air to settle before work resumed. Miners on the project worked 10- to 14-hour shifts, six days a week. The fourth bore project had an excellent safety record and no lost work days. (Both, courtesy California Department of Transportation.)

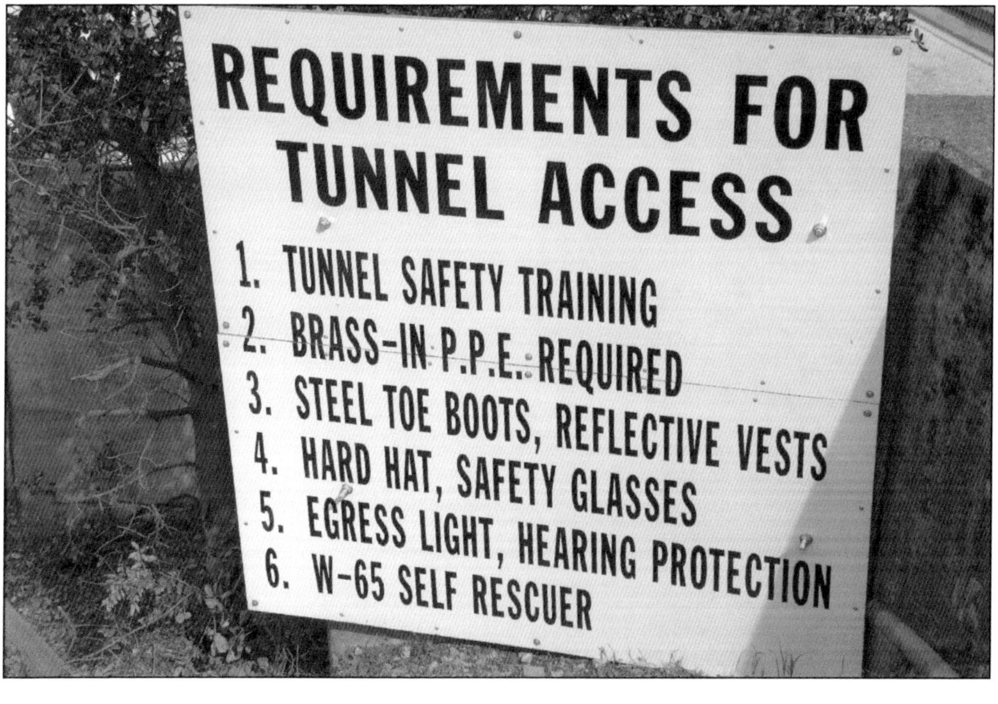

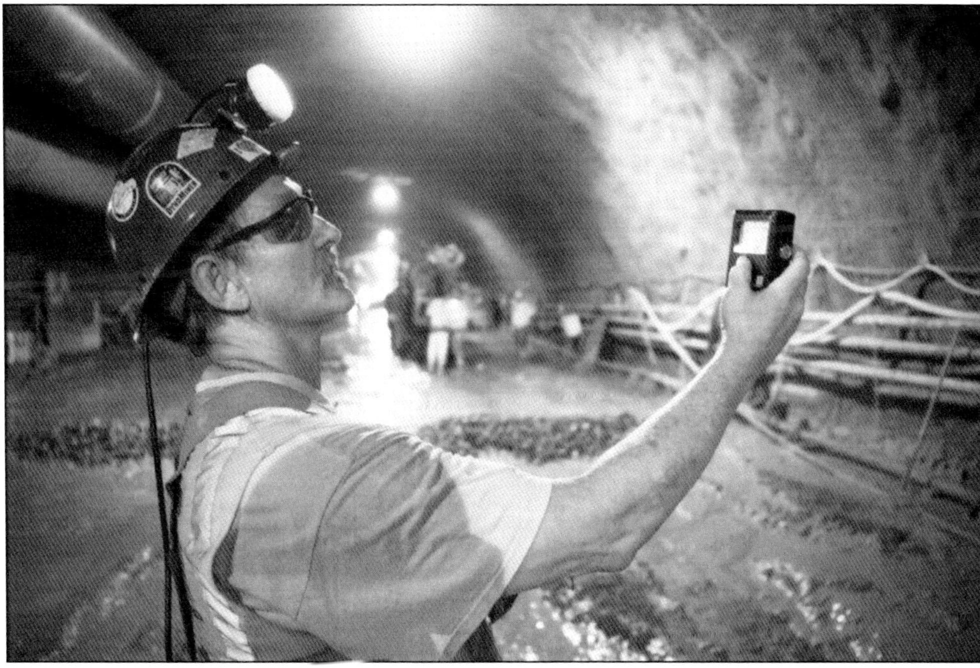

Safety officer Tom LeRoux (shown above) monitored the air quality inside the tunnel for combustible gases possibly released during the excavation. The California Division of Occupational Safety and Health classified the fourth bore as gassy due to trace amounts of methane. This classification required the use of tunnel-safe equipment, including a ventilation system, to maintain air quality in the tunnel, plus a special safety-training program and equipment for tunneling crews. (Both, courtesy California Department of Transportation.)

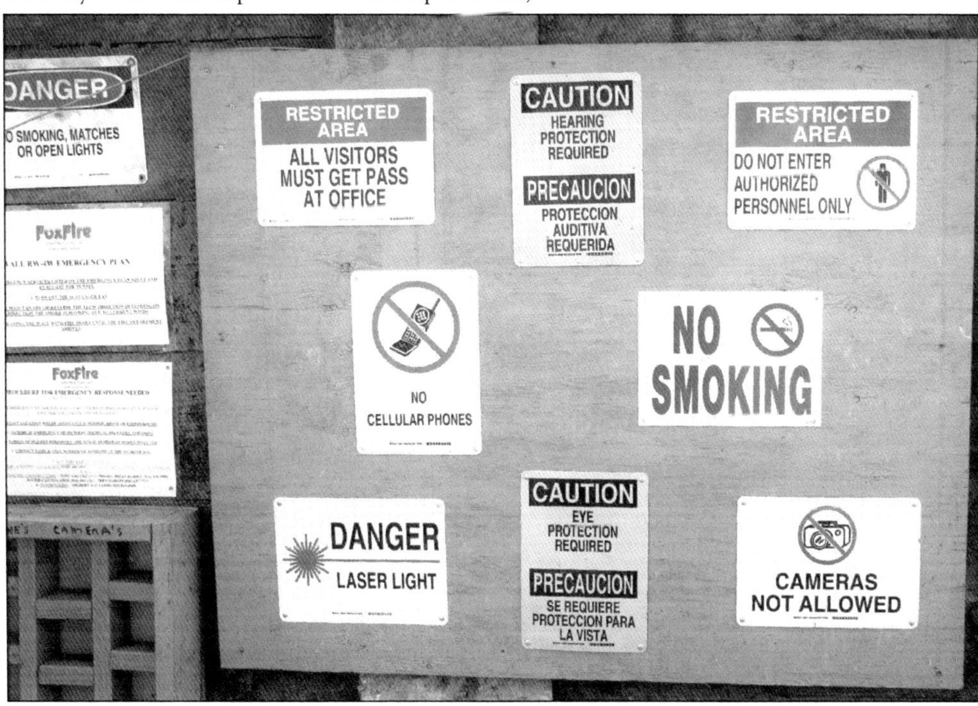

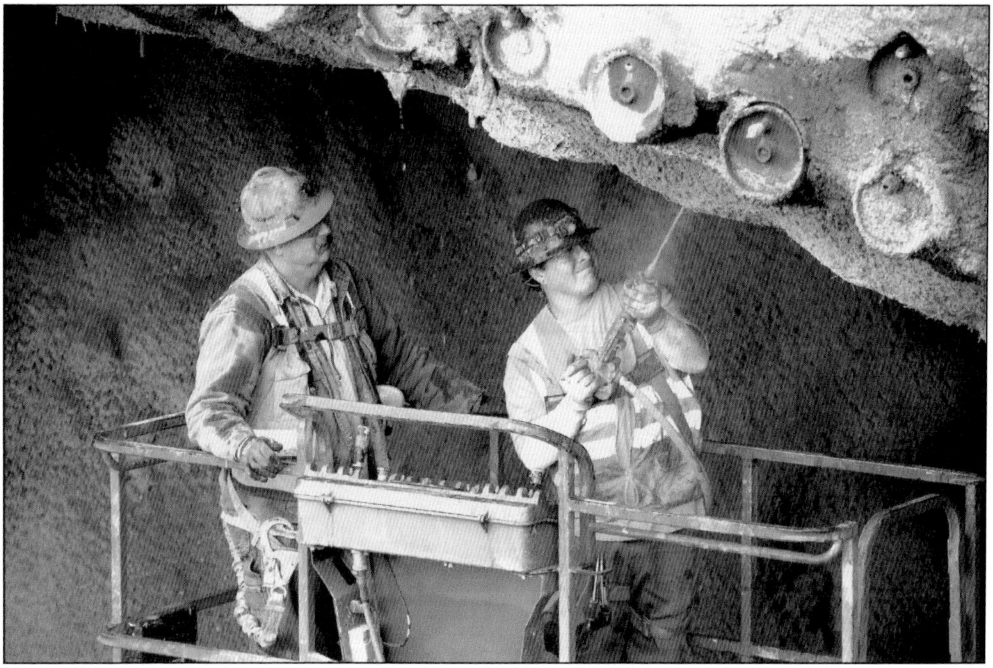

The depth and strength of the tunnel roof was tested after shotcrete had been applied and hardened. After some of the section was excavated, workers applied shotcrete to walls and installed steel rods around the perimeter of the excavation. The shotcrete and steel rods provided temporary support during construction. Workers gradually covered the entire length of the tunnel with shotcrete. (Courtesy California Department of Transportation.)

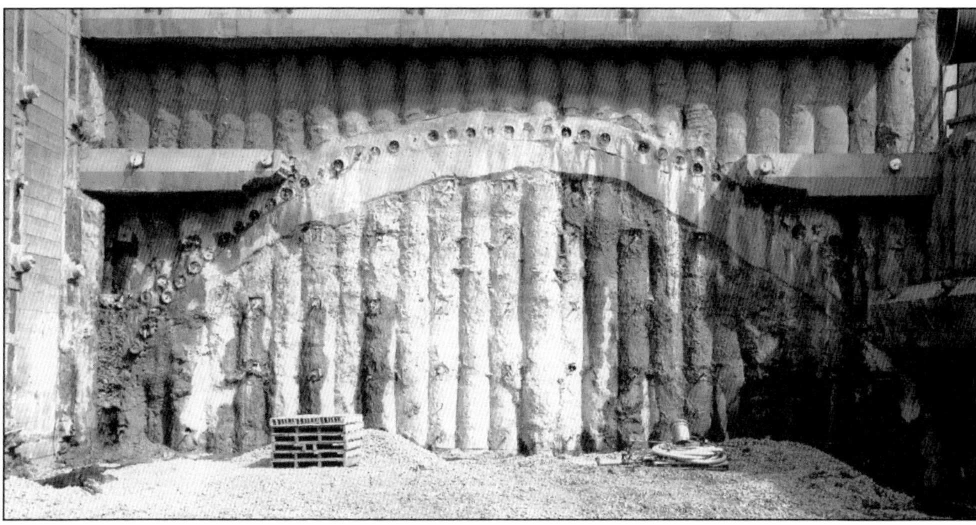

Each portal wall was built as a secant wall, a method in which the retaining wall is built underground and later excavated. A series of holes are drilled several feet apart in the earth. A steel cage is inserted into every other hole and filled with concrete, forming a "cast in drilled hole" pile. Once the piles have hardened, they overlap the existing piles by about six inches on both sides. When the new pile hardens, it will form a sturdy underground wall. The wall is strong enough that it can be drilled through to form an entrance to the tunnel. The tunnel wall is also supported by tiebacks above the section to be drilled through. (Courtesy California Department of Transportation.)

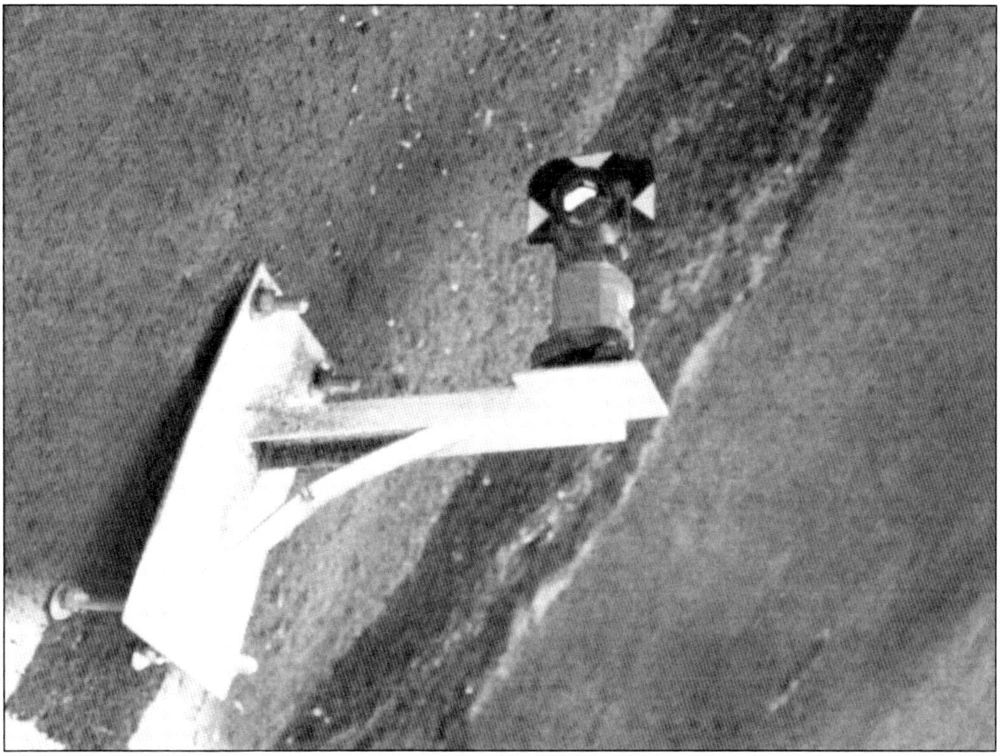

Lasers projected on the face of the tunnel outlined exactly where the roadheader needed to excavate. After each round of excavation, high-tech scanning equipment provided a 3-D profile to indicate how much ground had been excavated. Crews using standard survey equipment would crosscheck the alignment as excavation progressed. DIBITS (digital-in-band interswitch trunk signaling) surveying machines were used to measure the alignment in the tunnel and the thickness of the shotcrete. An assessment of the thickness took place after every round of excavation. When the two crews, coming from opposite directions, broke through in November 2011, the two sides of the tunnel were less than an inch apart. (Both, courtesy California Department of Transportation.)

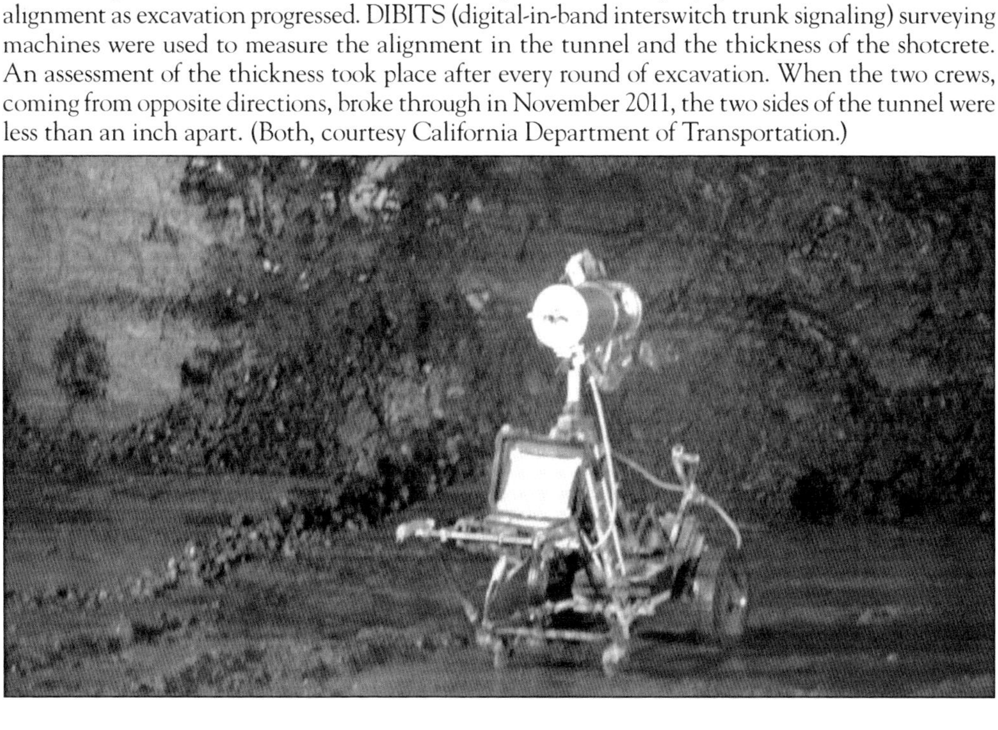

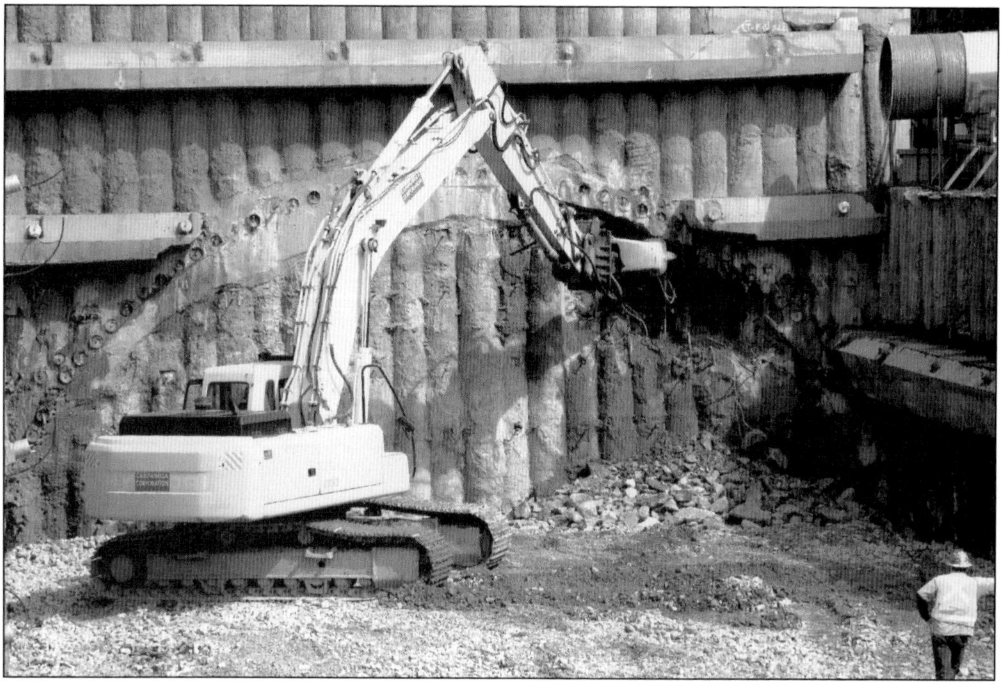

A Caterpillar Excavator 330 was used at the west portal to break up the concrete on the wall and create an entryway for the tunnel. The steel within the concrete was cut with blowtorches. After a tunnel-sized hole was made in the portal wall, the excavator, using a cutting head, began tunneling, gouging out chunks of dirt and rock from the face of the tunnel. Workers then sprayed the walls with shotcrete, installed steel lattice girders, and sprayed them with shotcrete. The excavator repeated the process through the tunnel. A view toward the outside of the east portal is shown below. (Both, courtesy California Department of Transportation.)

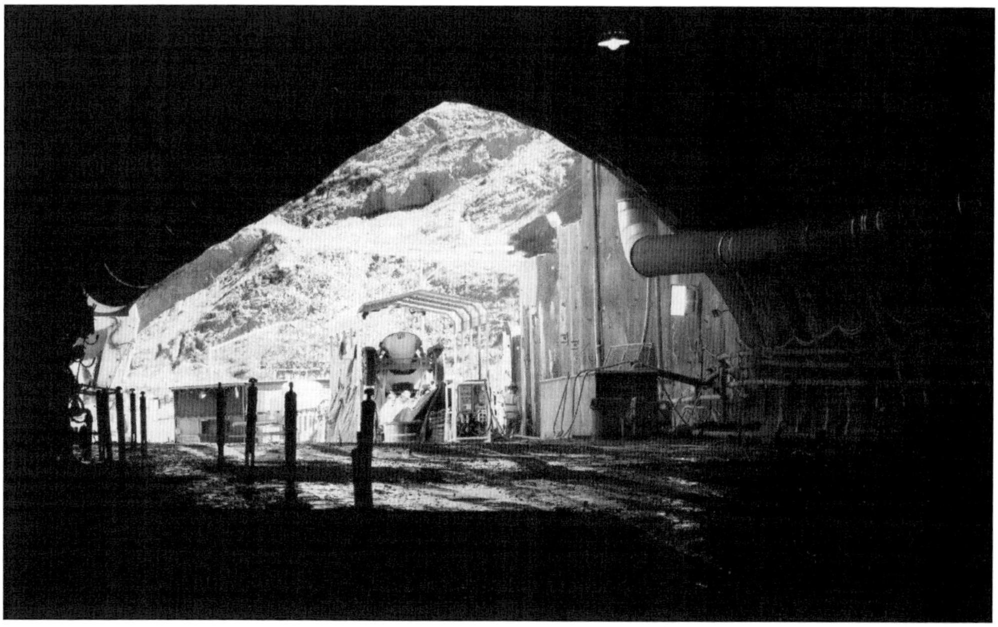

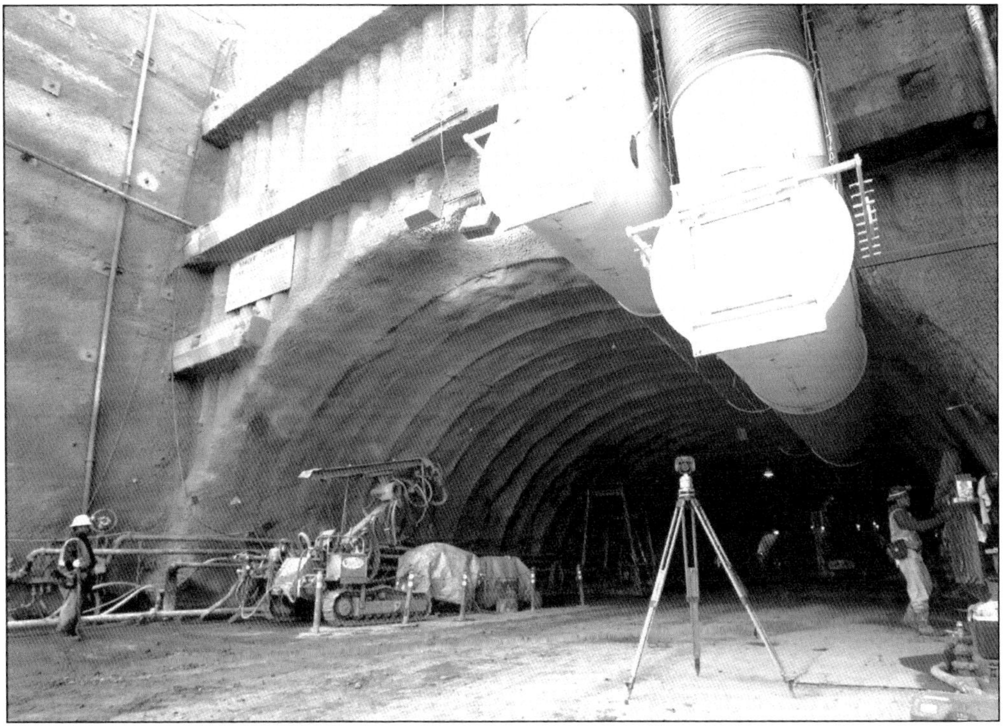

Large ventilation ducts removed tunnel air and replaced it with fresh air from the outside. In addition, workers were required to wear respirators when drilling due to the dust and silica in the air. A metal bulkhead separated the two converging crews digging in the tunnel. The bulkhead was at the site where the east and west tunneling crews met in November 2011. The wall allowed two separate ventilation systems to operate independently. (Courtesy California Department of Transportation.)

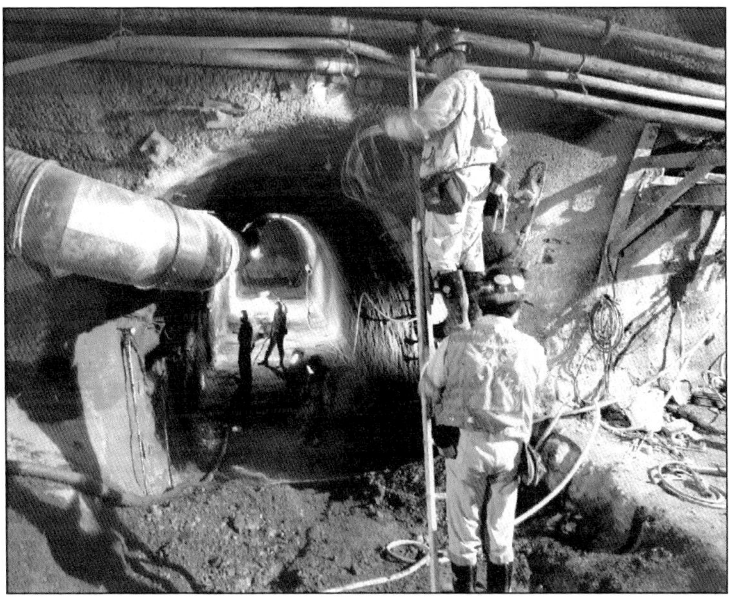

Seven cross passages, such as the one shown, were built to connect the fourth bore with the third bore, which runs next to it. Tunnel fires, such as those in the third bore in 1982 and in the St. Gotthard tunnel in 2001, have raised concerns about fire safety in tunnels, resulting in many countries adopting codes for exit routes and cross passages in tunnels. (Courtesy California Department of Transportation.)

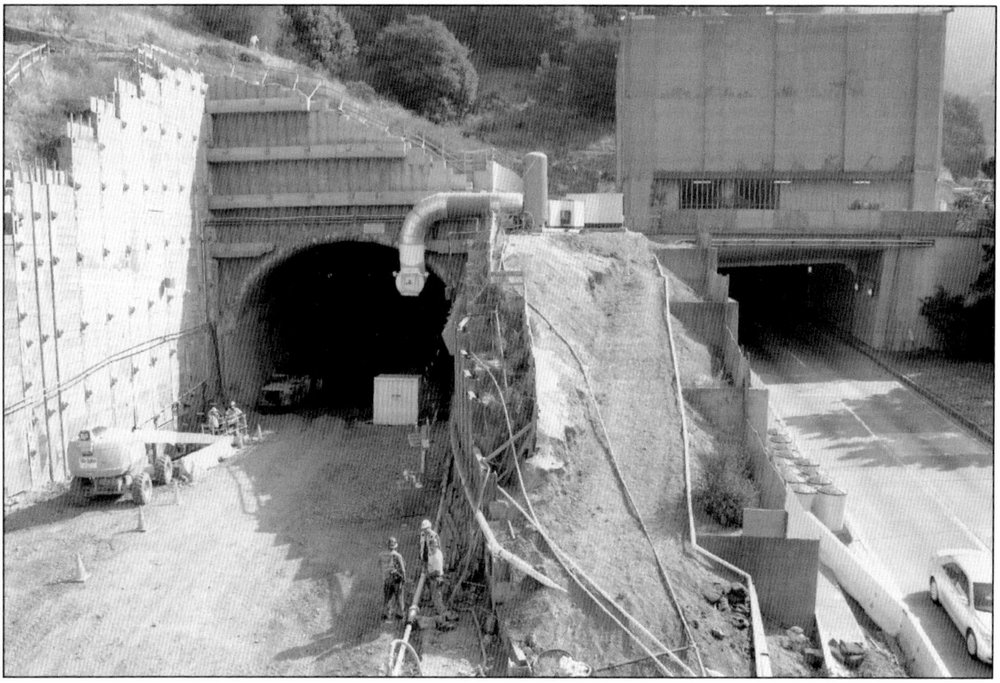

The portal walls were set back so far into the hillside that retaining walls needed to be built perpendicular to each portal wall to hold back the hillside. These walls, located on either side of the portal wall, were tieback walls built on the exterior of the hillside. Holes were drilled into the hillside, steel strands were inserted, and grout was injected into each hole and allowed to harden. The strands and bearing plate protrude through the face of the wall and were tightened, pulling the wall against the hillside. (Courtesy California Department of Transportation.)

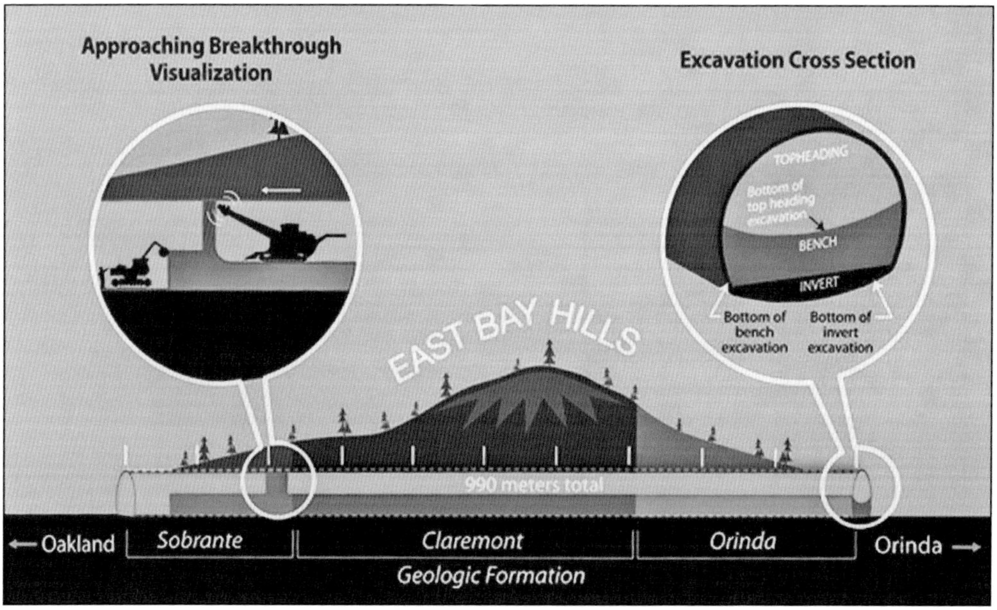

This schematic shows a cross section of the breakthrough of the excavation of the tunnel through the various geologic formations. (Courtesy California Department of Transportation.)

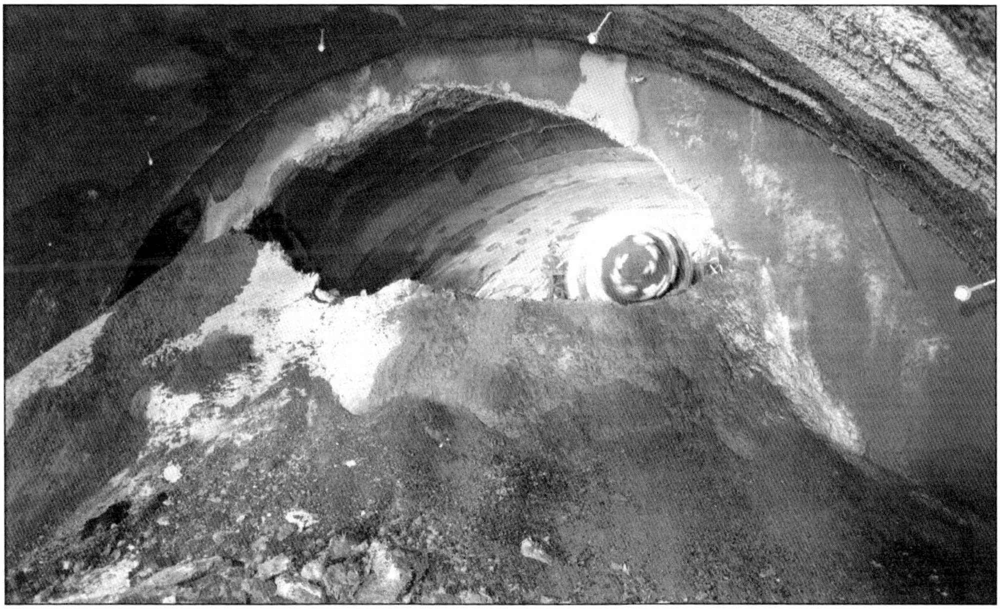

On November 29, 2011, at 2:37 p.m., crews operating the roadheader from the eastern side broke through the final chunk of rock to complete the excavation and join the top portion of the east and west sides of the tunnel. In this image, the rotary cutting head is emerging from the other side. At the time of the breakthrough, the tunnel was over 21 feet high. (Courtesy California Department of Transportation.)

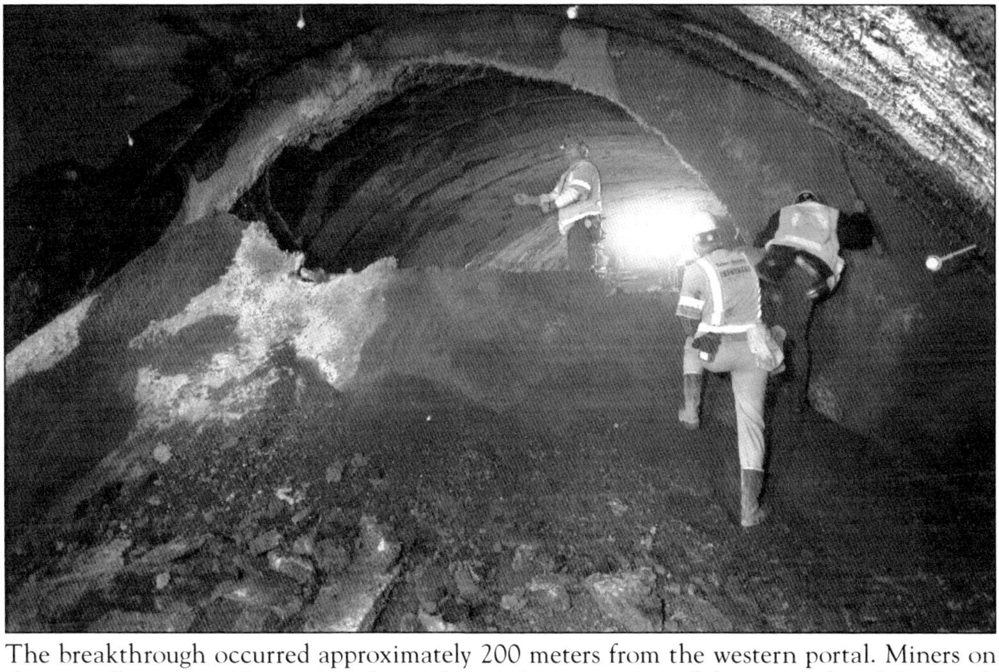

The breakthrough occurred approximately 200 meters from the western portal. Miners on the tunnel's eastern side continued completing the excavation of the remainder of the fourth bore's top heading. Following the breakthrough and removal of excavated rock, the roadheader continued excavation of the bench, traveling from west to east. (Courtesy California Department of Transportation.)

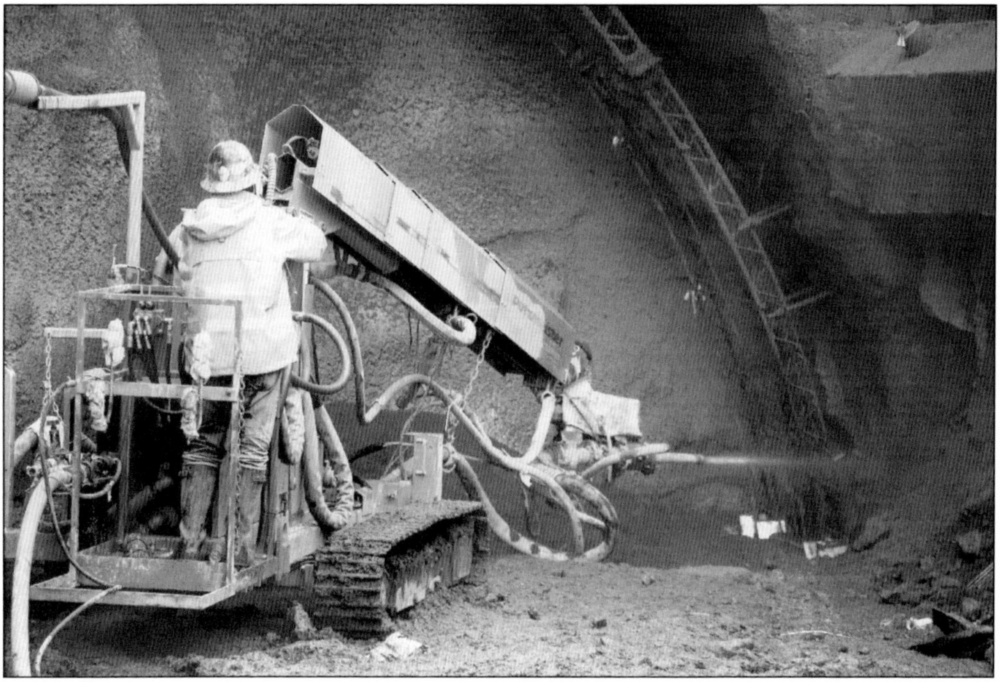

In the above image, a layer of fiber-reinforced concrete, called shotcrete, is sprayed over the newly exposed rock surface at the west portal. Shotcrete was always applied to the face or crown. Miners mixed thousands of batches of shotcrete during the construction of the tunnel, and each batch needed to be tested by being sprayed on test panels that could be adjusted to different angles to see how the shotcrete dried on the varying angles of the tunnel walls. Part of the tunnel arch pictured below had been reinforced with shotcrete before further excavation occurred. The reflective dots at the top of the face of the excavation were used by surveyors to align boring equipment. (Both, courtesy California Department of Transportation.)

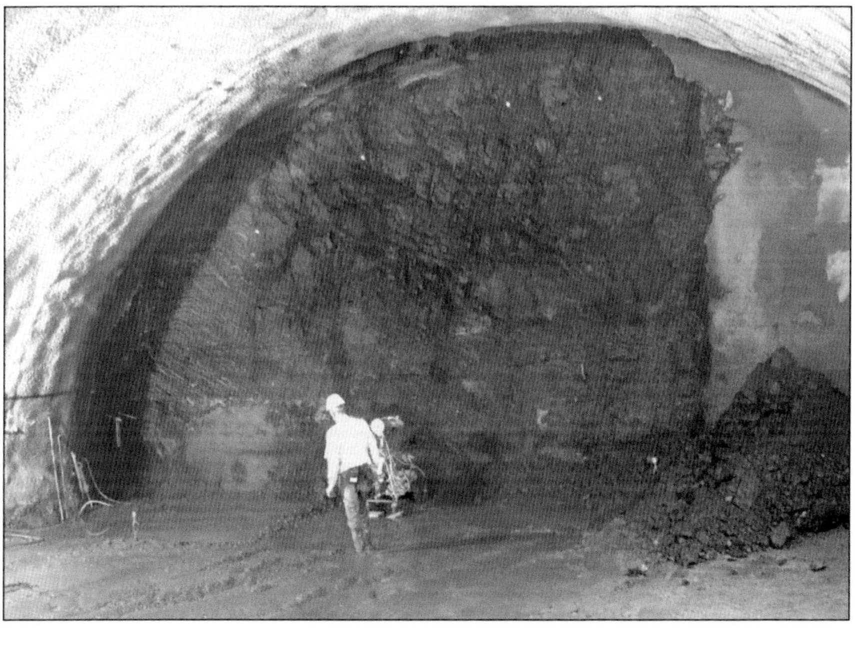

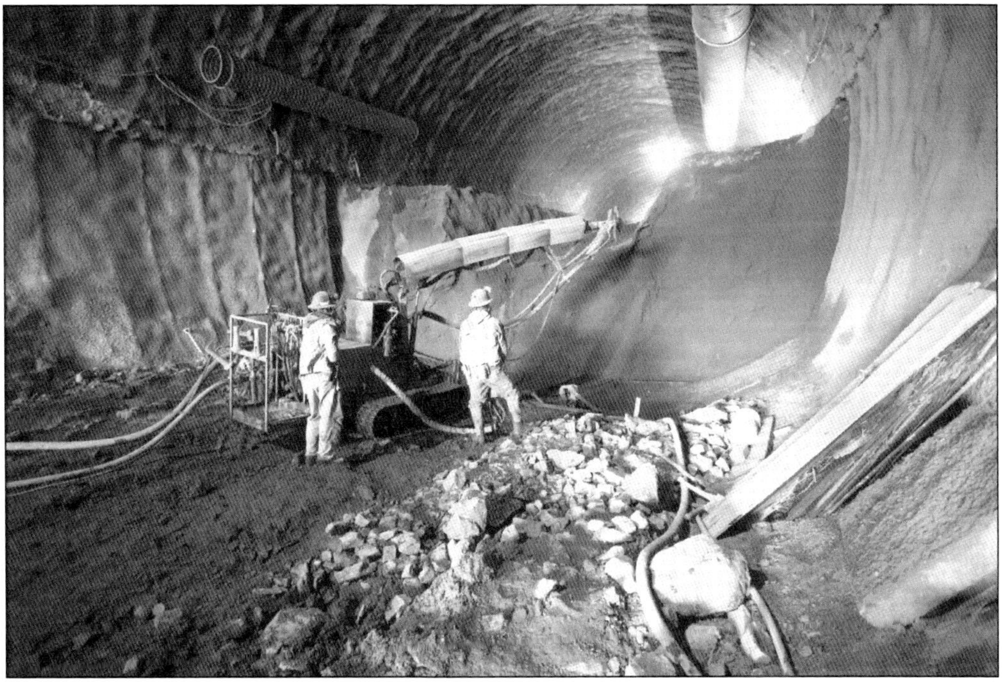

The upper portion of the crown of the tunnel was excavated first, before the bench and the invert. The bench is the middle portion of the tunnel (between the top heading and the invert). The invert is the lowest portion of the tunnel (below the bench). The arches transfer the surrounding overhead and lateral loads of the open tunnel cross section around the tunnel and into undisturbed ground. (Courtesy California Department of Transportation.)

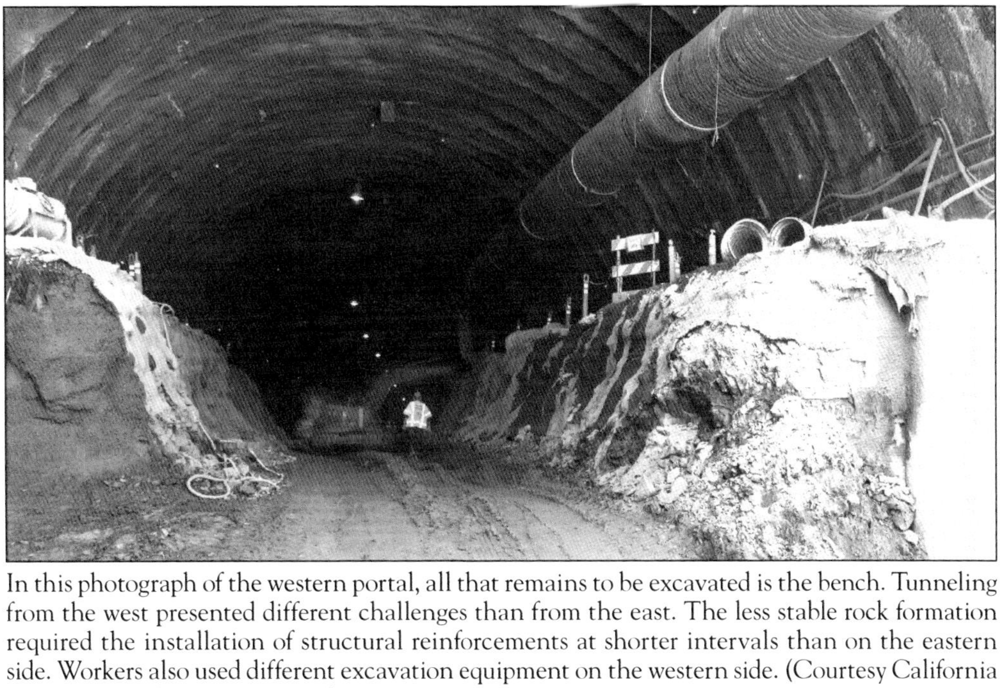

In this photograph of the western portal, all that remains to be excavated is the bench. Tunneling from the west presented different challenges than from the east. The less stable rock formation required the installation of structural reinforcements at shorter intervals than on the eastern side. Workers also used different excavation equipment on the western side. (Courtesy California Department of Transportation.)

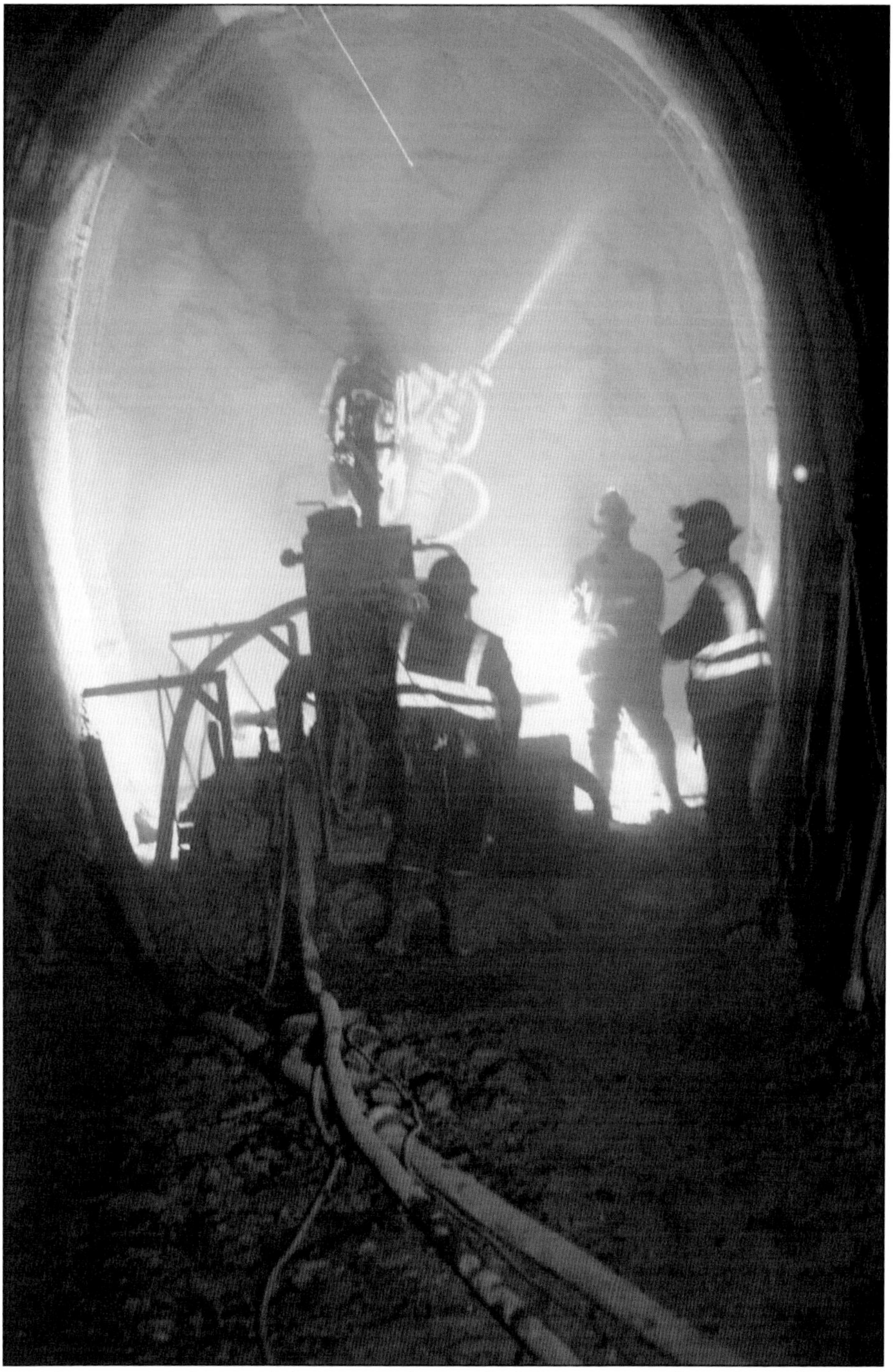

After workers excavated some of the section, they applied shotcrete to walls and installed steel rods around the perimeter of the excavation. The shotcrete and steel rods provided temporary support during construction. The entire length of the tunnel was gradually covered with shotcrete. The application of shotcrete to the walls and top of this cross passage is being guided by a laser beam to ensure accuracy. (Courtesy California Department of Transportation.)

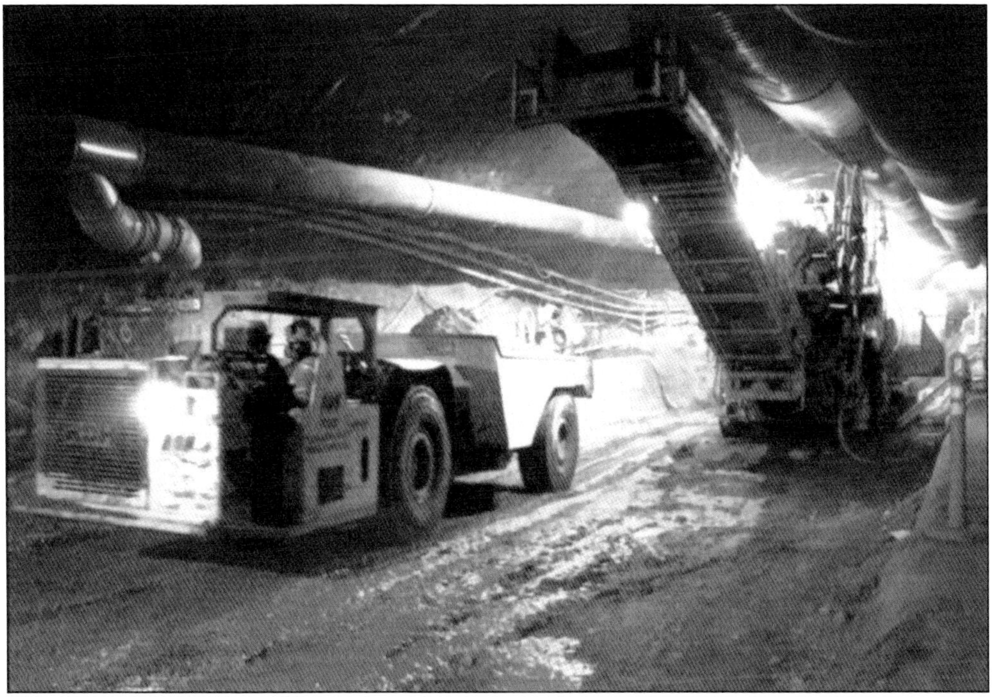

After a section had been tunneled, front-end loaders moved the tunnel spoil to long, flat mining dump trucks. Workers excavated 210,000 cubic meters during construction of the fourth bore. The trucks offloaded the spoil outside the tunnel portal. All spoils were tested for contaminated or hazardous materials before leaving the site. Loaders filled larger dump trucks with clean spoils that were hauled to Treasure Island in San Francisco. Any contaminated spoils were loaded into trucks and transported to appropriate disposal sites. The hazardous materials most likely to be found during testing were naturally occurring hydrocarbons. Paleontology samples from the fourth bore were sent to the University of California, Berkeley, for analysis. (Both, courtesy California Department of Transportation.)

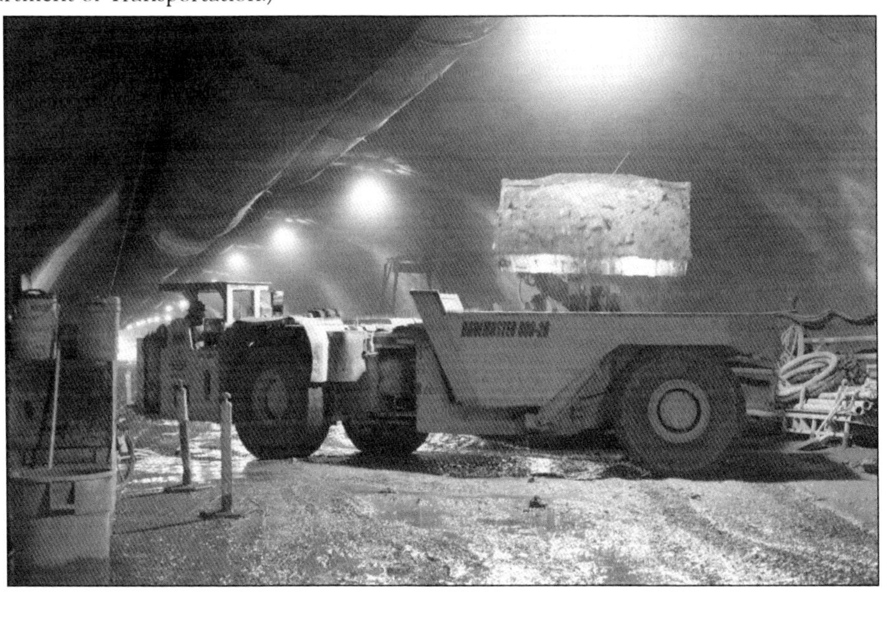

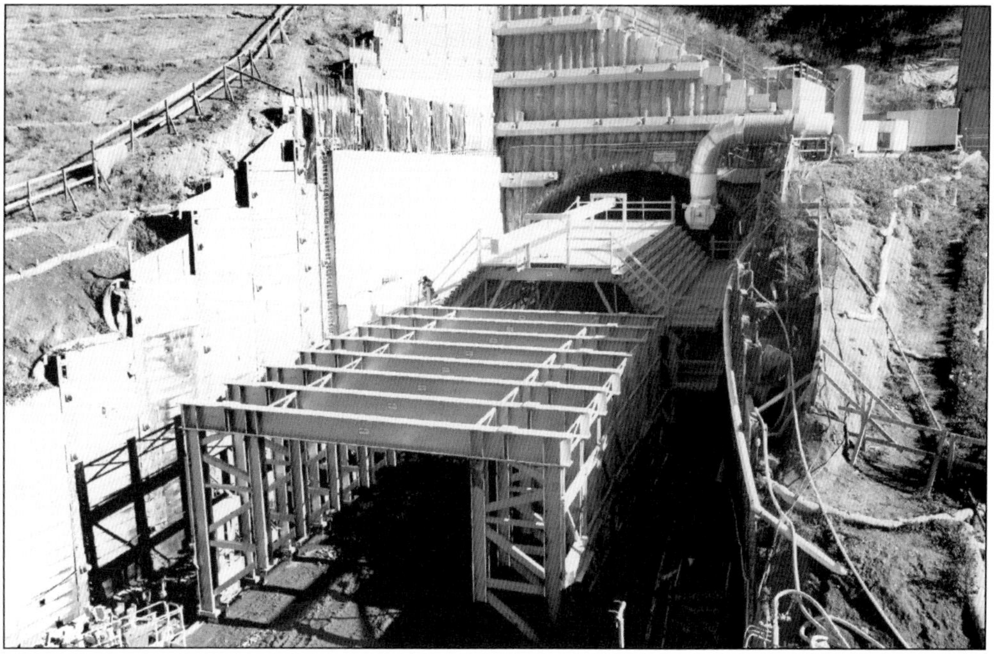

The gantry is a frame that slides on tracks to facilitate installation of the waterproofing and final lining at the western portal. The framework glided forward as work progressed on the lining. Workers used the gantry to hand-tie the rebar cage supporting the final lining. (Courtesy California Department of Transportation.)

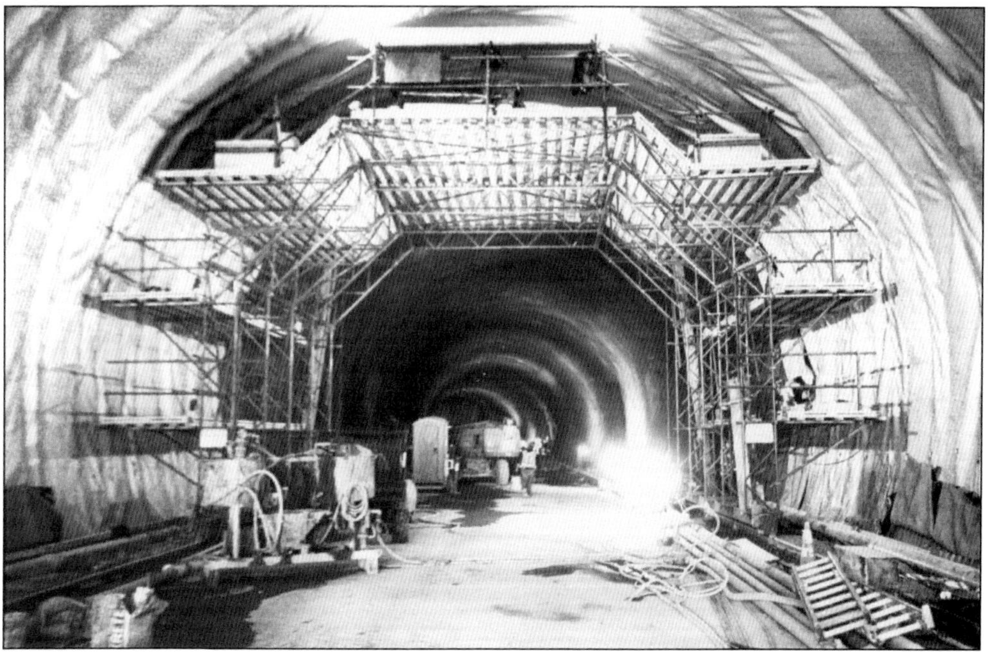

Work continues on excavating the invert (the trench), which was filled with concrete and rebar to compensate for groundswell on the east side of the hills. The tunnel's waterproof membrane, rebar cage, and final lining were installed from west to east. (Courtesy California Department of Transportation.)

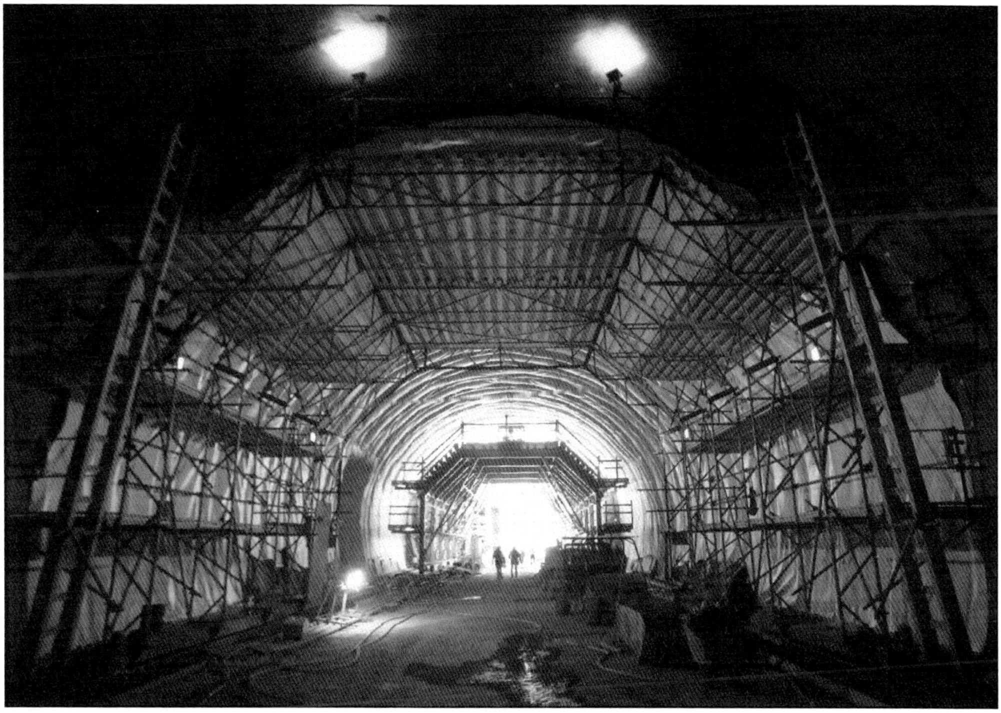

Seven millimeters of yellow waterproofing membrane, made of a polymer-based material, were applied over the top of the smoothed shotcrete (shown below) throughout the length of the tunnel. For the final lining, the contractor cast a wall of reinforced concrete by assembling a rebar cage, constructing formwork (shown above) to contain the concrete, pouring the concrete through holes in the form, then plugging the holes when the wall space was filled. (Both, courtesy California Department of Transportation.)

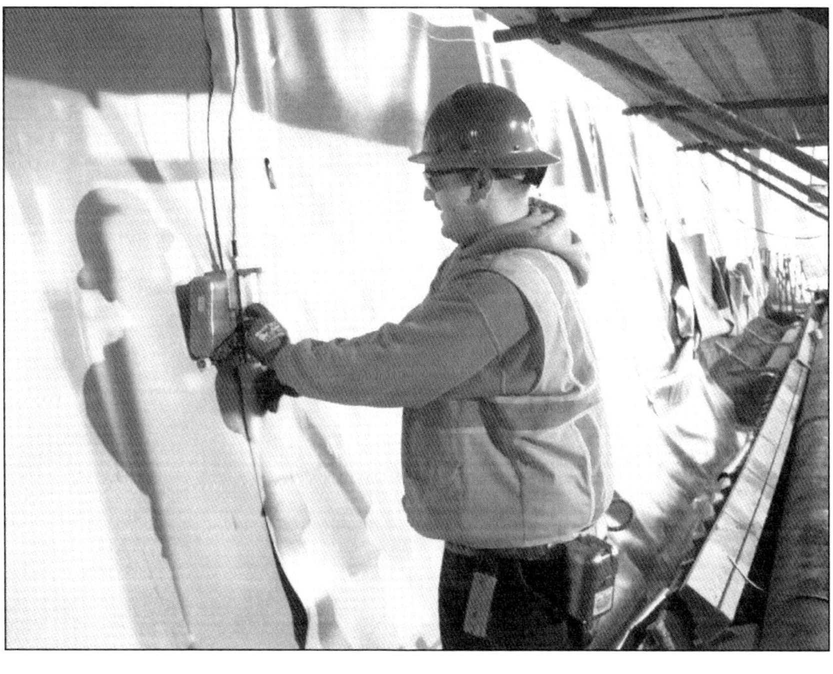

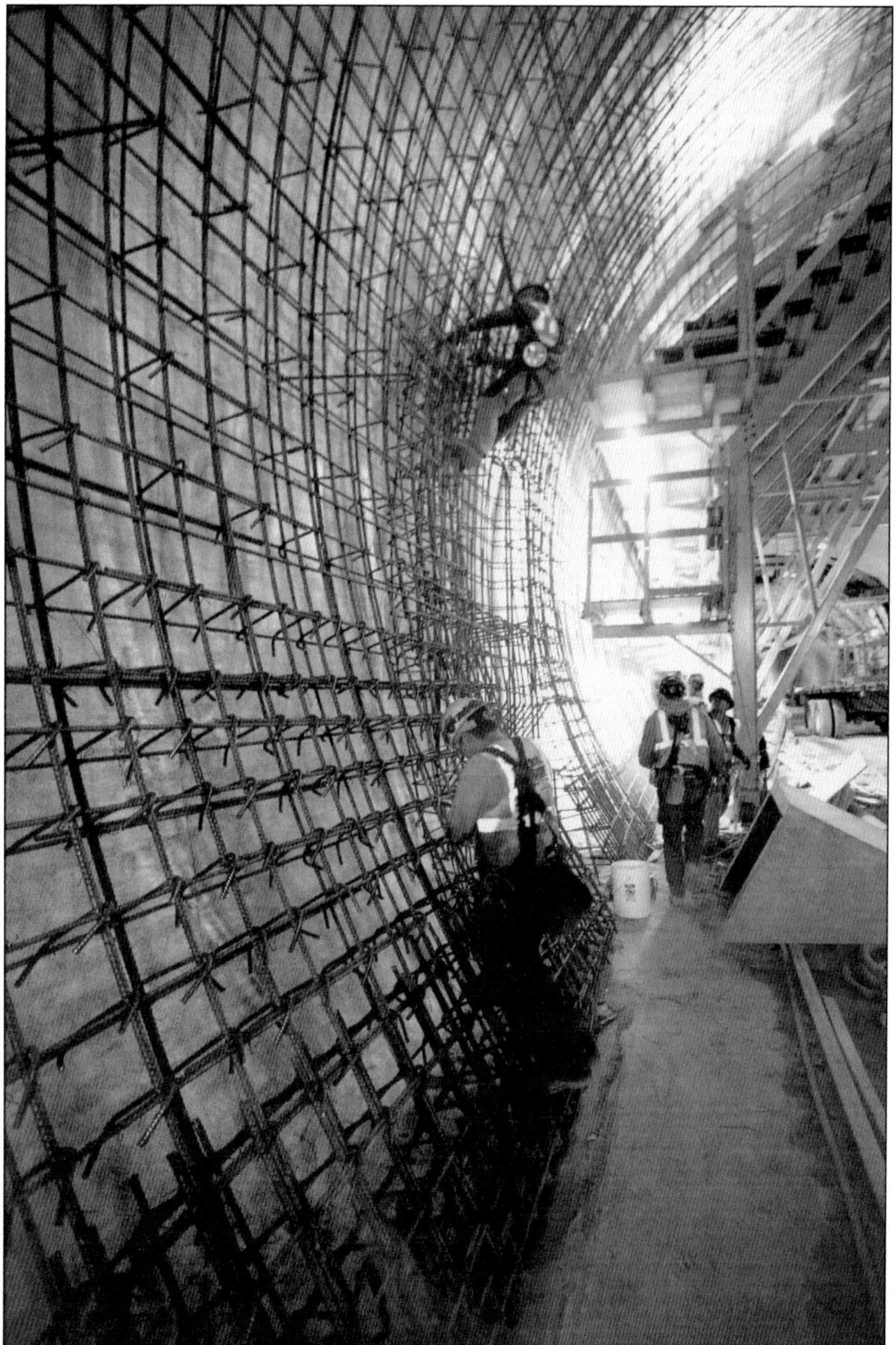

Workers used metal ties to fasten pieces of rebar that provided reinforcement and strength to support the final concrete lining. A cage made of rebar was installed over the waterproof membrane to provide structural support and deflect earthquake energy to maintain the tunnel's structural integrity. Over 3.5 million pounds of steel rebar were used while constructing the fourth bore, which should enable the tunnel to withstand a strong earthquake on the Hayward Fault. (Courtesy California Department of Transportation.)

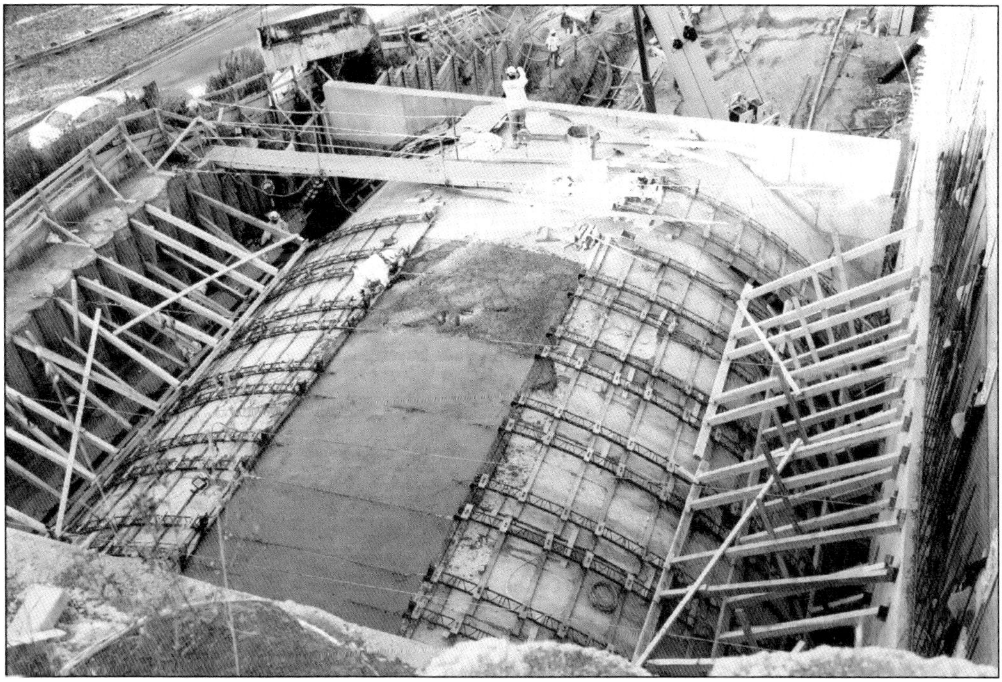

Concrete was applied to the outside of the tunnel to create a portal entrance. The workers climbed atop gantries to first build the forms to shape the domed arch before the concrete could be applied. Then, after it was spread, it needed to be hand-finished to create a smooth surface. This was the cut and cover section of the tunnel. It matched the same shape as the mined tunnel. The substation buildings were built near this section of the tunnel. (Both, courtesy California Department of Transportation.)

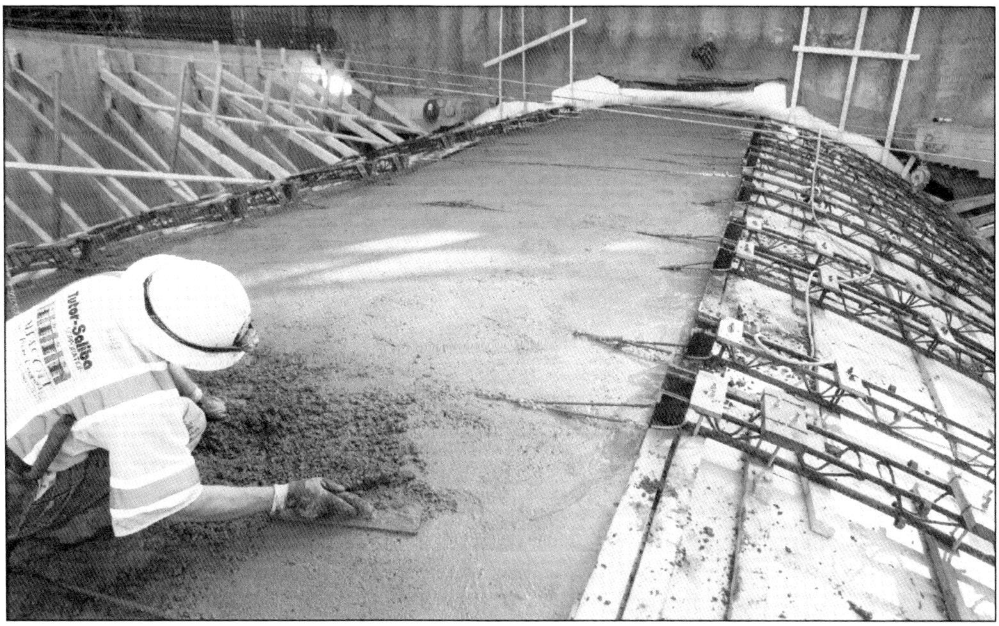

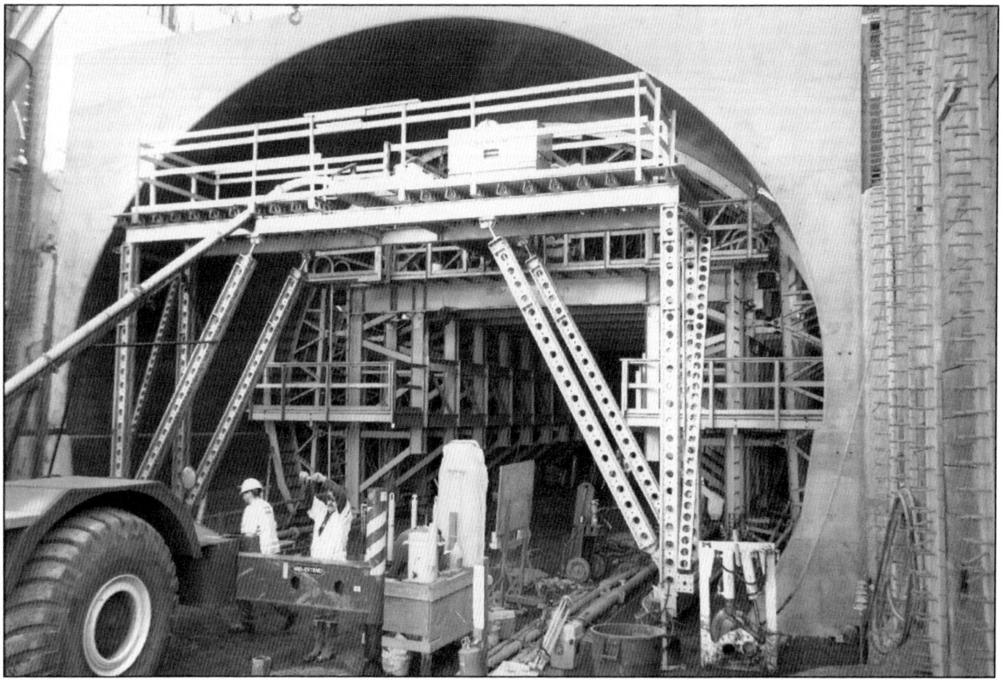

Once the tunnel excavation was completed, work on the outside and inside of the bores progressed. Outside, moveable work bridges offered an improvement over the jumbos used in the original Broadway Low Level Tunnel construction as work began on the portals in May 2012. Inside the tunnel, excavators removed the last of the bench so that they could begin work on preparing the roadway. (Both, courtesy California Department of Transportation.)

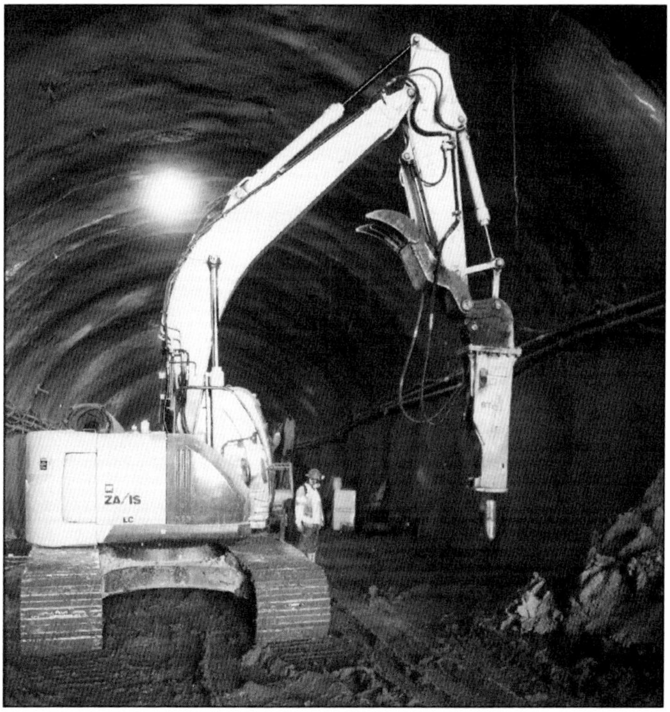

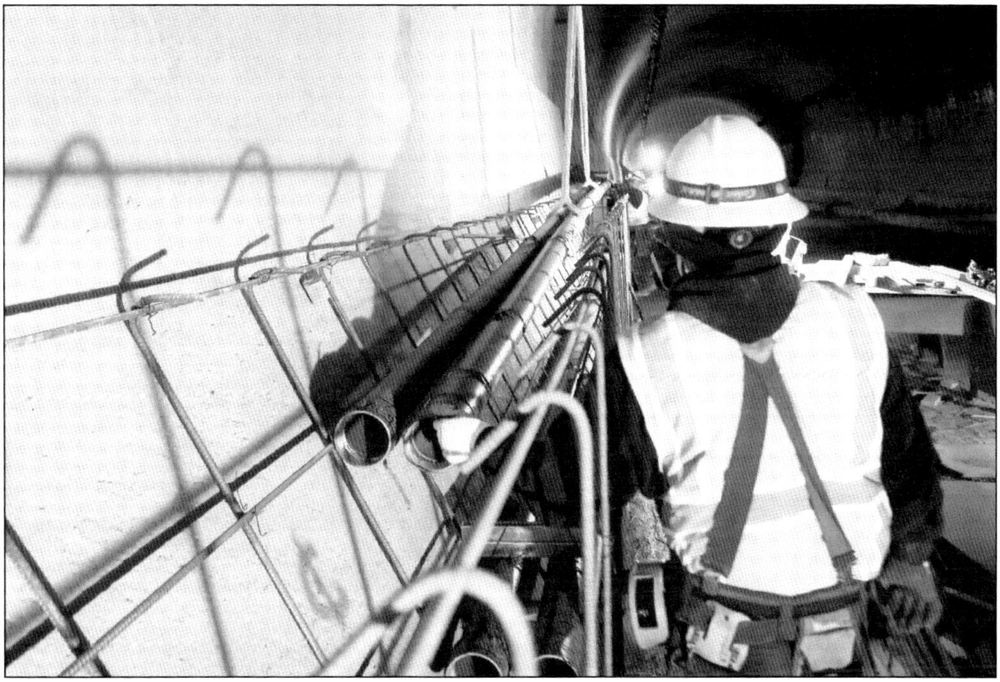

Workers install electrical conduits in a rebar cage along the walls of the bore in this November 2012 photograph. Once all of the pipes and wiring had been put into place, the cages were filled in with concrete to protect the utilities. (Courtesy California Department of Transportation.)

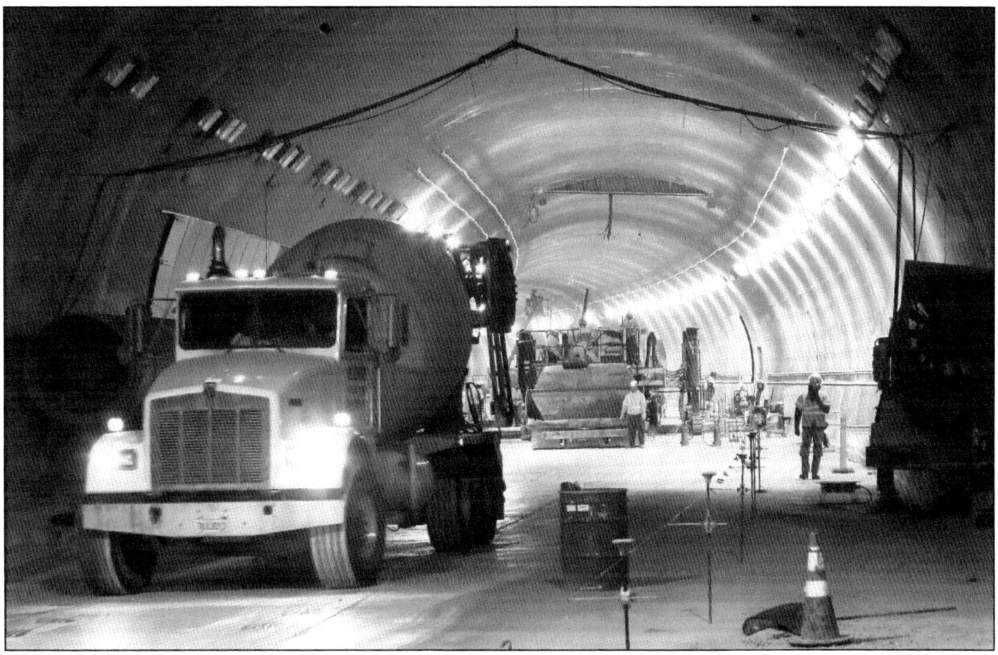

Workers used massive quantities of concrete, delivered day and night by trucks, to construct the fourth bore. Concrete was poured to form the exterior walls, tunnel final lining, curbs, roadway, and portals. In this image, a cement truck is leaving the west portal. (Courtesy California Department of Transportation.)

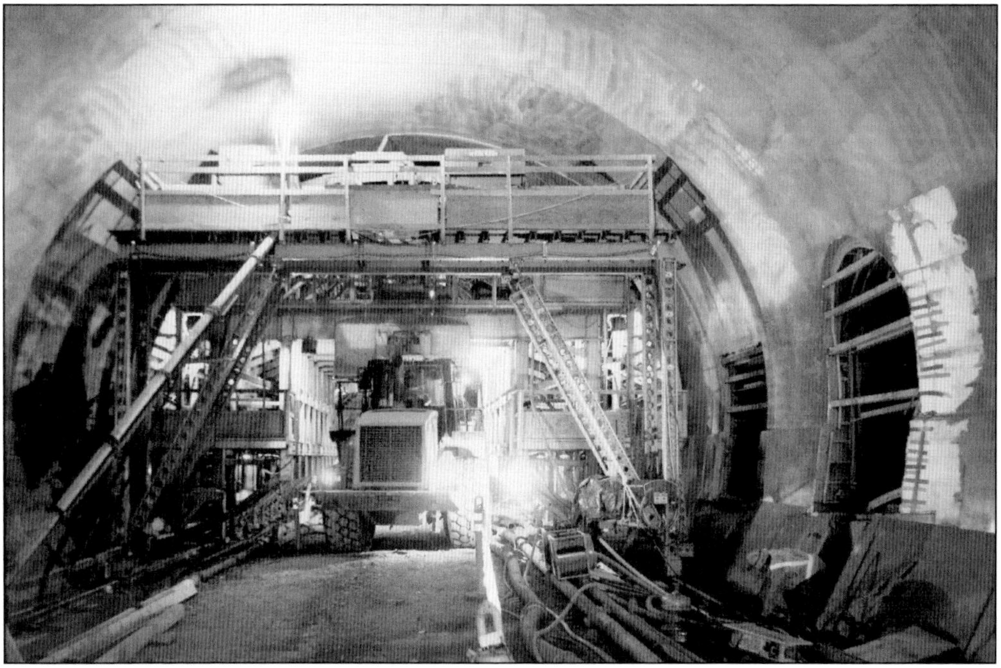

Finishing work in the tunnel included using a gantry to seal the roof with shotcrete while workers prepared shoulders and walkways for rebar installation. In the above image, the cross passage at right was excavated and awaited shotcrete and electrical work. Below, a worker measures the height of the opening in the concrete pipes set to become part of the drainage system. Even with the lighting provided in the tunnel, many miners wore headlamps. (Both, courtesy California Department of Transportation.)

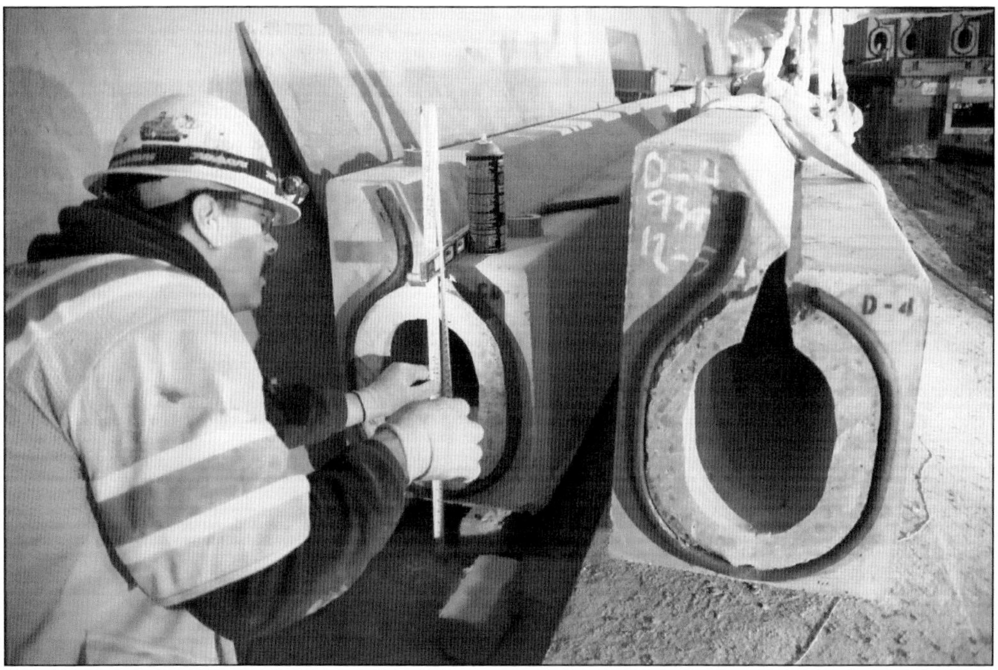

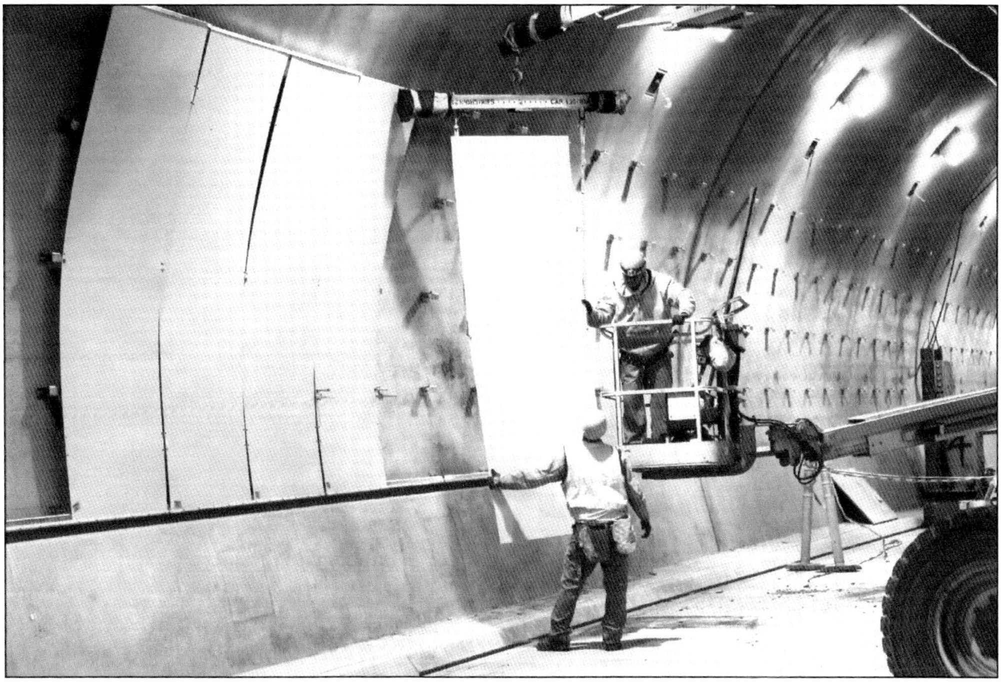

Stainless steel panels were installed along the entire length of the new tunnel. The panels, designed to be easily cleaned (in comparison to the concrete walls in the first and second bores), also help to create a tunneling effect that focuses motorists' attention on the road. (Courtesy California Department of Transportation.)

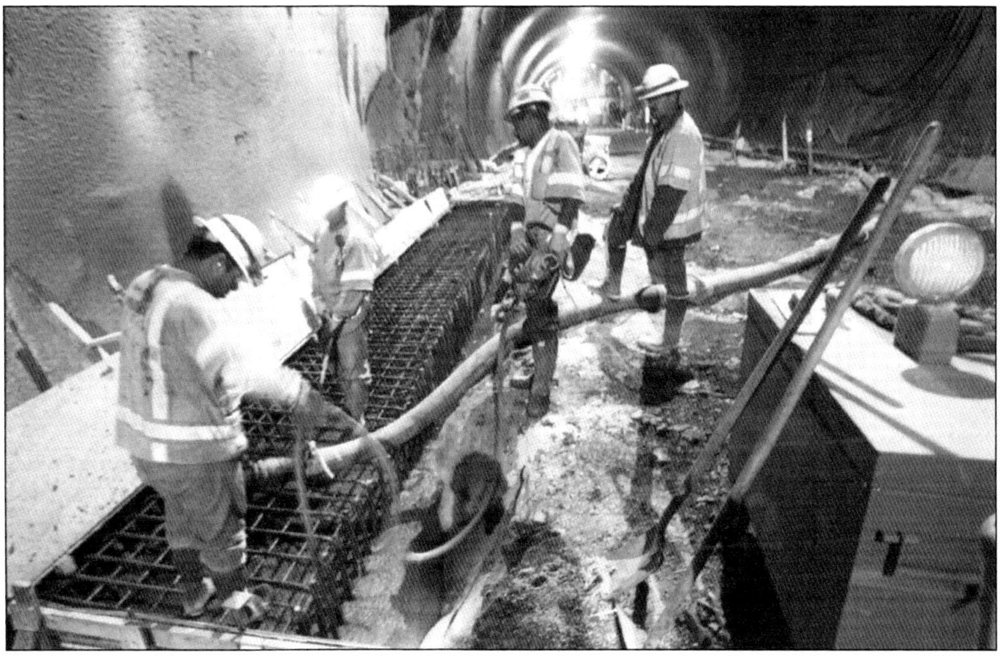

Workers pumped concrete into forms reinforced with rebar to complete the shoulders and walkways in the new bore. Trucks delivered concrete into the bore, where it was poured into pumps and then sprayed into the forms by hose. (Courtesy California Department of Transportation.)

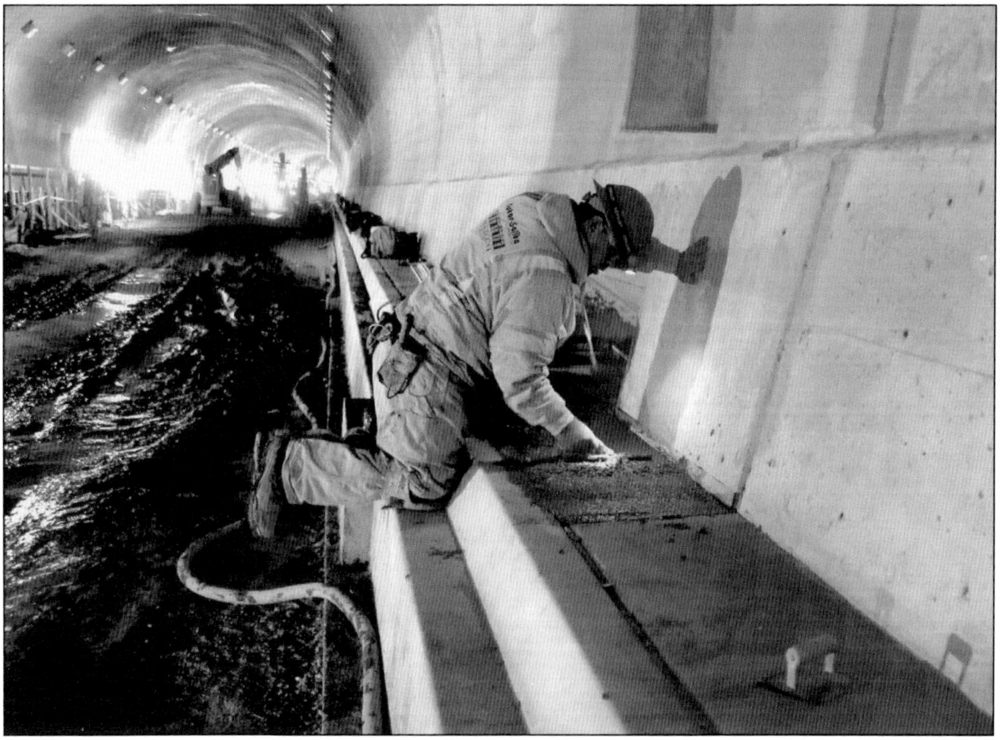

In the above image, a worker finishes the curb and walkway along the roadbed. Workers laid the concrete for the roadway by using a slip form paver (below) filled by a concrete truck. Progress was slow, and finishing was done by hand. (Both, courtesy California Department of Transportation.)

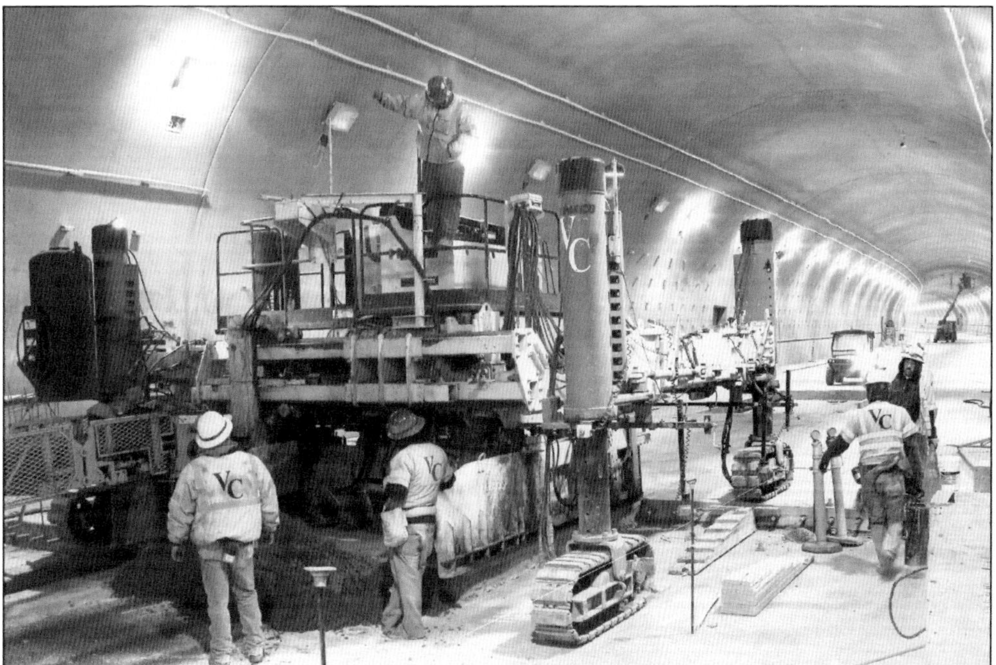

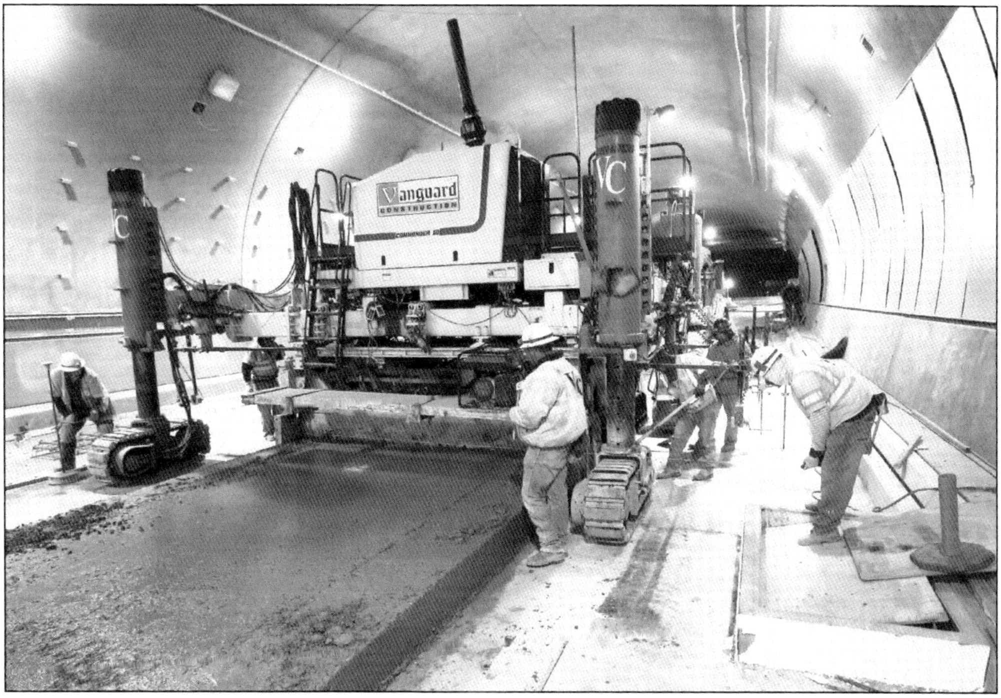

As the project moved towards completion in July 2013, workers laid concrete to complete the 3,348 feet of roadways and curbs in the new bore. They placed rebar in the roadbeds to increase the tunnel's strength. The fourth bore has a 10-foot shoulder on the right and a two-foot shoulder and three-foot walkway on the left, making it wider than any of the previous three bores. (Both, courtesy California Department of Transportation.)

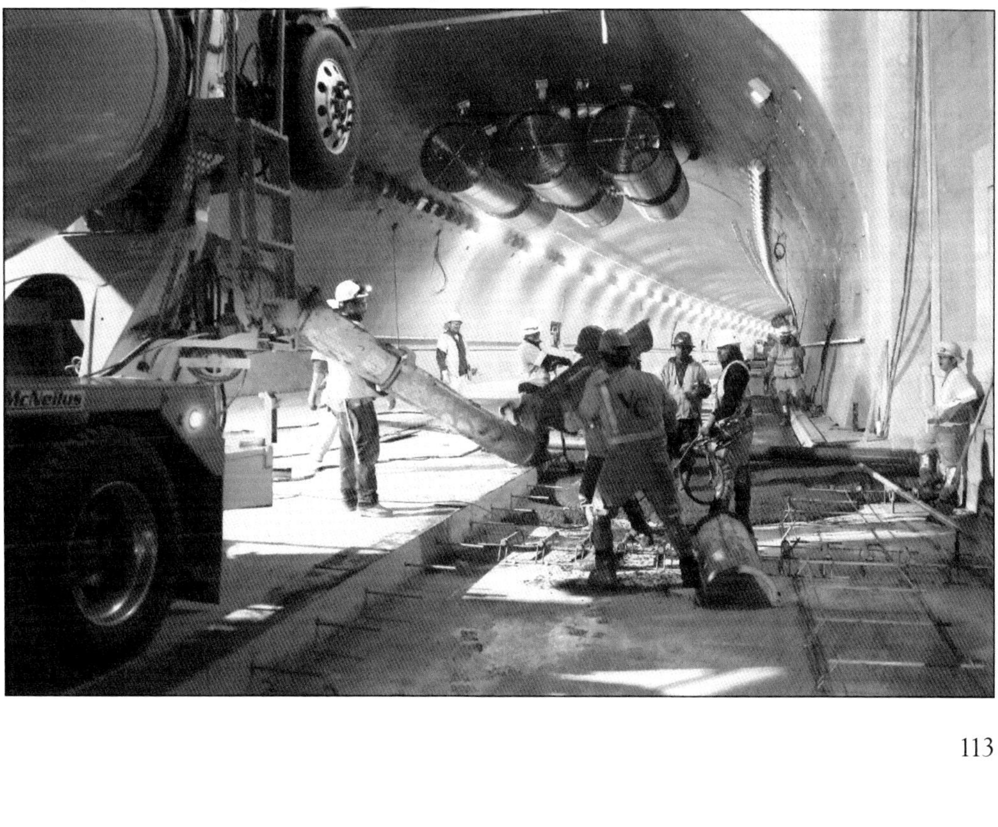

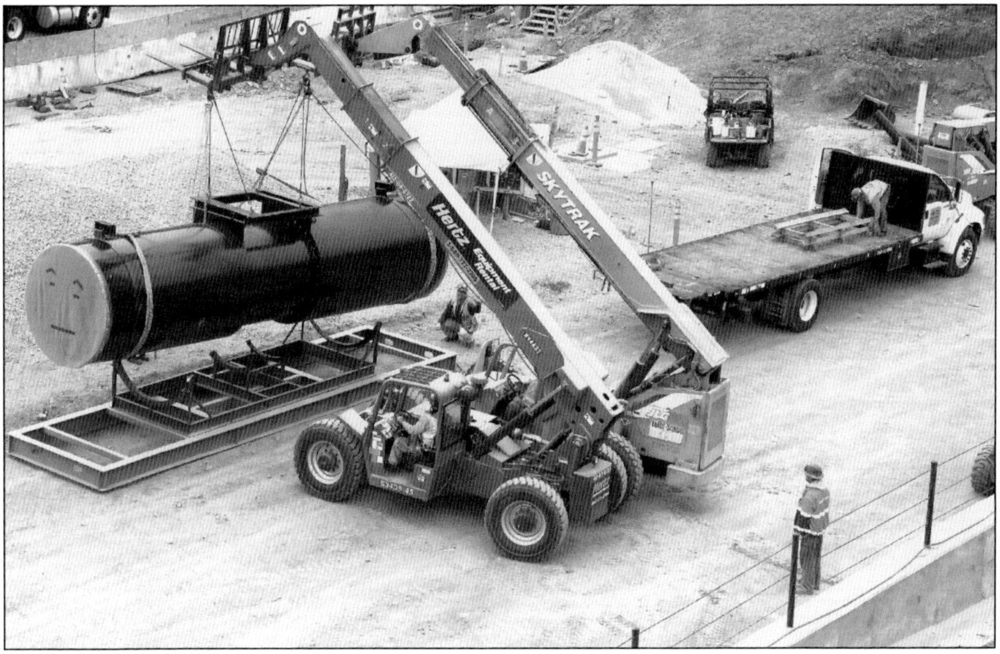

The installation of state-of-the-art fire and life safety systems meets the stringent requirements for tunnel safety that were established after the 1982 fire in the Broadway Low Level Tunnel. Nineteen jet fans were installed in June 2013 and will be able to remove smoke from the tunnel in the event of a fire. The fans can be operated manually or automatically and will be able to direct air flow in either direction in the event of an air-quality issue or emergency. The fans will be triggered by fire alarms, carbon monoxide detectors, and nitrous oxide detectors throughout the tunnel. All of the systems underwent extensive testing before the tunnel opened to traffic. Note the "face" drawn on the end of the jet fan in the above image. (Both, courtesy California Department of Transportation.)

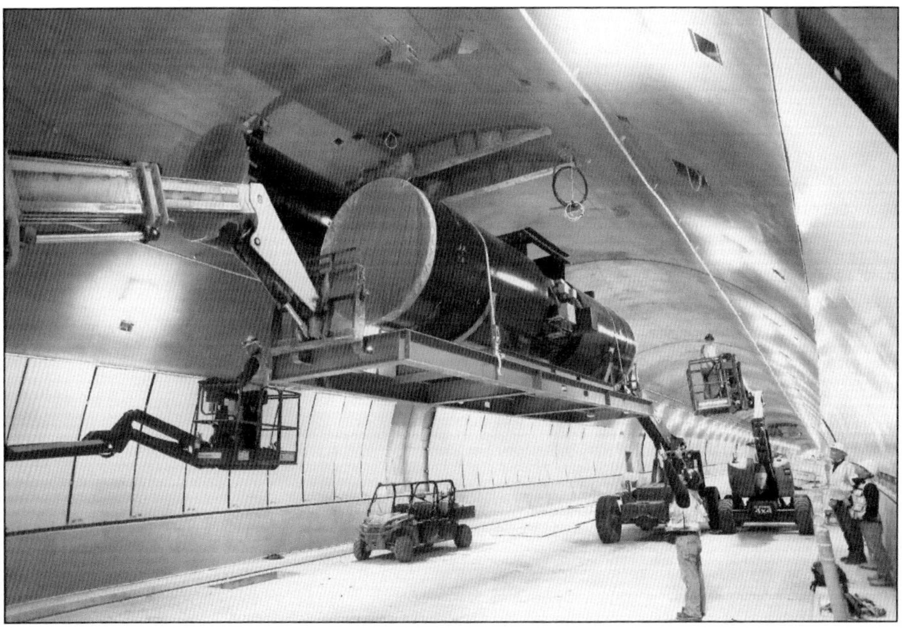

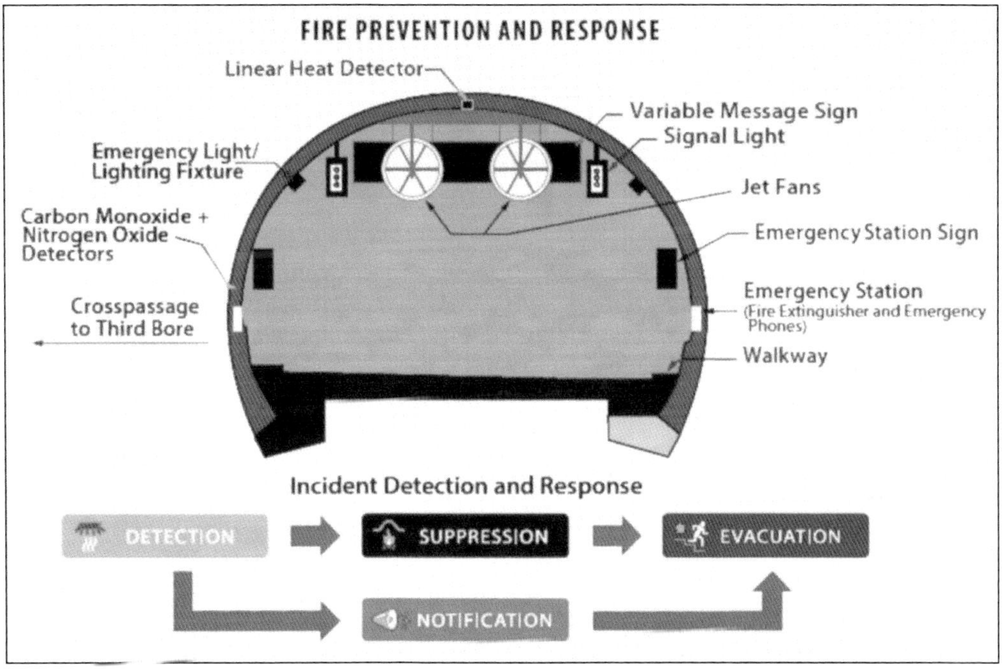

This image highlights the fourth bore's fire-life-safety systems, which include the fire prevention and response equipment in the tunnel. The linear heat detector runs overhead for the entire length of the tunnel. All of the other monitoring systems were designed based on knowledge drawn from previous tunnel fires and advancements in tunnel safety. (Courtesy California Department of Transportation.)

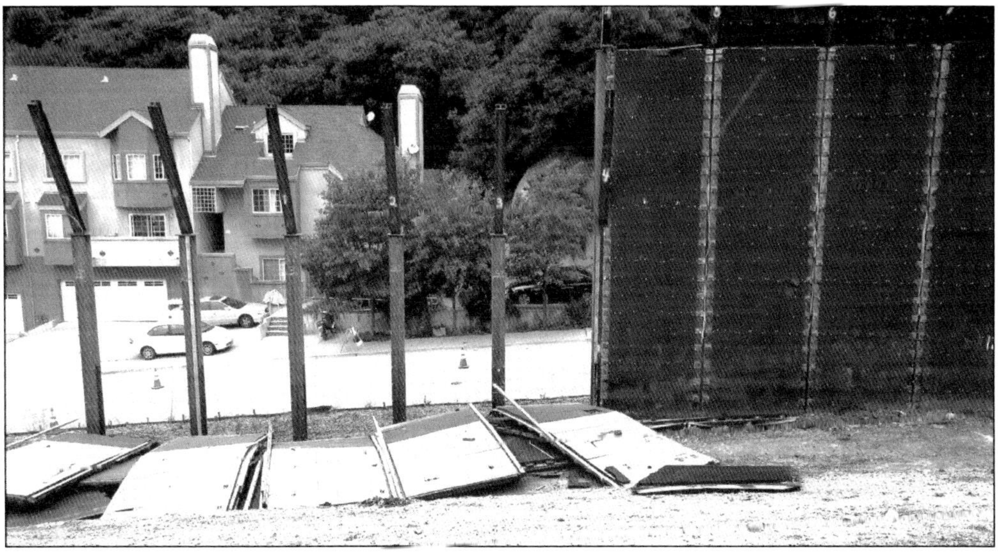

Workers built a temporary soundwall on the west side of the tunnel in Oakland; it was dismantled in the summer of 2013 and replaced by a permanent berm and soundwall. The wall trapped the noise, light, and dust generated during construction; trucks used the approach between the freeway and the wall as a staging area that contained a concrete plant, water-treatment facility, and dumping area for soil excavated from the Oakland hills. This was the largest temporary soundwall ever used on a state highway project. (Courtesy California Department of Transportation.)

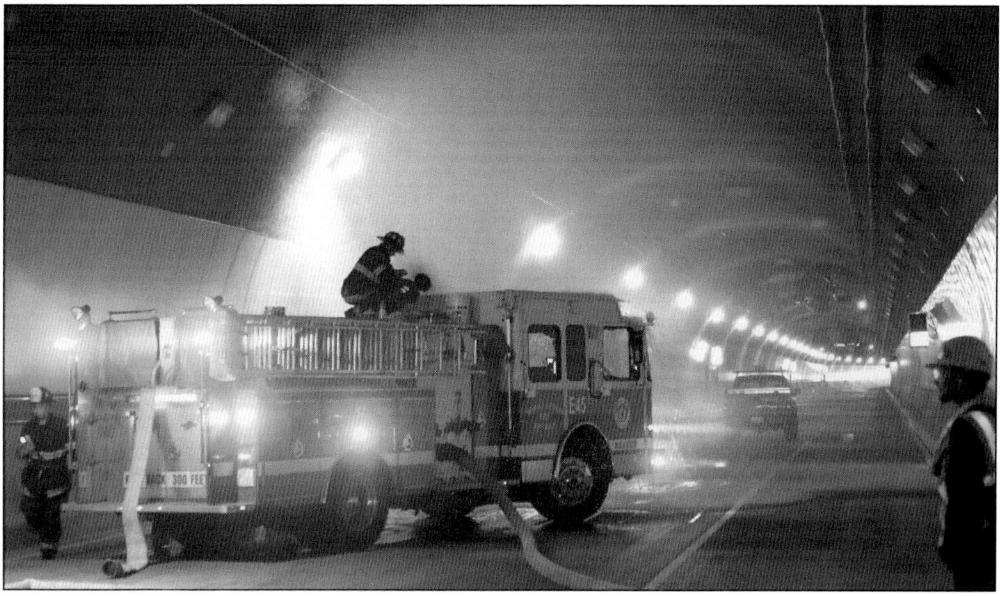

Two days before the tunnel opened, local fire departments conducted drills in the fourth bore. Both the Oakland and Moraga-Orinda Fire Departments are slated to respond to tunnel fires. To shut down the tunnel, operators activate stop lights outside the tunnel entrances and lower a gate. After fire crews completed successful drills in mid-November 2013, representatives from the state fire marshal, the California Highway Patrol, the Moraga-Orinda Fire District, and the Oakland Fire Department signed the emergency response plan to authorize the state to open the tunnel to traffic. (Above, courtesy California Department of Transportation; below, (Courtesy Lafayette Historical Society.)

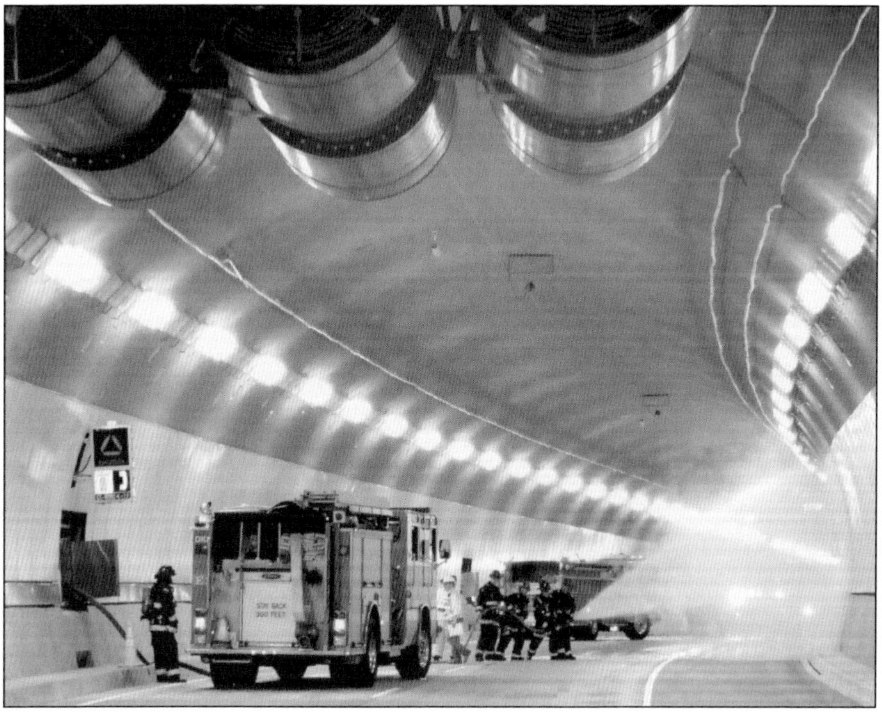

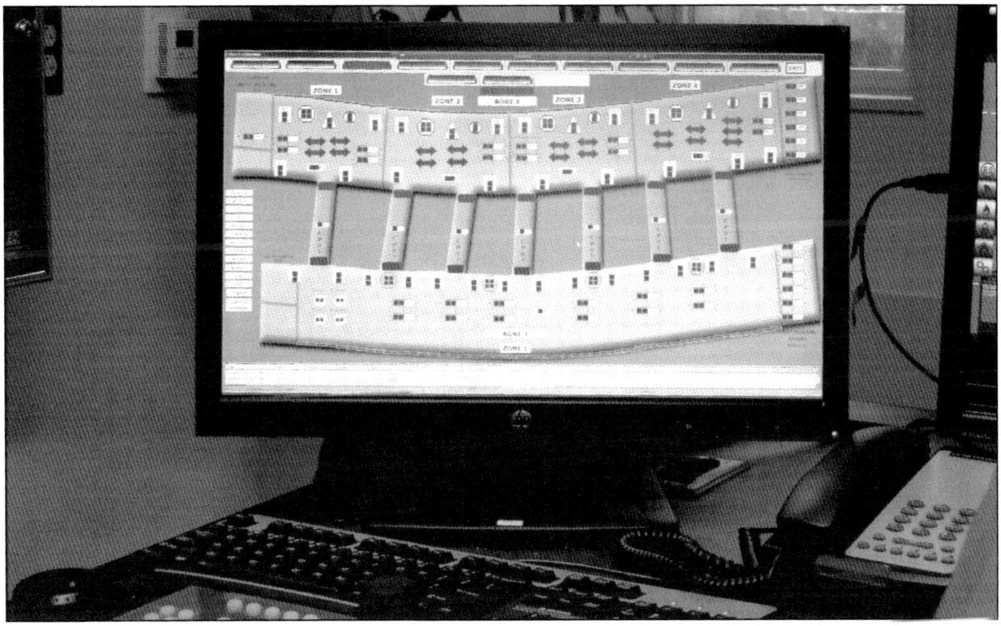

The Caldecott Fourth Bore is designated as a regional lifeline structure and was designed to reopen to emergency traffic within 72 hours of a major earthquake. Tunnel systems will help with traffic management. The VID (Video Image Detection) cameras will monitor traffic patterns and alert an operator if there is a slowdown or accident. Variable-message signs at the portals and within the tunnel will display pre-programmed messages when there is an event. A tunnel radio system will be able to override other radio stations to give emergency messages to motorists. (Both, courtesy Lafayette Historical Society.)

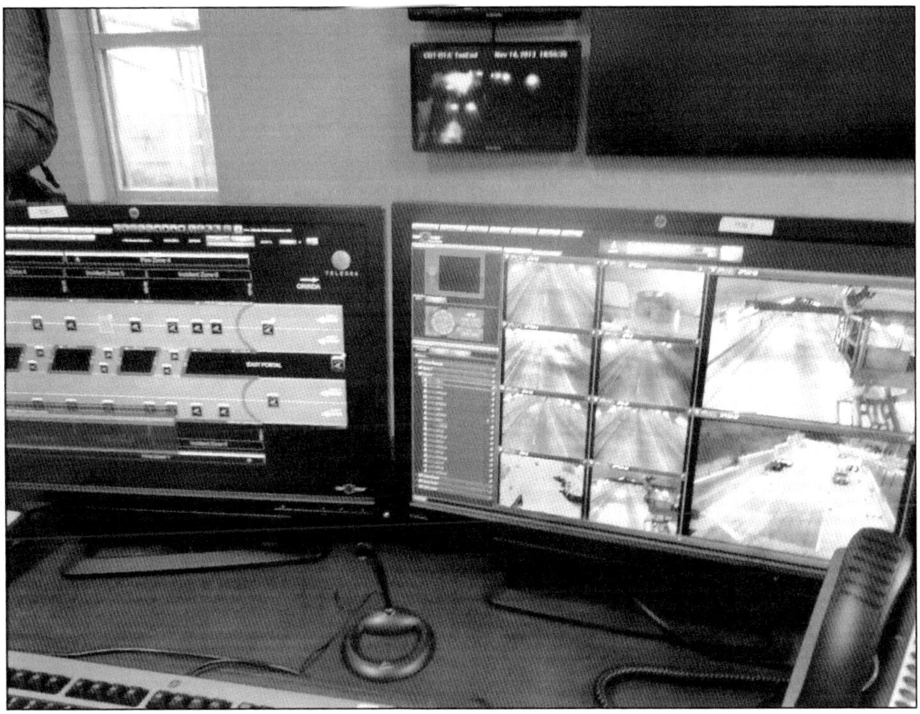

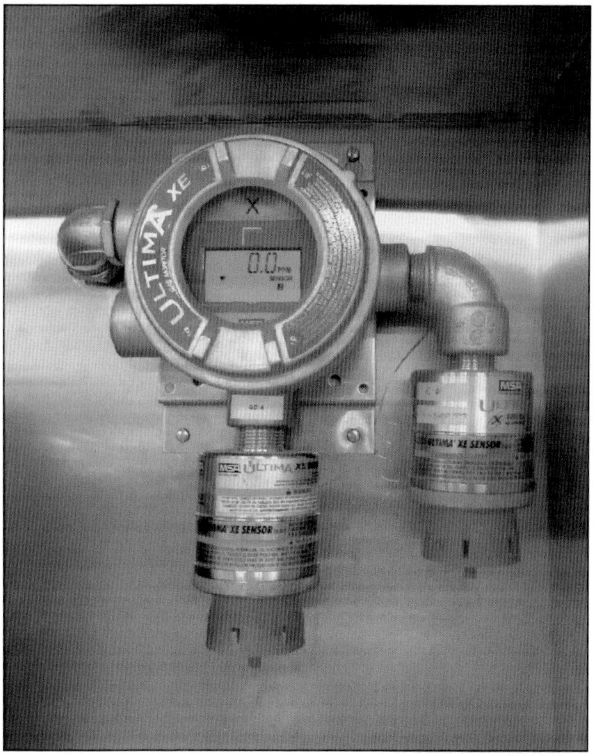

Emergency stations in niches throughout the tunnel house fire extinguishers, manual fire alarms, and emergency phones. Gas sensors can alert tunnel employees to the presence of toxic materials. Traffic signals and variable-message signs reside along the lengths of the third and fourth bores. The variable-message signs will only be illuminated if there is an incident in one of the tunnels and will provide real-time information and directions for motorists. The gates at the eastern portals of the third and fourth bores will lower if there is a serious incident inside in order to keep vehicles from entering the tunnel. (Both, courtesy Lafayette Historical Society.)

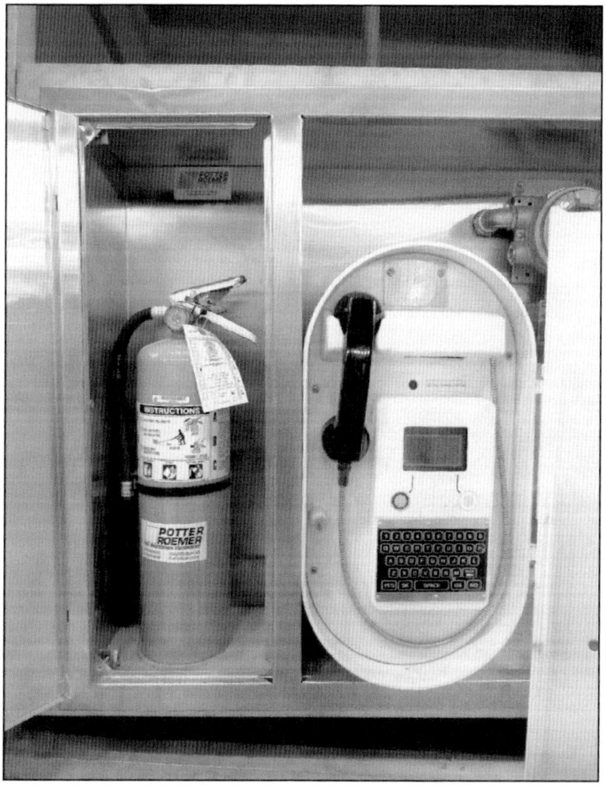

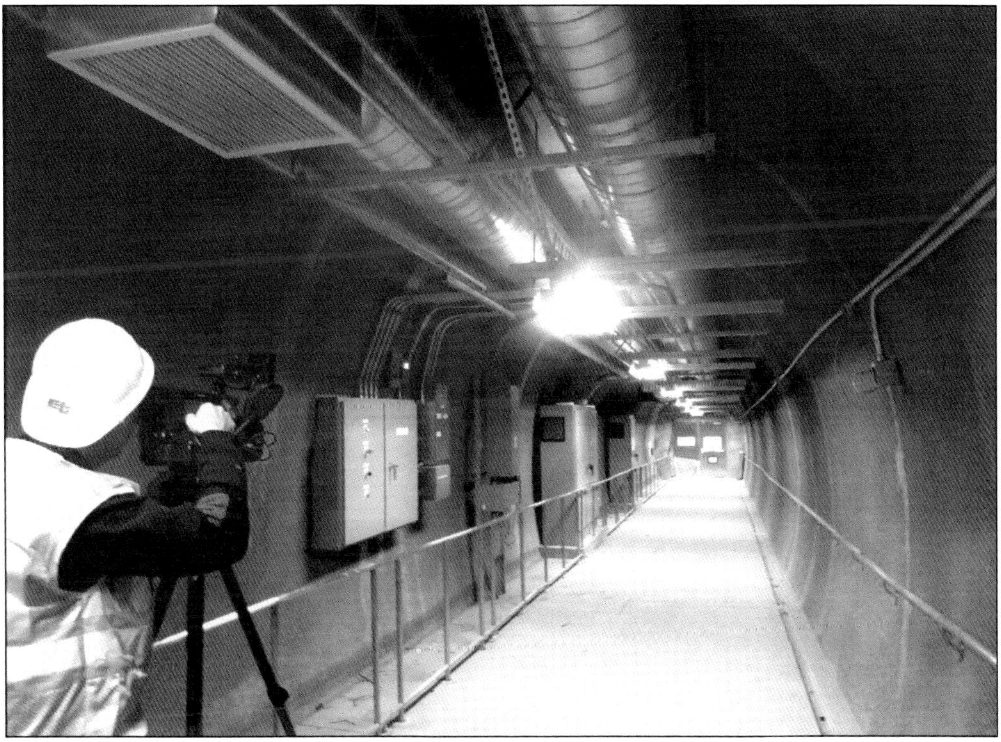

Cross passages like the one shown above allow access between the third and fourth bores for evacuation purposes (both bores will be shut down if there is an incident in either bore). These cross passages have closed-circuit televisions and intercoms, so operators can monitor and communicate with anyone inside the tunnels. The passages also have a ventilation system that will create positive pressure inside to prevent smoke and flames from entering. A state-of-the-art operations and maintenance control (OMC) building (shown below) is the "nerve center" for the four Caldecott tunnels, as well as the Webster and Posey Tubes in Alameda County. The OMC is staffed 24 hours a day, seven days a week, by specially trained operators who passed a rigorous test administered by the state fire marshal before the tunnel opened to traffic. (Above, courtesy Lafayette Historical Society; below, courtesy California Department of Transportation.)

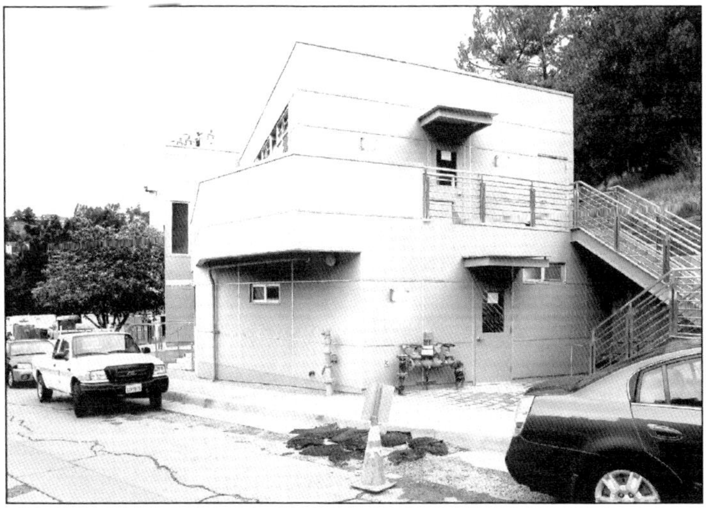

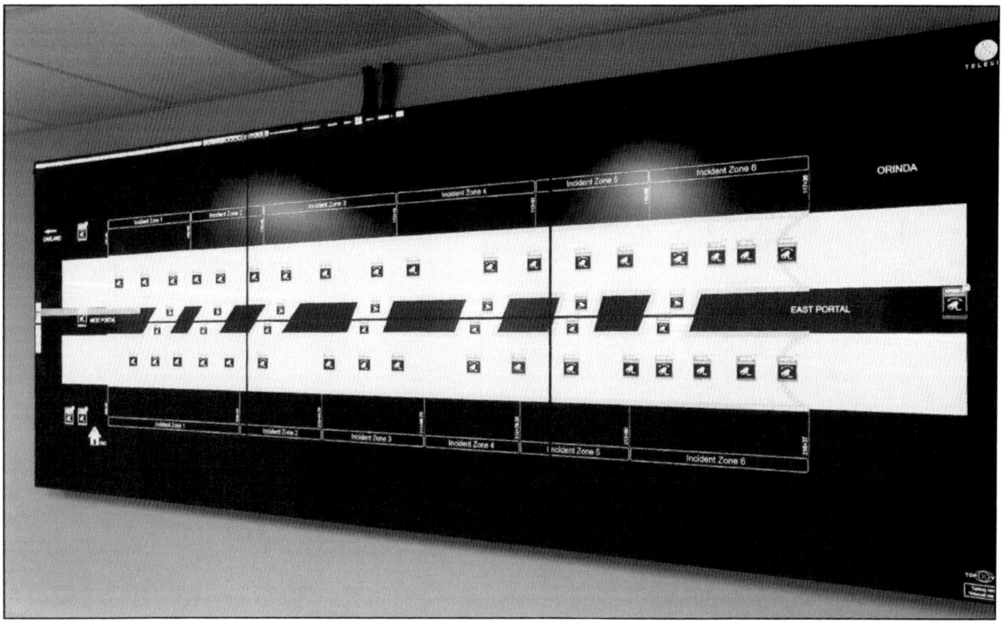

The Caldecott Tunnel's Traffic Operating System (TOS) is a state-of-the-art fire and safety system that includes fire detection and suppression systems. These systems provide operators with real-time information and management capabilities for traffic, fire detection, power supply, and ventilation and lighting systems in the four tunnels. The TOS is located in the operations and maintenance control facility near the western portals. (Above, courtesy Lafayette Historical Society; below, courtesy California Department of Transportation.)

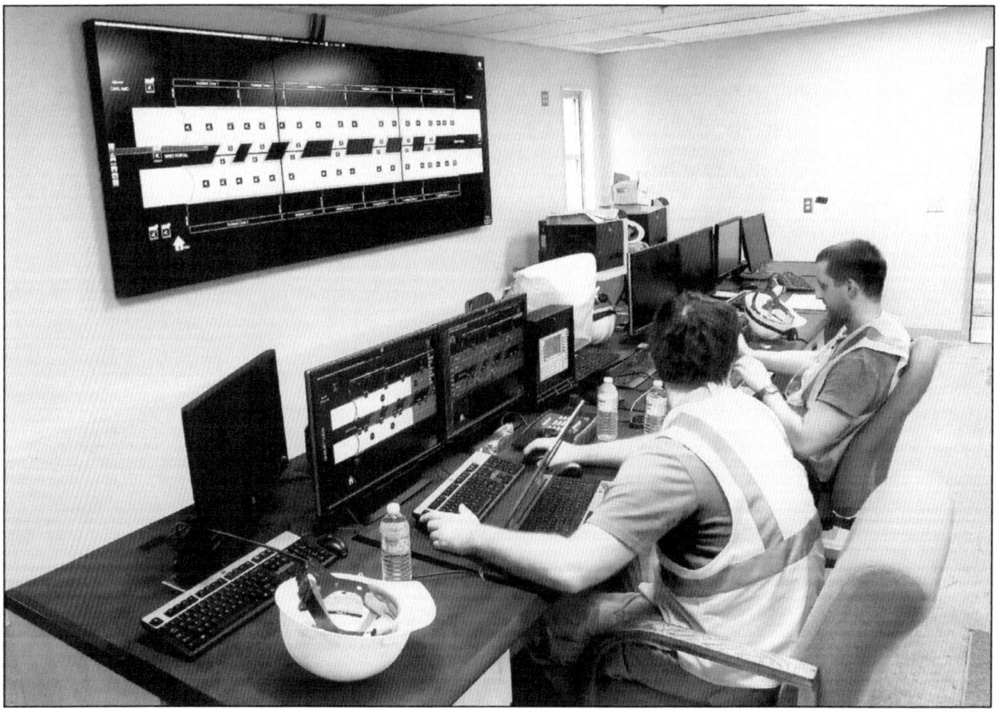

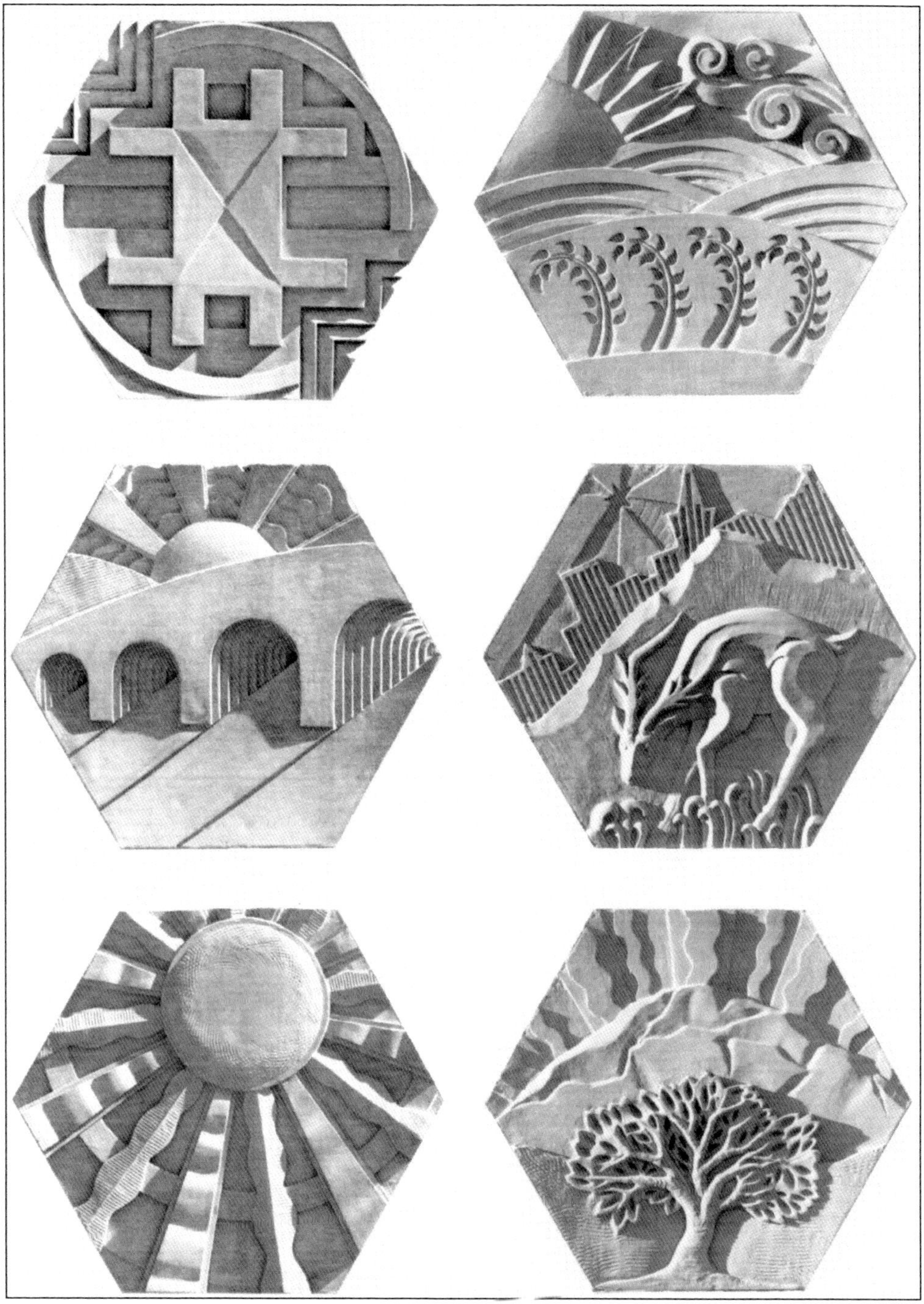

The Fourth Bore Project sponsored a contest for Alameda and Contra Costa County students, asking them to design a medallion for the new tunnel portals using the same Art Deco style of the medallions on the original Broadway Low Level Tunnel portals. There were over 300 entries submitted. The winning designs are pictured here—the medallions from Alameda County are on the left, and the ones from Contra Costa County are on the right. (Courtesy California Department of Transportation.)

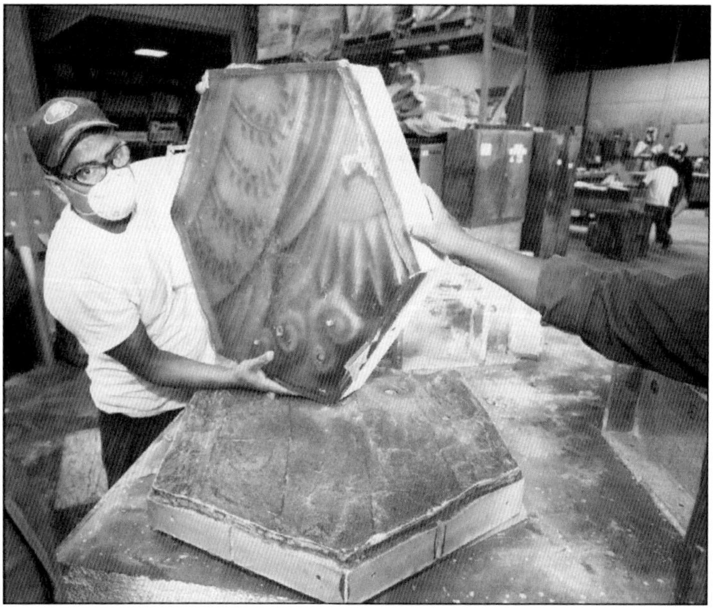

After Caldecott Tunnel Fourth Bore Project judges chose the winning designs from those submitted by Alameda and Contra Costa County students, professional sculptor Johnathan Roberson-Beery (not shown) adapted the winning drawings into 3-D models from which the portal medallions were cast. (Courtesy California Department of Transportation.)

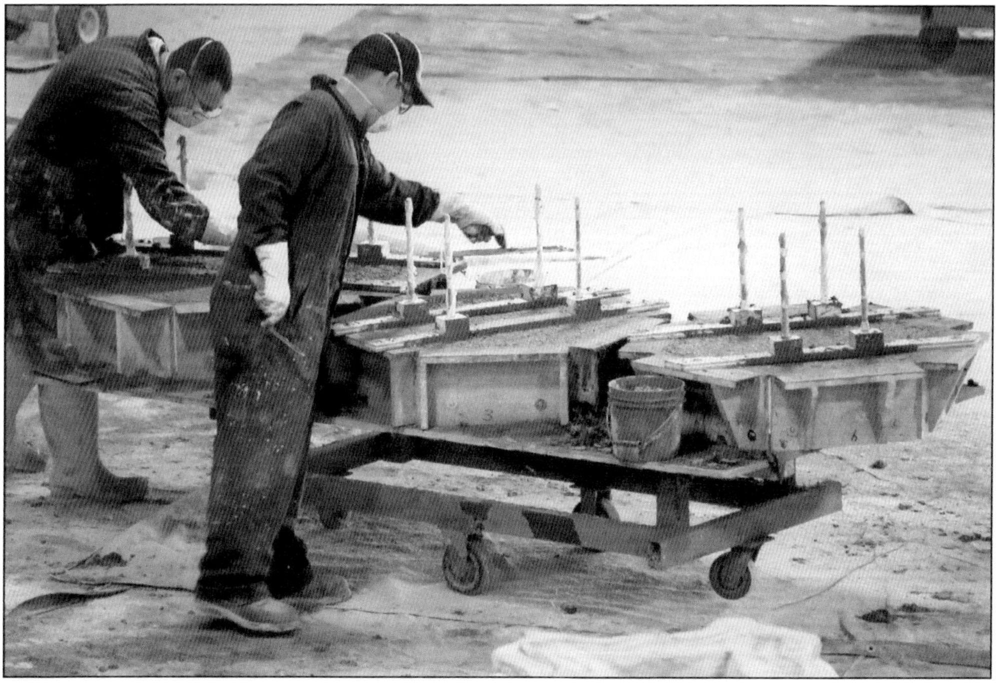

Employees at Architectural Facades Unlimited in Gilroy, California, attached screws and bolts to the backs of the medallions after the students' designs were cast from glass-fiber-reinforced concrete. (Courtesy California Department of Transportation.)

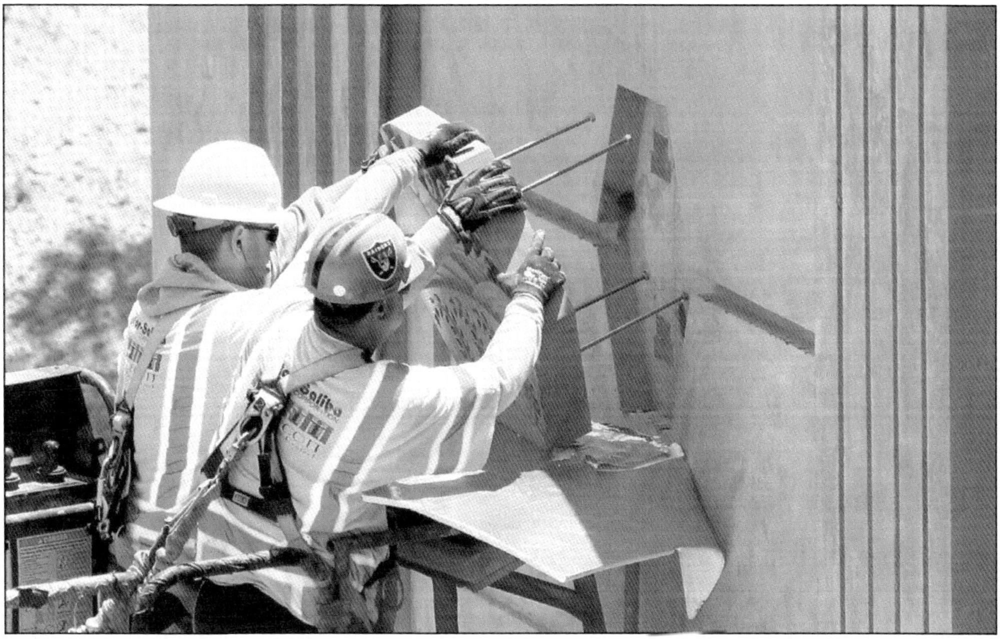

Workers installed the medallions on the faces of the tunnel portals. Three students from Contra Costa County have their medallions displayed on the eastern portal, and three Alameda County students' medallions are displayed on the western portal. (Courtesy California Department of Transportation.)

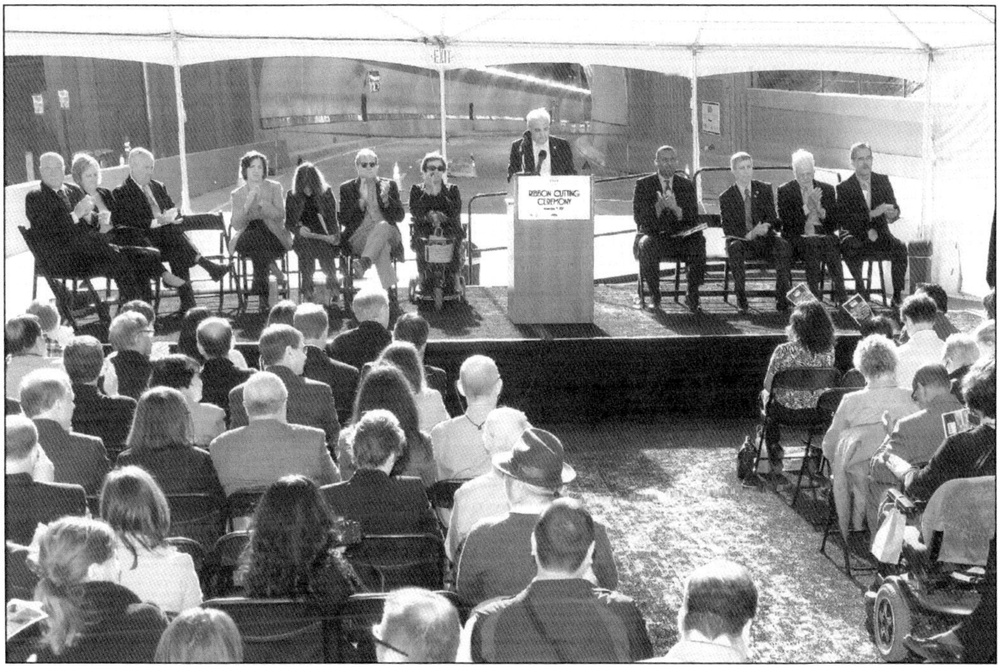

Local officials, politicians, tunnel workers, transportation agencies, and members of the press met in a tent on the approach to the new bore to celebrate the impending opening of the fourth bore on November 15, 2013. Those in attendance were allowed to wander halfway through the tunnel the day before it officially opened. (Courtesy California Department of Transportation.)

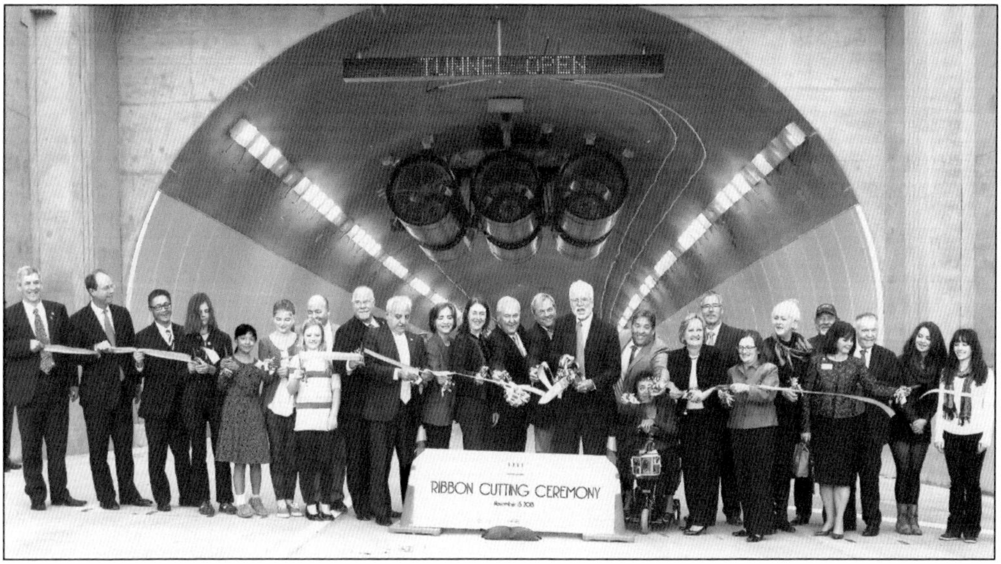

On November 15, 2013, a ribbon-cutting ceremony officially marked the opening of the fourth bore. Notable people made speeches and the medallions were unveiled, and those present gave thanks to those who made this project a success, as it came in on time and under budget! The tunnel officially opened to traffic on Saturday, November 16, 2013 at 4:25 a.m. (Courtesy California Department of Transportation.)

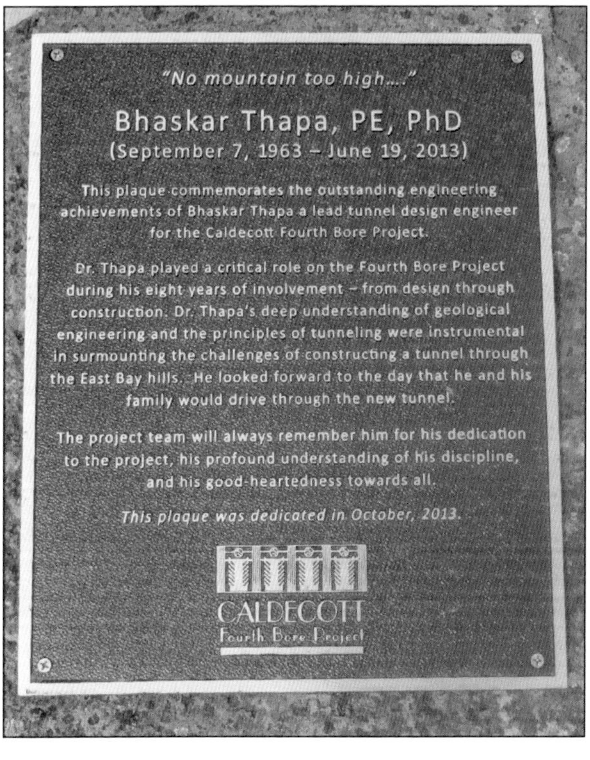

"This plaque [dedicated in October 2013] commemorates the outstanding engineering achievements of Bhaskar Thapa a lead tunnel design engineer for the Caldecott Fourth Bore Project. Dr. Thapa played a critical role on the Fourth Bore Project during his eight years of involvement—from design through construction. Dr. Thapa's deep understanding of geological engineering and the principles of tunneling were instrumental in surmounting the challenges of constructing a tunnel through the East Bay hills. He looked forward to the day that he and his family would drive through the new tunnel. The project team will always remember him for his dedication to the project, his profound understanding of his discipline, and his good-heartedness towards all." (Courtesy Lafayette Historical Society.)

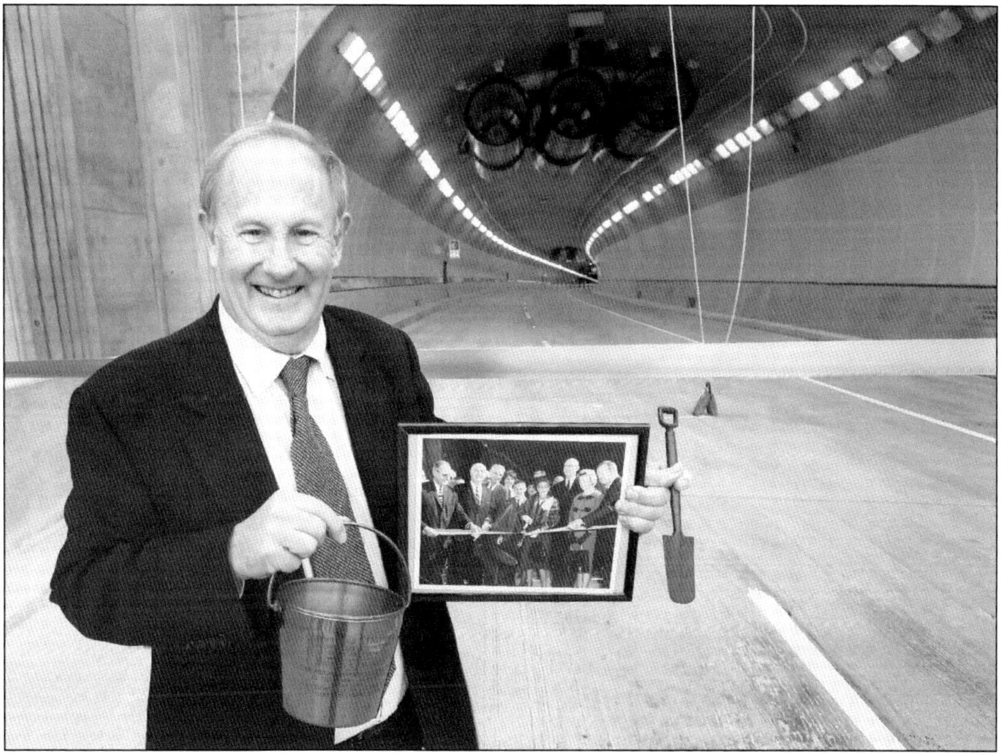

Thomas P. Caldecott holds a photograph of his family taken when the Caldecott Tunnel was named after his grandfather Thomas E. Caldecott in 1960. The shovel and pail shown below were given to his grandfather at the ground-breaking ceremony of the Broadway Low Level Tunnel in 1934. The inscription on the pail reads "Broadway Low Level Tunnel Ground Breaking Ceremonies, Sunday, June 17, 1934, presented to Thomas E. Caldecott by the Oakland Jr. Chamber of Commerce at the tunnel dedication Dec. 5, 1937, in recognition of his untiring efforts to make the tunnel a reality." (Above, courtesy California Department of Transportation; below, courtesy Lafayette Historical Society.)

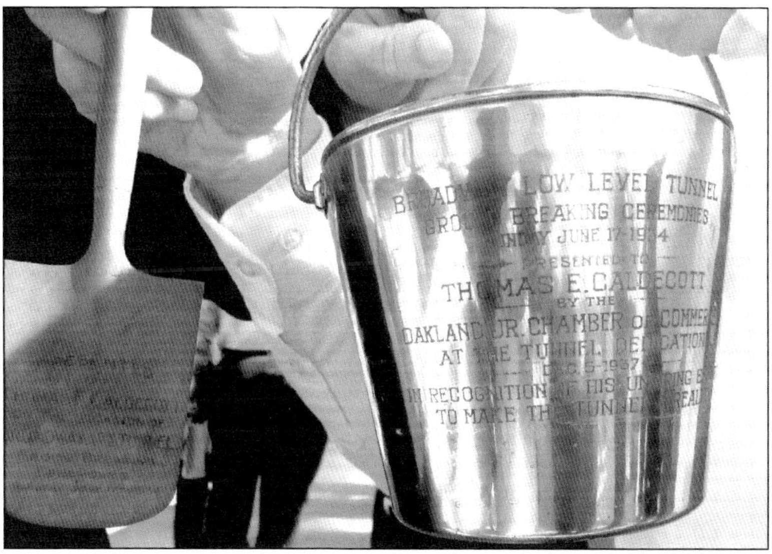

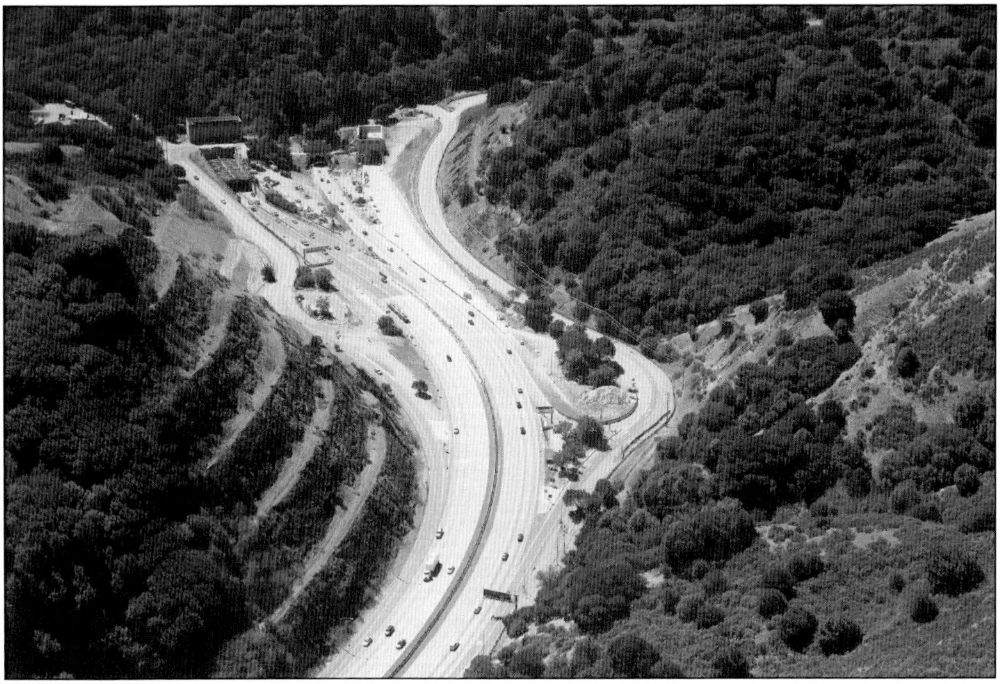

These aerial photographs show the eastern and western portals of all four bores of the Caldecott Tunnel in November 2013. (Both, courtesy California Department of Transportation.)

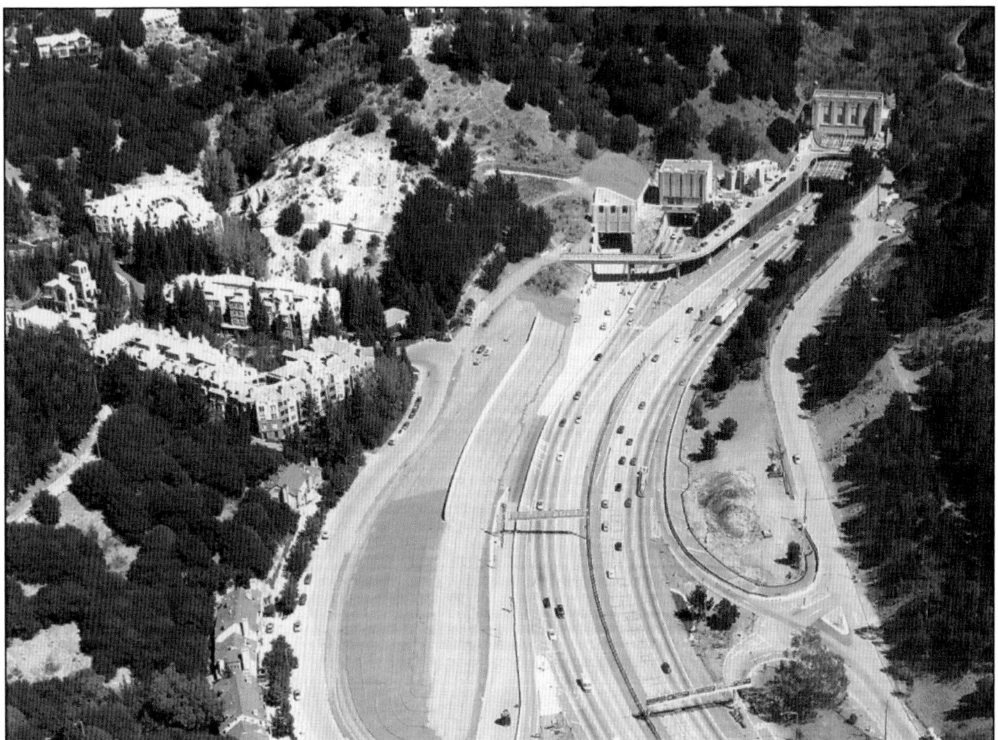

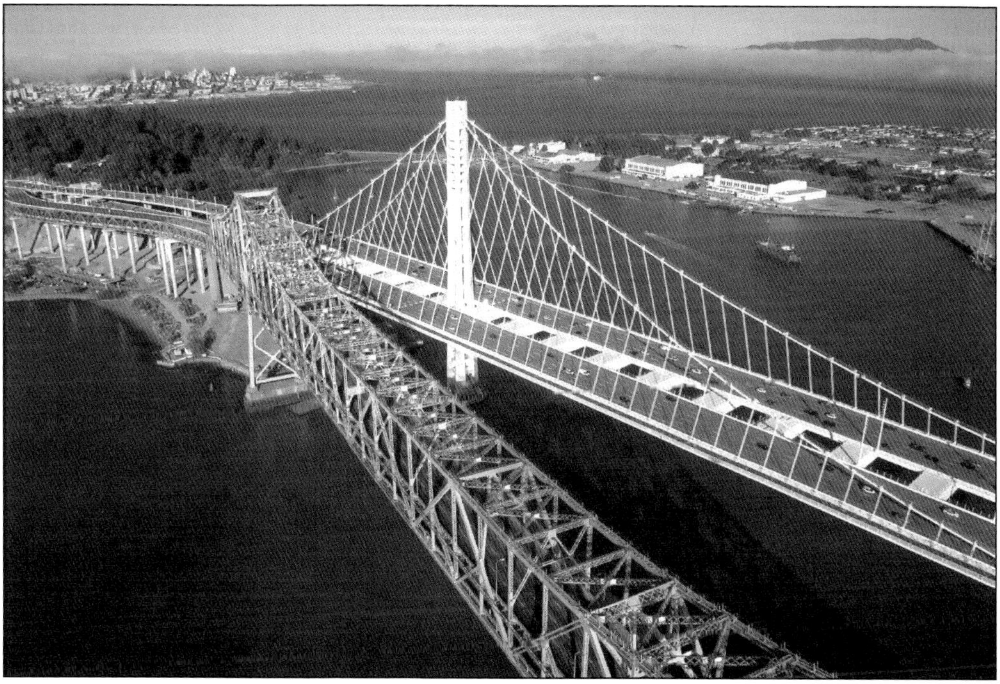

San Francisco Bay Area commuters witnessed major milestones in 2013. With the opening of the new span of the San Francisco/Oakland Bay Bridge in August and the opening of the fourth bore of the Caldecott Tunnel in November, driving times between Contra Costa County (in the east) and Alameda and San Francisco Counties (in the west) were noticeably shortened. Much like the opening of the Bay Bridge in 1936 and the Broadway Low Level Tunnel bores in 1937, the 2013 transit improvements continue to open the towns and cities east of the Oakland/Berkeley hills to travel and living—a far cry from the early wagon trips taken over winding dirt roads. (Above, courtesy California Department of Transportation; below, Bay Area News Group.)

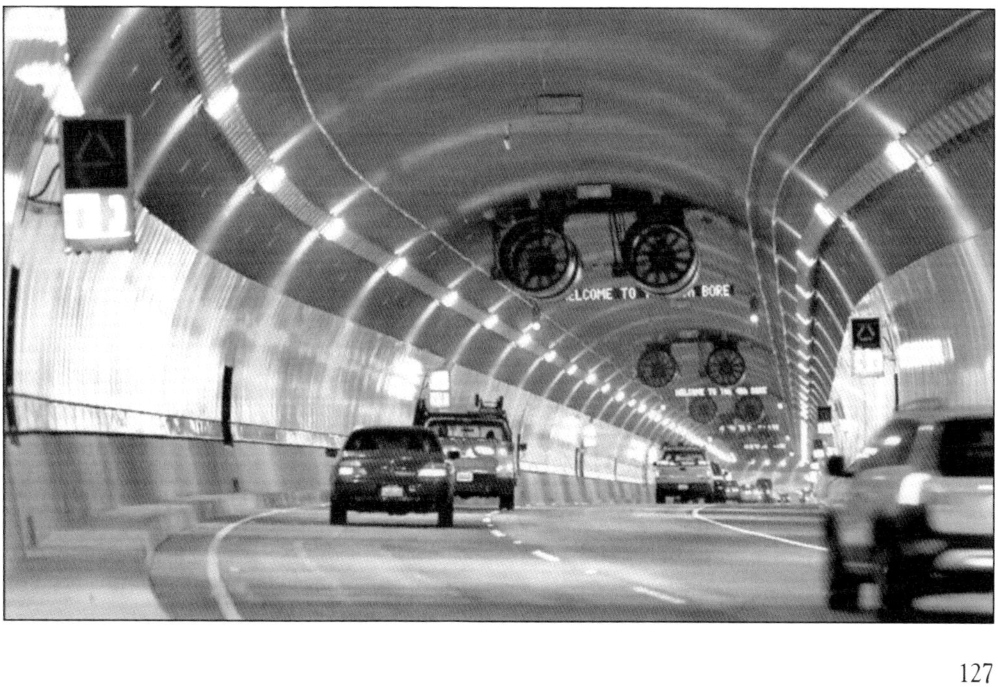

Discover Thousands of Local History Books Featuring Millions of Vintage Images

Arcadia Publishing, the leading local history publisher in the United States, is committed to making history accessible and meaningful through publishing books that celebrate and preserve the heritage of America's people and places.

Find more books like this at
www.arcadiapublishing.com

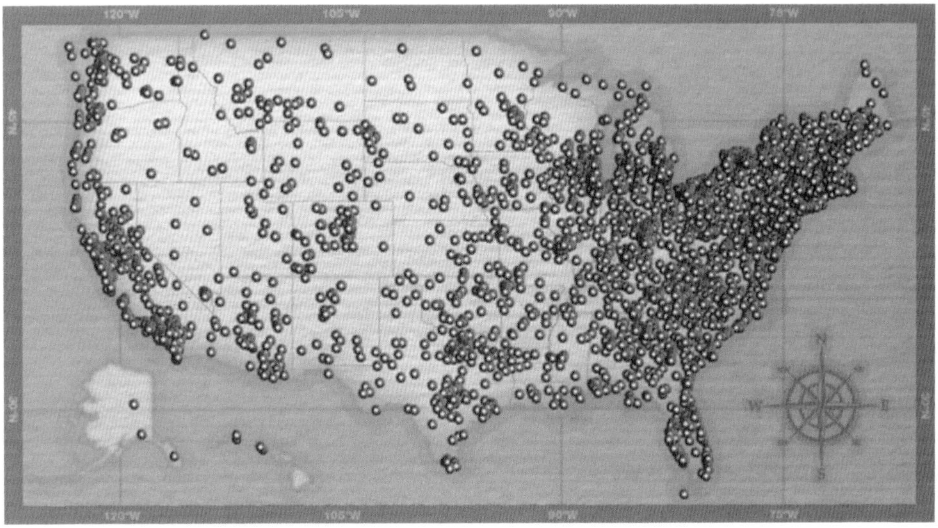

Search for your hometown history, your old stomping grounds, and even your favorite sports team.

Consistent with our mission to preserve history on a local level, this book was printed in South Carolina on American-made paper and manufactured entirely in the United States. Products carrying the accredited Forest Stewardship Council (FSC) label are printed on 100 percent FSC-certified paper.

MADE IN THE USA